DogLife ❧ Lifelong Care for Your Dog™

GOLDEN RETRIEVER

tfh

Susan McCullough

GOLDEN RETRIEVER

Project Team
Editor: Stephanie Fornino
Indexer: Ann W. Truesdale
Design: Mary Ann Kahn
Series Design: Mary Ann Kahn, Angela Stanford

T.F.H. Publications
President/CEO: Glen S. Axelrod
Executive Vice President: Mark E. Johnson
Publisher: Christopher T. Reggio
Production Manager: Kathy Bontz

T.F.H. Publications, Inc.
One TFH Plaza
Third and Union Avenues
Neptune City, NJ 07753

Printed and bound in China

10 11 12 13 14   3 5 7 9 8 6 4 2

Library of Congress Cataloging-in-Publication Data
McCullough, Susan.
  Golden retriever / Susan McCullough.
    p. cm.
  Includes bibliographical references and index.
  ISBN 978-0-7938-3607-9 (alk. paper)
  1. Golden retriever. I. Title.
  SF429.G63M33 2010
  636.752'7--dc22
                        2010001279

This book has been published with the intent to provide accurate and authoritative information in regard to the subject matter within. While every reasonable precaution has been taken in preparation of this book, the author and publisher expressly disclaim responsibility for any errors, omissions, or adverse effects arising from the use or application of the information contained herein. The techniques and suggestions are used at the reader's discretion and are not to be considered a substitute for veterinary care.
If you suspect a medical problem consult your veterinarian.

Note: In the interest of concise writing, "he" is used when referring to puppies and dogs unless the text is specifically referring to females or males. "She" is used when referring to people. However, the information contained herein is equally applicable to both sexes.

The Leader In Responsible Animal Care for Over 50 Years!®
www.tfh.com

CONTENTS

INTRODUCING THE GOLDEN RETRIEVER

When was the first time you saw a Golden Retriever? For many people, that first sighting came in a television commercial that featured a large, mellow dog with a glorious sunshine-colored coat. The dog may have been lying at the feet of his human companion, holding a leash and trotting over to that person or trying to score some baked beans. Or perhaps your initial acquaintance with a Golden came in a movie theater, where you saw a wise dog named Shadow lead his compatriots Sassy the Siamese cat and Chance the Bulldog across the mountain range to reunite with their family in the classic movie *Homeward Bound: The Incredible Journey.*

Golden Retrievers certainly can be large, mellow, and wise. But as with any other breed, there's much more to the Golden than the stereotypes we see on any screen. All too many dog lovers who welcome their first Goldens into their homes are surprised to find that their new friends differ considerably from what they expected. To understand this gap between expectation and reality—and to better appreciate your new Golden for who he really is—it's important to learn about his history.

HOW DOGS BECAME DOMESTICATED

The history of Golden Retrievers starts many centuries before the breed even existed. That said, scientists don't agree on a single event or even a single place that started the evolution of wild animals into the canine companions we know and love today. The one principle upon which scientists do seem to agree is that today's domestic dog—whether that dog is a Golden Retriever, a Dachshund, a Dalmatian, or any other breed or mixture of breeds—can claim the wolf as his earliest ancestor.

But where that wolf and his compatriots began to evolve into domestic dogs is open to question. Until recently, scientists had agreed that the domestic dog had originated in eastern Asia. However, in the summer of 2009 that consensus was called into question when two anthropologists from the University of California, Davis, and a biologist from Cornell University collected and analyzed blood samples from village dogs in Egypt, Namibia, and Uganda. The samples revealed that the African dogs have just as much genetic diversity as the East Asian dogs do. That doesn't mean that domestic dogs originated in Africa—for one thing, there were no wolves there—but

The history of the Golden Retriever starts many centuries before the breed even existed.

scientists are now wondering whether the domestic dog's beginning was somewhere in between east Asia and east Africa, such as the Caucasus mountains, and whether there were multiple domestication events.

Scientists also aren't sure when the domestication process began. Current theories place the start of the process at anywhere between 15,000 and 40,000 years ago. Much more testing and study will be needed to determine a more precise figure.

But wherever and whenever dogs began to become part of people's lives, the process probably began in hunter–gatherer societies, where dogs would huddle on the outskirts of villages to eat the skin, bones, and other leftovers from human hunts. Psychologist Stanley Coren, in his classic book *The Pawprints of History*, theorizes that the human villagers valued the presence of the dogs because their consumption of what the humans discarded kept away insects and diminished odors of what was discarded. Then, when the dogs barked, humans realized that the dogs' vocalizations could keep predators away from the village. To keep the dogs and the protection they offered within the village, the villagers began giving extra food to them. Eventually, they might have taken some of the dogs' puppies and raised them in their own homes. As time went on, people began to learn more about breeding dogs for the traits they wanted, such as docility, trainability, herding ability, and hunting prowess.

EARLY DEVELOPMENT OF THE GOLDEN RETRIEVER

But while people realized that dogs might be useful hunting companions, breeding for hunting prowess was no simple matter. That's because as humans evolved, their hunting techniques became more sophisticated and specialized. Some hunters required large, powerful dogs to help them chase down their prey; among the dogs these hunters developed were the Rhodesian Ridgeback and the Mastiff. Others were fishermen who wanted dogs who could herd fish into nets, and they developed breeds such as the Portuguese Water Dog and the Newfoundland. Meanwhile, other hunters wanted canine assistants who could point themselves in the direction of birds being hunted; consequently, they developed the Pointer and the Viszla, among others. Then there were those hunters who needed dogs who could flush game from bushes; these dogs became our modern-day spaniels.

However, still another type of hunter wanted still another type of canine assistance. This hunter wanted a dog who was strong enough to slog with him through marshland, even-tempered enough to not be fazed by the sound of gunfire, keen enough to tear through the marsh to retrieve any birds felled by that gunfire, and gentle enough to take the fallen bird in his mouth, bring the bird back to the hunter, and place that bird intact at the hunter's feet. From this set of requirements, 19th-century breeders and hunters in England and Scotland developed that subset of hunting dogs known as retrievers. Today's retrievers can all bring birds back to hunters and also fetch tennis balls and other paraphernalia for their people. These retrievers include the Flat-Coated Retriever, the Curly-Coated Retriever, the Chesapeake Bay

Today's retrievers can bring birds back to hunters and also fetch items.

Retriever, the Nova Scotia Duck Tolling Retriever, the Labrador Retriever, and of course the Golden Retriever.

THE GOLDEN RETRIEVER IN SCOTLAND

Among the 19th-century Scotsmen who were instrumental in developing working retrievers was Sir Dudley Marjoribanks (later known as

Both the United States and Canada played a large part in the development of the Golden Retriever.

Lord Tweedmouth). He wanted to produce a yellow retriever who could work in the sometimes severe Scottish climate, rugged terrain, and game available there. Toward that end, in 1865 Sir Dudley purchased "Nous," a yellow retriever puppy, from a cobbler in southern England. Sir Dudley then took Nous to his estate in Scotland and bred him to Belle, a Tweed Water Spaniel he already owned. (This breed is now extinct.) That mating produced four yellow female puppies. He subsequently bred these four and their progeny to dogs from other breeds, including Wavy-Coated Retrievers (an ancestor of the Flat-Coated Retriever), Irish Setters, and even, reportedly, a Bloodhound. Sir Dudley kept mostly yellow puppies, along with a few black puppies, to continue developing his breed.

By the early 20th century, a few dogs who resemble today's Golden Retriever had begun to appear at dog shows—but not as Golden Retrievers per se. Instead, the show catalogs designated them as either "Retriever-Wavy or Flat-Coated" or "Golden Flat-Coat." According to the American Kennel Club (AKC), devotees of these golden dogs finally formed the Golden Retriever Club of England in 1913. The Kennel Club of England officially recognized the breed under its new name, "Golden Retriever," in 1920.

THE GOLDEN RETRIEVER IN THE UNITED STATES

Meanwhile, breed devotees were bringing the Golden Retriever across the Atlantic to North America. The first Golden to step onto Western Hemisphere shores did so in Canada in 1881, courtesy of the Honorable Archie Marjoribanks, grandson of Sir Dudley. Three years later, the younger Marjoribanks registered a dog named Lady with the AKC in the United States. Interest in the breed grew in both

Canada and the United States over the next several decades.

RECOGNITION BY MAJOR CLUBS

By late 1925, the AKC had registered its first Golden Retriever, signifying its official recognition of the breed. The Canadian Kennel Club (CKC) followed suit two years later.

The Golden Retriever Club of America (GRCA)

Enthusiasts in the United States formed the Golden Retriever Club of America (GRCA) in 1938. This formation was a significant development for the breed in the land of Old Glory. Formation of the GRCA gave enthusiasts a platform upon which to educate the American public about Golden Retrievers and to hold events that would showcase not only the beauty but also the versatility of the breed. To that end, the GRCA holds an annual national specialty show that includes not only conformation (show) events but also agility trials, competitive obedience trials, hunting trials, and other events. In addition, regional clubs hold their own specialty events, giving Golden Retriever devotees lots of opportunities to develop and exhibit the versatility of their breed.

Finally, the GRCA confers special recognition upon highly accomplished Goldens. Outstanding show dogs can qualify for the GRCA Show Dog Hall of Fame and either Outstanding Sire or Dam status if they produce offspring who also do well in conformation and/or performance competition. There's also an Obedience Hall of Fame, Field [Hunting] Dog Hall of Fame, and Agility Dog Hall of Fame. Golden Retrievers also compete in other activities such as tracking and rally obedience.

The GRCA places great emphasis on making sure that the Golden, as gorgeous as he is, is known as much for his brains and athleticism as for his good looks. The organization has established several types of recognition, including the Versatility and the Dual Dog Hall of Fame programs. Versatility awards are given to Goldens who excel in the show ring and in performance events (agility, obedience, and/or tracking) and field trials. The Dual Dog Hall of Fame is open to Goldens who excel in both conformation and field trials.

The Golden Retriever Club of Canada (GRCC)

Canadian enthusiasts formed the Golden Retriever Club of Ontario in 1958, which was renamed the Golden Retriever Club of Canada (GRCC) in 1960. The GRCC offers opportunities for Canadian Goldens and their people similar to those offered by the GRCA.

INFLUENTIAL GOLDEN RETRIEVER PEOPLE

A number of people have contributed to the development of the Golden Retriever. Here are just a few.

Sir Dudley Marjoribanks

If any single person can be considered to be the creator of the Golden Retriever, this is the guy.

Archie Marjoribanks

The grandson of Sir Dudley, Archie brought the first Golden Retriever into the United States.

Robert Appleton

This East Hampton, New York, resident registered the very first Golden Retriever with the AKC in 1925. The dog was Lomberdale Blondin, whom Appleton had imported from England. He later mated the dog with a female Golden Retriever named Dan Hill Judy, whom he'd also imported. The resulting litter was the

The Golden Retriever is one of the most popular breeds in the United States.

first Golden Retriever litter registered with the AKC, also in 1925.

Samuel Magoffin

Samuel Magoffin was the first president of the GRCA and owner of the first Golden Retriever to win a Best in Show ribbon, Speedwell Pluto. Today the GRCA is one of the largest national breed clubs in the United States.

Elma Stonex

A longtime Golden Retriever breeder, judge, historian, and enthusiast, Mrs. Stonex gave the lie to the legend that Sir Dudley had developed Golden Retrievers by importing Russian circus dogs. Her findings appeared in a classic book called, appropriately, *The Golden Retriever*, published in 1952, and in subsequent writings for various British and American dog publications.

Rachel Paige Elliott

A world-famous authority on canine body structure in general and Golden Retrievers in particular, "Pagey" Elliott was also an award-winning author. She and her husband, Dr. Mark Elliott, raised more than 50 litters of Golden Retrievers. At her funeral in 2009, 50

Golden Retrievers with tartan bandanas around their necks walked (with human handlers, of course) in a procession until they reached the site of the funeral. In recognition of the breed's Scottish origins, a bagpiper played while the procession wound its way through town.

MEMORABLE GOLDEN RETRIEVERS

Because the Golden Retriever is one of the most popular breeds in the United States—not to mention a versatile, fun-loving companion—plenty of Goldens have imprinted themselves onto the collective memory of the public. Some of these renowned dogs have distinguished themselves in the show ring and/or in dog sports. Others have made themselves memorable through their appearances in television or film. Still others have made their mark by giving selflessly of themselves to save human lives. Here's a by no means comprehensive listing, in no particular order, of Golden Retrievers who have shown us many sides of this wonderful breed.

OTCh. Moreland's Golden Tonka

OTCh. Moreland's Golden Tonka, a Golden Retriever who in 1977 was the first dog of any breed to win the AKC's Obedience Trial Champion (OTCh) title. A dog who earns this title must perform a series of highly complicated exercises that the AKC itself calls a Ph.D. exam for dogs. Other than the National Obedience Championship, which only one dog may earn each year at a special event held by the AKC, the OTCh is the highest obedience honor a dog can

Part of the Golden's popularity stems from the fact that he is such a versatile, fun-loving companion.

Today's Golden Retrievers have many influential ancestors.

earn. (The next two dogs to earn the title were Goldens too.)

Ch. Amberac's Asterling Aruba

Ch. Amberac's Asterling Aruba was a great Golden Retriever of the 1980s who, more than almost any other Golden, is responsible for beginning America's love affair with blond, fluffy Golden Retrievers. Not only did Aruba clean up in the show ring, but among her 38 puppies were 32 breed champions, many of whom produced scores of additional breed champions. Many Golden Retriever experts believe that Aruba is among the most influential bitches in the history of the breed.

Buddy

Buddy is the Golden Retriever character who was at the center of the Air Bud movie franchise. Five movies were made about Bud between 1997 and 2003, and several others about his offspring were made between 2006 and 2009. The dog who played Bud in the original movie, *Air Bud* (1997), also starred in the movie *Fluke* (1995), although in that movie he portrayed a mixed-breed dog.

Kelsey

Kelsey is the only Golden Retriever to have won the AKC National Agility Championship. That win occurred in 1997. Kelsey's owner and handler was Maggie Downie.

Polly

Polly is the Golden Retriever who belongs to fictional New York advertising executive Don

Draper and his family on the award-winning television show *Mad Men*. During the first season, a single scene showcases the breed's hunting roots, particularly its affinity for birds. In that scene, Polly is outside playing with the two Draper children, Bobby and Sally, when the next-door neighbor releases his pigeons. When she sees the pigeons, Polly takes a flying leap and grabs one in mid-air. Polly's leap—and the horrified pigeon owner's subsequent threat to kill the dog—may have inspired the children's mother, the usually prim and proper Betty Draper, to grab a rifle and start shooting at the neighbor's remaining pigeons later in the episode.

Shadow

Shadow, from the movie *Homeward Bound: The Incredible Journey* (1993), is another well-known Golden Retriever. He is clearly the leader in the intrepid trio of animals that make their way home over extremely rugged terrain. The movie is based on the novel *The Incredible Journey* by Sheila Burnford.

Duke

Duke is one of two dogs from the Bush's Baked Beans commercials that are seen on television. Yes, there are two such dogs. According to the company website, the decision to showcase company spokesperson Jay Bush and his Golden Retriever, Duffy "Duke" of Castlebury, in the commercials ran into trouble when Duke turned out to be uncomfortable performing in front of a television camera. For that reason, another Golden was hired to portray Duke in the commercials.

Liberty

Liberty is the Golden Retriever who resided with President Gerald Ford and his family during their tenure in the White House in the mid-1970s. When Liberty produced a litter of puppies during her stay at 1600 Pennsylvania Avenue, the resulting publicity ramped up the breed's popularity. Today, more than 30 years later, Goldens remain among the five most popular breeds in the United States.

Rookie

Rookie is a Golden Retriever who almost singlehandedly brought the sport of canine freestyle (choreographed movement of dogs and people to music) to the world. His human partner, Carolyn Scott, founded the Musical Dog Sport Association (MDSA), and both Carolyn and Rookie appeared on countless television programs demonstrating their sport. Their performance to the music of "You're the One that I Want" from the musical *Grease* was recorded for posterity and has drawn millions of looks via YouTube. Rookie died of cancer in July 2008 at the age of 15.

Riley

Riley is the Golden Retriever who was photographed lying calmly on a basket-like platform that was suspended above a 60-foot (18.5-m) canyon created by the collapse of the World Trade Center after the September 11, 2001, attacks. In the photo, Riley was being sent across the canyon to search the rubble. He and his handler/trainer, Chris Selfridge, were members of a Federal Emergency Management Agency (FEMA) Task Force from Pennsylvania. Riley retired from search-and-rescue work a little more than one year after the attacks, but lived a long and happy life with Selfridge and his family. He died on February 26, 2010, at the age of 13.

PART I

PUPPYHOOD

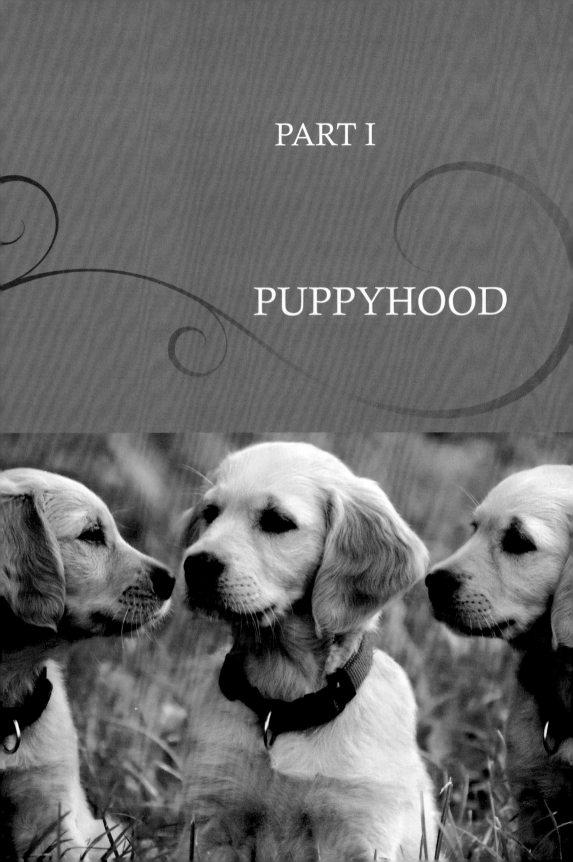

CHAPTER 1

IS THE GOLDEN RETRIEVER RIGHT FOR YOU?

The Golden Retriever's glorious good looks, outgoing nature, and ability to perform many tasks captivate many people—including, perhaps, you. And like many other people, you might think that raising a Golden Retriever from puppyhood will not only maximize the amount of time you have with a Golden but also allow you to have a dog with whom you can build a bond almost from the very start of his life.

However, enchantment with a breed and being able to live successfully with an individual dog of that breed are two entirely different things. That's just as true with a Golden Retriever as with any other dog. Moreover, when it comes to Golden Retrievers, puppyhood lasts a long time. At least from the vantage point of temperament, most Golden Retrievers remain puppies until around the age of two. Physical maturity generally occurs around that time too—although, as countless car commercials warn, your mileage may vary.

This chapter will help ensure that, as you consider whether to add a Golden Retriever puppy to your life, your fantasies will not collide with reality.

BREED CHARACTERISTICS

Just watching a Golden Retriever can be a like taking a happy pill. What's not to like? The adult Golden looks majestic but is fully capable of behaving clownishly. He's happy to be wherever his people and their friends are. He'll put everything he has into whatever he's doing, be it playing, eating, chewing, cuddling, retrieving, or otherwise working. As you watch him sprinting in the afternoon sunlight, running as fast as he can to find the tennis ball you've thrown and to bring that ball back to you, you can't help but smile over his wholehearted ability to live in the moment and to look wonderful doing so. And as he places the tennis ball at your feet or in your hand and looks up at you expectantly, waiting for you to throw out that ball for him to retrieve yet again, you may wonder where he gets all his energy.

The Golden Retriever Club of America (GRCA), like all other breed clubs, maintains a detailed written description of how the ideal Golden should act and look. This description is called a breed standard. Very few Goldens totally conform to this standard, but it does provide a blueprint for recognizing a healthy, well-bred representative of the breed.

Golden Retrievers remain puppies for a relatively long time—until the age of two.

The standard states that a Golden should be friendly, reliable, and trustworthy. He shouldn't be quarrelsome or exhibit hostility toward other dogs or toward people in normal situations. He shouldn't be excessively shy or nervous either.

Of course, every Golden Retriever is an individual. For example, some are energetic to the point of being almost hyper; this is especially true of Goldens bred especially to be hunting dogs (or in "breeder speak," field dogs). Others, such as those who are bred from dogs who have competed in the show ring, may be a little mellower. While many Goldens instinctively take to retrieving and swimming, others may need to be shown the joys of such pursuits. And while quite a few Goldens love participating in dog sports and other structured

By the Numbers

Golden Retrievers don't start looking like adults until they're at least one year of age and more likely closing in on their second birthdays. For the first few months of their lives, they look like furry little butterballs that most people can't resist cuddling. From about four months of age on, though, those butterballs begin morphing into the powerful, athletic dogs we know and love.

The Golden's Hunting Heritage

Neither the Golden's affability, wholeheartedness, nor stamina should be surprising. After all, this breed was bred to hunt birds in water and marshland under sometimes severe weather conditions and to work as a partner with a human being. To succeed at what he was bred to do, the Golden needed to have enough stamina to work with a hunter an entire day. He needed enough enthusiasm and drive to swim or slosh through the wetlands time after time to bring those birds back to his person. And he needed to enjoy this work enough in order to remain unfazed whenever that person fired his shotgun.

You may not plan to hunt birds with your Golden (although you certainly could). But whether you hunt or not, it's important to realize how big a role the Golden Retriever's hunting heritage plays in who he is, how he looks, how he behaves, and whether he's suitable for you and your family.

activities with their people, others are more individualistic and prefer to devise their own forms of entertainment.

Despite such individualism, though, most Goldens do carry quite a few traits in common. Those include:

Love of All People

Goldens adore any and all human beings. If you want a watchdog, do not get a Golden Retriever. These happy-go-lucky individuals are more likely to bestow kisses on an intruder than to stop that intruder from making off with your possessions. That said, Goldens can and do sense true danger and will act upon it; plenty of stories recount tales of Golden Retrievers saving their people from peril.

Love of You

Goldens are nothing if not loyal, and they bond easily and deeply to the people who take care of them. A human member of the household who's under the weather can count on a Golden Retriever to stick close by her—next to or even on the bed—until that person is feeling like herself again.

Lots of Energy and Stamina

Like other sporting breeds, the Golden Retriever has energy to spare—and he was developed to be that way. A hunter who's counting on a canine partner to accompany him through the wetlands all day needs to be sure that the dog won't wimp out or crash mid-afternoon. That's why this breed needs plenty of regular exercise, particularly in the first few years of their lives. Failure to give a young Golden his daily aerobic workout could put your furniture in peril, not to mention your sanity.

Oral Fixation

Goldens love to put anything and everything in their mouths. Furniture, soap, matches, knives, pillows, clothes, you name it—anyone who chooses to live with a Golden Retriever needs to count on having to puppy-proof her home until he has been taught house manners and has developed mature self-control, which in some instances could take the dog's entire lifetime. Neglect such puppy-proofing and you're likely to lose precious possessions and face repeated veterinary bills in order to remove the unauthorized objects that have lodged themselves in your inquisitive Golden's digestive tract.

Eagerness to Learn

Golden Retrievers are known for their strong desire to learn new tricks. They're among the most intelligent and trainable of all dog breeds. If you want a dog who will enthusiastically embrace all you can teach him—and who will teach you quite a few life lessons in return—the Golden may well be the right breed for you.

PHYSICAL APPEARANCE

Here, in laymen's terms, is what the American Kennel Club's (AKC) breed standard for the Golden Retriever specifies an ideal Golden should look like. Keep in mind that no Golden Retriever will perfectly reflect these specifications, and you shouldn't reject a dog simply because he's oversized, his ears are a bit too long, or he has other similar imperfections. Nevertheless, the breed standard provides a good guide as to what a healthy Golden Retriever looks like and can, to some extent, aid you in your search for the right Golden for you.

General Appearance

The Golden should look well proportioned and have a powerful, active appearance. He should project an eager, kindly personality but also appear alert and confident. He should look as though he could work all day gathering

The Golden puppy you choose should look well proportioned and have a powerful, active appearance.

The Golden's body should convey an impression of power and athleticism.

birds for a hunter on challenging terrain or in cold marsh water amid sometimes difficult weather conditions.

Size

When measured from the floor to the top of the shoulder, an adult male Golden Retriever should be from 23 to 24 inches (58.5 or 61 cm) tall and weigh between 65 and 75 pounds (30 and 35 kg). Female Goldens should be 21½ to 22½ (54.5 cm to 57 cm) inches tall and weigh between 55 and 65 pounds (25 and 30 kg). That said, plenty of gorgeous Goldens deviate from these specifications; for example, the female Golden Retriever to whom this book is dedicated is nearly 25 inches (63.5 cm) tall and weighs 70 pounds (31.5 kg). Despite the fact that she's lean, muscular, and has an impressive pedigree filled with show dogs, she is too big to conform to the breed standard and would be disqualified in any show ring. That said, she is more than qualified to be a beloved member of her family.

Neutering either males or females prior to sexual maturity (approximately one year of age) may cause them to grow taller than their natural genetic potential and take on a lankier appearance.

Coat Type

Golden Retrievers are double-coated dogs. As such, their fur can be compared to a person's winter coat that has a lining. The outercoat, also known as the topcoat, should be firm and resilient and neither coarse nor silky to the touch. The outercoat should also lie close to the body and may be either straight or wavy.

The thicker coat surrounding the neck (also known as the ruff) shouldn't be trimmed. Longer strands of hair, or feathering, should appear on the backs of the front legs and under the body. Heavier feathering should appear on the front of the neck, backs of the thighs, and the underside of the tail. By contrast, the coat on the head, paws, and fronts of the legs is short and even.

Training Tidbit

Golden Retrievers are far easier to train when they get sufficient exercise. Consider carefully whether you can provide a Golden with the regular exercise opportunities he needs to be the best—not to mention happiest—dog he can be.

Multi-Dog Tip

Golden Retrievers generally get along well with other dogs—but before you add one to your multi-dog household, consider whether your current canine companions are ready to welcome a Golden puppy into the family.

Color

The Golden comes in a wide range of golden shades, ranging from light blond to almost russet. In some dogs, the feathering may be lighter than the rest of the coat. No matter what the dog's overall coat color is, though, there should be no white hairs (other than graying or whitening of the face due to age or a few white hairs on the chest) or black hairs on the coat.

The undercoat should be full and thick and is generally a much paler color than the outercoat. Together, both coats should be dense and water repellent.

General Body Structure

A Golden Retriever's body should convey an impression of power and athleticism; this is a dog who's been bred to work all day without tiring. The dog's topline—the line the back forms from the top of the shoulders to the pelvis—should be level, while the line from the pelvis to the base of the tail should have a slight slope.

The body should look well balanced and not be disproportionately long in length. (Golden Retrievers should *not* look like long-legged blond long-haired Dachshunds.) The Golden's chest should be deep; the width of the chest between the forelegs should at least equal the width of a man's hand, including the thumb. The dog's chest area and ribs should be long and deep but not exaggerated in shape and should extend well toward the hindquarters. The area from the dog's rib cage to the pelvis— in breeder speak, the loin—should be short, muscular, wide, and deep and should show little upward slope or tuck-up.

A Golden Retriever's tail should be thick and muscular at the base and follow the slope that began at the top of the pelvis. The dog should carry the tail in a way that reflects his generally merry disposition: at the level of the back or with a moderate upward curve but never curled over the back or drooping between the back legs.

The dog's forequarters should look as though they go with the hindquarters—in other words, as though both the forequarters and hindquarters belong to the same dog—and look limber. The shoulder blades are not prominent. The dog's upper arms appear about the same length as the blades, and the elbows should be directly beneath the upper tips of the blades. The forelegs, when viewed from the front, are straight with good bone but not to the point where the bone looks coarse. The pasterns (breeders peak for the area where the foot blends into the leg) should be short and strong and slope slightly with no suggestion of weakness. The feet should be medium sized, round, compact, and well knuckled, with thick pads. Excess hair at the nails and between the paw pads may be trimmed to show natural size and contour and also to prevent stones, seeds, ice or other debris from getting stuck in the feet.

The hindquarters should be broad and strongly muscled. In a natural stance, the upper leg joins the pelvis at approximately a 90-degree angle and the knees are well bent. The hocks (the joints between the lower thigh and the rear pasterns) are well let down with short, strong rear pasterns. The back feet should look the same as the front feet, and the legs should be straight when viewed from behind the dog.

A sound structure such as what's described in this section should produce a gait that is free, smooth, powerful, well coordinated, and showing good reach forward of the forelegs when the dog is trotting. When viewed from any position, the legs should turn neither in nor out, nor should the feet cross or interfere with each other. As the dog's speed increases, the feet tend to converge toward a center line of balance.

Head and Neck
A Golden Retriever's head is relatively broad across the skull, with a slight arch when viewed in profile. The area between the eyes, where the top of the nose meets the forehead (in breeder parlance, the stop) is well defined but not abrupt. The front of the face (the foreface) is deep, wide, and nearly as long as the skull. The muzzle is straight when viewed in profile or from above and is slightly deeper and wider at the stop than at the tip. The flews, also known as jowls, shouldn't be heavy. The teeth should meet in a scissors bite; the outer sides of the lower incisors touch the inner sides of the upper incisors.

The neck should be medium long and should merge gradually into the shoulders to give the dog a sturdy, muscular appearance.

Eyes
A Golden Retriever's eyes should have a friendly, intelligent expression. They should be medium large with dark, close-fitting rims

The Golden's eyes should have a friendly, intelligent expression.

and should be set well apart and reasonably deep in the sockets. The preferable color (according to the standard) is dark brown, but medium brown is acceptable. The dog's eyes shouldn't be slanted, narrow, or triangular, and neither the whites nor lining inside the lower lid should show when the dog is looking straight ahead. In other words, even though the Bloodhound may be one of the Golden Retriever's forebears, the Golden's eyes should not resemble those of a Bloodhound.

Ears

A Golden Retriever's ears should be rather short, with the front edge attached well behind and just above the eye and falling close to the cheek. When pulled forward, the tip of the ear should just cover the eye. The nose should be black or brownish black in color but may fade to a lighter shade in cold weather. That said, the normal color of the dog's nose should not be pink or otherwise light in color.

CAN A GOLDEN FIT INTO YOUR LIFE?

The Golden Retriever is a very adaptable dog if you're willing to meet him halfway. But that doesn't mean that he's right for every person or in every environment. Just as with every other breed, the Golden is more likely to thrive in some scenarios than in others. This section discusses where a Golden is most likely to live happily ever after—and where his people will be happiest too.

Think carefully before adding a Golden puppy to your family.

Goldens and Other Dogs

Got other dogs? Your new Golden Retriever will probably enjoy playing with them and being part of their pack. Some like to play rather roughly—wrestling and body slamming are often the Golden's preferred play maneuvers—but during such canine smackdowns, the Golden will often roll over before his playmate does. That said, any addition of a Golden Retriever to a multi-dog household needs to be okay not just with the Golden but also with the other dogs, no matter what their breeds are. After all, they were in the household first.

not happy, his person won't be happy either.

The Golden should not be left alone all day when the family is at work or school. Such an environment spells disaster for the sociable, active Golden Retriever. These dogs are intensely active and intensely sociable. Failure to meet a Golden's needs for exercise and for company can lead to boredom and loneliness, which in turn may well prompt that Golden to take drastic steps to amuse himself and engage in some sort of physical activity. Such steps include ripping up cushions, excavating holes in carpets, and eating through drywall—none of which will be to the liking of most owners.

Bottom line: A Golden Retriever can live almost anywhere as long as he gets to spend plenty of time with people and can get enough exercise each day to tire him out.

Environment

Repeat, repeat, repeat: the Golden Retriever was bred to be a hunting dog and to work closely with another person. This means that he needs to be in an environment where he has plenty of human companionship and where he has opportunities to get strenuous exercise on a regular basis.

The ideal environment for a Golden, then, is in an active household where someone is home during at least part of the day and can give the dog the opportunity to run and fetch or perform some other task until he's panting. That said, with a bit of ingenuity, a person who's committed to building a happy life for a Golden (and for herself) can create that environment. Whether you're in an urban, suburban, or rural environment, plenty of contact between person and dog and plenty of opportunities for the dog to have regular strenuous exercise is extremely important. Without those two elements, it's hard to keep a Golden Retriever happy. And if the Golden's

Exercise

Some dogs are happy to be couch potatoes, but the Golden Retriever is not one of them. Until he reaches seniorhood, a Golden needs regular strenuous exercise just to stay sane.

A couple of walks around the block each day are not going to cut it with this active dog. To the Golden Retriever, those walks are like mere appetizers at a meal. A Golden won't be satisfied unless he gets not only the appetizer but also the main course.

Of course, exercise does more than just keep your Golden sane. A daily workout also helps burn off the extra calories that this food-loving dog is all too likely to accumulate in his endless quest to score another goodie.

Moreover, exercise helps your dog to behave better—mainly because he's too tired to misbehave. Dog trainers often tell their clients that "a tired dog is a good dog," and they often ask their clients to make sure their dogs have had some exercise before coming to obedience classes. They know that if a dog has a chance

Until they're seniors, Goldens need regular strenuous exercise.

to let off some steam, he's more likely to be able to focus on learning to sit or come when called.

Among the physical exercises that adult Golden Retrievers thrive on are running, swimming, participating in various dog sports, and engaging in mental exercise.

According to psychologist Stanley Coren, the Golden Retriever ranks fourth in intelligence out of 110 breeds. Only the Border Collie, Poodle, and German Shepherd Dog consistently show more smarts than the Golden. But those smarts need nurturing. Regular positive training sessions can help keep that Golden brain nimble; so, too, can indoor games such as hide-and-seek and hide the toy. Another mental exercise option is to give your dog an interactive treat-dispensing toy that requires him to think in order to figure out

how to get the toy to dispense the treat.

Any way you look at it, though, providing physical and mental exercise is crucial to living happily with a Golden Retriever. If you can't provide such exercise opportunities on a regular basis, you might want to reconsider whether this breed is right for you.

Grooming Needs

That glorious Golden Retriever coat doesn't happen all by itself. As mentioned earlier, the Golden has a double coat, which means that underneath the outercoat of long, sturdy guard hairs is a soft, downy coat. This undercoat helps protect the dog from excessive cold and heat. The undercoat is constantly replenishing itself. Old hair sheds—copiously—to allow new hair to grow in. That's why, if you want your house to stay free of dog fur-induced dust bunnies, you should reconsider your choice of a Golden Retriever.

That said, there's plenty an owner can do to keep a Golden's shedding under control. Among the most effective steps are regular brushings of the dog's coat with the right kind of brush, good nutrition, and regular cleaning of the house with a powerful vacuum cleaner. None of those steps is difficult to take, and they need not take up a lot of time. But if you're looking for a wash-and-wear dog—well, the Golden Retriever is not that animal.

Health Issues

Like most other purebred dogs, Golden Retrievers have their share of health concerns. Among the health issues that would-be Golden owners need to be aware of include hip dysplasia, cataracts, allergies, hypothyroidism, subaortic stenosis, and different types of cancer.

Sociability

A sociable dog is a dog who enjoys being around people and other dogs. He just generally likes having company, and he meets new individuals with ease and aplomb. That being the case, if you are looking for a truly sociable dog—well, look no further. For the most part, Golden Retrievers epitomize sociability.

Got kids? Your Golden probably will not only like them but love them. In fact, he might love them too much—as in he might become so enthusiastic playing with them that he might accidentally knock one of them over, particularly if they're small. Appropriate supervision is crucial if your children and your Golden are to live happily together. Teach your children how to behave and interact appropriately with the dog, train your dog in basic good manners—and never let children under six years of age play with your Golden (or any other dog, for that matter) without your direct supervision.

Got company? Your Golden will play the role of canine host with the utmost enthusiasm. He'll not hesitate to greet anyone who enters your home, whether he knows the person or not. The challenge you're most likely to face in dealing with your Golden and strangers won't be fear; instead, it will be excessive zeal: jumping up on people and otherwise endlessly soliciting attention. Appropriate training will teach your Golden how to greet people politely and get more attention than he could ever get by just demanding it.

Want to Know More?

For more detailed information on Golden health concerns, see Chapter 8: Golden Health and Wellness.

Trainability

If you're looking for a canine companion who's not only capable of working closely with you but also really wants to do so, a Golden Retriever may be perfect for you. These dogs are rated among the most intelligent of all breeds, and they pair that intelligence with a willingness to cooperate. It's no accident that Golden Retrievers can be found performing such sports, activities, and tasks as conformation, obedience, agility, flyball, canine freestyle, animal-assisted therapy, service, and search and rescue.

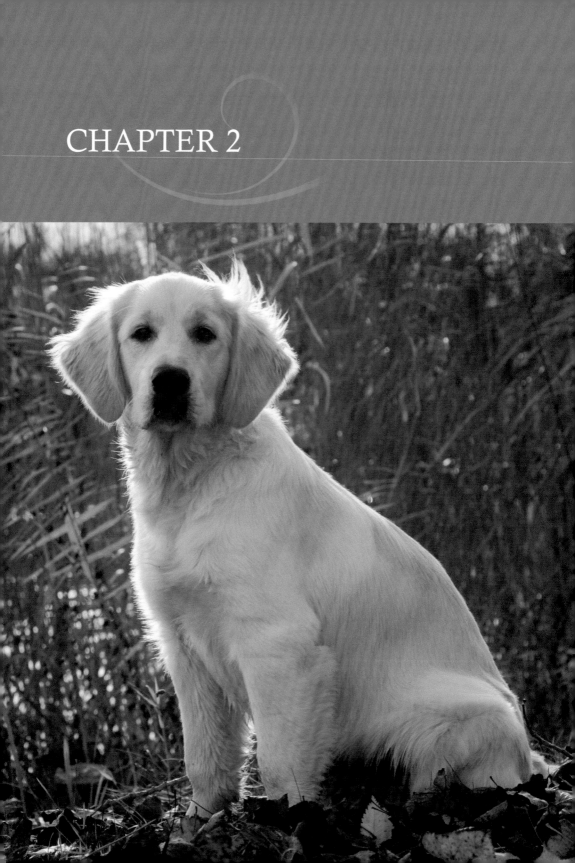

CHAPTER 2

FINDING AND PREPPING FOR YOUR GOLDEN RETRIEVER PUPPY

Now that you've decided that you're ready to add a Golden Retriever to your household, you need to start searching for the dog of your dreams and making your home Golden Retriever-friendly. But even before you take up those tasks, you need to make one last decision whether your new Golden should be a puppy or an adult.

WHY GETTING A PUPPY IS A GOOD IDEA

Who can resist getting a cuddly, teddy-bear-like Golden Retriever puppy? More to the point, why would anyone want to? Acquiring a Golden while he's still a baby has definite pluses.

First, you'll be treated to perpetual cuteness for a few months. Few experiences are more endearing than playing with your fuzzy Golden butterball as he romps in the living room or backyard, except for cuddling that little butterball in your arms after he tires himself out.

Second, by starting off with a well-bred puppy, you get a dog with no baggage. Not that he's a blank slate—to the contrary, he's a unique individual with his own very special personality. However, he probably is a *clean* slate. He hasn't had the negative experiences that an older dog might have sustained. He also hasn't had time to develop the bad habits that an older dog might have had time to cultivate—things like raiding the garbage can or gouging craters into the carpet.

With a puppy you can start fresh and start right. And that's true of any puppy from a reputable breeder, not just a puppy who's destined for the show ring. In fact, your best bet might be to buy a puppy whom a breeder has determined won't show well because he doesn't quite conform to the breed standard. Maybe the breeder thinks he'll grow too big or that his ear flaps won't reach the proper place when pulled toward the face. But while such features disqualify him from the show ring, they don't disqualify him as a companion. In that respect, he has the potential to be just as wonderful as his ribbon-winning littermate.

Want to Know More?

If you're more interested in adopting an adult Golden, see Chapter 5: Finding Your Adult.

But adding this puppy paragon to your life depends on your buying him from a reputable breeder. How do you find one?

WHERE TO FIND THE PUPPY OF YOUR DREAMS

Finding a reputable breeder requires a little research and perhaps some patience!

Finding the Breeder

Fortunately, the Golden Retriever Club of America (GRCA) can help cut your research time. Just log onto the club's website at http://www.grca.org/allabout/puppyreferrals.html, and you'll find a state-by-state listing of GRCA members who refer prospective Golden owners to breeders who will soon have or who already have litters. These individuals are called breeder referral coordinators. Find the breeder referral coordinator for your state

The breeder should ask you questions to determine which Golden Retriever puppy is right for your home.

or region, and contact her by either phone or e-mail. Depending on the information your coordinator gives you, you can then either e-mail or telephone the breeders themselves to learn more about any puppies they have.

Another way to find a breeder is to log onto the GRCA's listing of member clubs at http://www.grca.org/thegrca/member_clubs.html. There you'll find a searchable database of state and regional Golden Retriever clubs. Click on the appropriate links to get you over to one of these local club websites, and you're likely to find listings and contact information on breeders who belong to that club—either a breeder referral coordinator or an online listing of breeders who have litters available.

Some experts suggest attending a dog show and chatting up breeders there as a way of finding a new puppy. However, this method can be problematic. If you approach a breeder before her dog is scheduled to go around the ring and be judged, she may be too distracted to talk with you. If you wait until after the dog competes, though, the breeder may be packing up and getting ready to go home—and, again, be too distracted to answer your questions thoroughly.

The parents of the breeder's Golden puppies should be more than two years old.

What to Ask a Breeder

In your initial contact with the breeder, tell her that you're interested in welcoming a Golden Retriever puppy into your household, and ask whether she has any puppies available. If that's the case, the breeder will say so and is likely to ask you a few questions about your home, your lifestyle, and your dog-owning experience. Don't worry, though; you'll get a chance to ask questions too. Among those you should pose are the following:

Are the Parents of the Puppies More Than Two Years Old?

Parents who are younger than two years of age may lack the physical maturity necessary to sire or give birth to healthy puppies. Plus, a breeder who's not willing to wait until the parents are at least that age may be more interested in making money than in raising healthy Golden Retriever puppies.

How Many Litters Do You Breed Each Year?

A breeder who raises more than two or three litters a year may be breeding more for profit than to improve the breed.

Do the Parents Have Final Health Clearances?

Because Golden Retrievers—like all purebred dogs—have some inherited health challenges, conscientious breeders have their dogs evaluated for possible problems before they breed them. If the evaluation determines that the dogs don't have these problems, the evaluating organization issues clearances certifying that the dog is healthy. Clearances for Goldens should include one from the Orthopedic Foundation for Animals (OFA) certifying that the dog's hips and elbows are normal, or the University of Pennsylvania Hip Improvement Program (PennHIP), which can also issue hip (but not elbow) evaluations. The dogs should also receive clearances from the Canine Eye Registry Foundation (CERF) certifying that the dog's eyes are problem-free. In addition, a breeder should have breeding dogs evaluated for sub-aortic stenosis (SAS) by a veterinary cardiologist.

How Many Years Have You Been a Breeder?
Ideally, your breeder has had plenty of experience raising Golden Retriever puppies. If the breeder responds that this is her first litter, ask who is mentoring the breeder—that is, providing advice on how to breed Goldens. A response that includes the names of experienced Golden breeders should offset the breeder's own inexperience, at least to some extent.

How Do You Raise Your Puppies?
The ideal answer here is "In the house with my family." Home-raised puppies are likely to be better socialized than those raised in outdoor kennels.

What Do You Charge for Puppies?
Be prepared for sticker shock here. A pet-quality Golden Retriever puppy from a good breeder is likely to cost between $1,000 and $1,500. A show-quality Golden will probably cost considerably more.

Do You Guarantee the Health of Your Puppies?
A reputable breeder will allow you to return a puppy for a full refund (or if you prefer and one is available, a replacement puppy) if a post-purchase vet check within about one week reveals that the dog has a serious medical condition. Such guarantees should be included in the purchase contract.

What the Breeder May Ask You
The breeder is likely to ask you some questions too. Don't be offended by any of these queries, even if they seem a little personal. The breeder simply wants to determine whether one of her puppies would be a good fit for you and your family. Among the questions asked may be:

Why Do You Want a Dog?
There are lots of right answers here, such as wanting to give and receive unconditional love; wanting to have someone to nurture; and wanting company. Wrong answers include

Your new Golden puppy will need plenty of outdoor exercise.

wanting to teach the kids responsibility (they shouldn't be practicing on a helpless dog) and looking for protection (there are better ways to protect one's property than trying to turn a dog into a living security system).

Why Are You Interested in a Golden Retriever?

The answer to this question will help the breeder determine whether you understand and appreciate the Golden's unique temperament and needs.

Have You Owned a Dog Before?

It's okay if your answer here is no. Your response simply gives the breeder an important clue as to what type of dog is best for you. If you haven't had a dog before, the breeder is likely to pick the calmer puppy for you rather than a more energetic, challenging one.

How Will You Exercise the Dog?

Good answers: playing with him in our fenced yard so that he can run; taking him for long hikes; teaching him canine sports. Bad answer: letting him out in the morning to run around the neighborhood.

Do You Have Children—If Yes, How Old Are They?

This is another question where the answer simply helps the breeder pick the right puppy for you. That said, she may hesitate to sell you a dog if your children are under the age of six because 1) children that age need closer supervision around dogs than many parents can give, and 2) a big, exuberant Golden could easily knock a small child over.

Does Your Living Situation Permit a Dog?

In other words, does your lease allow you to have a dog in your apartment? There's only

When selecting a dog from the breeder, ensure that he has a healthy skin and coat.

one right answer here: yes. And you should be prepared to show the breeder written documents indicating that you either own your home or that your landlord allows you to keep a dog who will reach an adult Golden's size.

How Many Hours a Day Will the Dog Be Alone?

A puppy who's home alone all day while everyone is at school or work is going to be a very unhappy puppy. A good breeder will want the puppy's new home to have people around for at least some of the work day. If you can't provide that kind of company for a puppy, the breeder is likely to suggest that you consider looking for an older dog and perhaps a different, less people-oriented breed.

Who Will Be the Dog's Primary Caregiver?

If the answer is "my kids," don't be surprised if the breeder says that she won't sell any of the puppies to you. Although children can and should participate in a dog's care, a responsible adult needs to be a puppy's main caregiver, no matter what the child's age is.

Where Will Your Dog Sleep at Night?

The breeder wants to know whether you understand that Goldens need lots of human company. The ideal answer is "in my room with me." Not so okay is "in the kitchen" or "in the basement."

How Do You Feel About Training Classes?

The answer should be a resounding "Just fine, as long as the trainer uses positive methods." No matter what his age, every dog lives more happily with people when he has at least a little training in basic manners—but that training needs to be given in a gentle, dog-friendly manner with no harsh corrections or aversive practices.

Visiting the Breeder

Once you and your breeder answer each other's questions to your mutual satisfaction, you can make an appointment for a visit. At the breeder's place, you should be able to meet the puppy's mother and see the litter. The breeder should allow you to interact with any available puppies if they are old enough to have had their first puppy shots. As you do, check for the following:

Clear, Bright Eyes

Make sure that the puppy can follow a moving object with his eyes; failure to do so may indicate blindness. Look, too, for discharge or cloudiness, both of which may signal an infection or other eye problem.

By the Numbers

Golden Retriever puppies are usually ready to go home with their permanent owners at around eight weeks of age.

Dry, Odorless Ears

If the puppy's ears smell like bread, they may have a yeast infection; other odors also may indicate that infection is present. Check for deafness, too, by clapping your hands to see whether the pup responds to the sound.

Healthy Skin and Coat

A puppy shouldn't have any scabs or dirt on the skin, nor bald spots on his coat. Check the mother, too. Although she probably won't be sporting her usual gorgeous Golden tresses (nursing a litter takes a lot out of a gal!), she should also have no scabs, bald spots, or rashes. Check for fleas (little dark specks that hop around on the coat) as well; if the mother or the puppies have them, they may not have gotten the level of care they should have.

Normal Movement

Watch to see how each puppy moves. If one limps or seems to lack energy, he may have health problems that you probably don't want to take on.

Sound Temperament

Even happy-go-lucky Golden Retrievers have their own special personalities. Some are more reserved than others; some are more active than others; some are more people-oriented than others. Look for a puppy who's curious enough to approach you but calm enough to not be bouncing off the walls when you interact with him.

Documents and Guarantees

When you pick up your Golden Retriever puppy from the breeder's, you won't be bringing home just your puppy; you'll be bringing home some papers too. The documents you bring should include:

The Contract

Your breeder should give you a copy of the contract you signed when you placed a deposit on your puppy. The contract should not only specify the puppy's purchase price but also include a health guarantee, requirements to spay or neuter the pup by a certain age (if you and your breeder don't intend to the show the dog), and requirements to return the pup to the breeder if you find that you can't keep him for any reason.

Registration Papers

If the puppy's parents are registered with the AKC, the breeder should give you a signed AKC litter registration certificate that you can use to register the puppy. This will include the puppy's breed, date of birth, sex, AKC registered names of the parents, AKC number, the breeder's name, date that the puppy was sold to you and the breeder's signature. AKC registration allows your puppy to compete in AKC events such as agility, obedience, field trials, and tracking. The fee you pay to register your puppy helps to support AKC-funded research and other activities sponsored by the organization.

The Pedigree

The breeder should also include a copy of your puppy's pedigree—or put another way, his family tree. By reading the pedigree from left to right, you can see the names of your new puppy's parents, grandparents, and even great-grandparents and beyond, depending on how many generations the pedigree includes.

Health Records

A copy of your puppy's health records—including date of birth, visits to the veterinarian, and immunizations—should be among the papers your breeder gives you. Bring the health records to your own veterinarian when you bring your puppy for his first checkup, which should take place within a few days of his arrival in your household. The records will then become part of your puppy's permanent health file.

Help keep your new Golden out of trouble by puppy-proofing your home and yard.

If you plan to exercise your Golden in your backyard without a leash, you'll need secure fencing.

Health Clearances

In addition to health records, the breeder should give you copies of all of the health clearances of the puppy's parents.

Care Instructions

The breeder should also provide written instructions on basic puppy care, including when and how much to feed him, plus a small amount of his regular dog food to help you get started.

BEFORE YOUR PUPPY COMES HOME

Now that you've picked your puppy, you may think that you can sit back and relax until the day comes when you can bring him home. Think again.

Now's the time to prepare yourself and your home for the arrival of the newest family member. Here's how to do just that.

Puppy-Proof Your House and Yard

If you have children, you know all about baby-proofing your home. You studied your home carefully, looking for hazards that could spell trouble for your child if the child started messing around with them. You installed door guards on the cabinets where your cleaning products are kept, placed child-proof locking devices on toilet seat lids, and put covers on electrical outlets. You knew that taking such steps would maximize the odds that a curious, mobile baby or toddler would stay safe.

The same principle applies when preparing your home for a new puppy's arrival. Before he crosses your threshold, you need to study your home's layout and remove as many hazards as possible, or at least keep them out of his reach.

Indoors

Start by conducting a sweep of the inside of your home. That means getting down on all fours and crawling around every room of your house so that you can get a puppy's-eye view of the mischief-triggering items those rooms contain. Among the items you should stash: shoes, socks, underwear, kids' toys, books, and magazines—all of which will be shredded or swallowed if they come into contact with your puppy's teeth.

Next, look for items that your puppy can get into, and block off his access to them. Put open wastebaskets up on bookshelves. Block off the kitchen garbage can with chairs, or install a lid guard. Close your bathroom doors, and for good measure, install toilet lid locks. Put covers on your electrical outlets and install door guards on your kitchen cabinets. Additionally, pay special attention to dangling electrical cords. A curious Golden Retriever might find such objects way too interesting to resist chewing—with potentially disastrous results. Finally, block off access to staircases until your Golden puppy has learned to navigate the stairs. Close any doors that lead to flights of stairs; if that's not possible, place baby gates at both ends of the staircase.

Outdoors

The outside of your house needs attention too. First, if you plan to exercise your Golden outdoors in your back yard without a leash, you need to invest in secure fencing—installed by either you or a fencing professional. Make sure, too, that the fencing doesn't contain any crevices or openings that your puppy can slip through.

You might be tempted to install an electronic fence, which can be much less expensive and certainly looks much nicer. After a technician installs underground wiring on your property, you buckle an electronic collar around your dog's neck. If your dog crosses the area of your property where the wiring is installed,

he receives a mild electric shock. However, most experts don't recommend these fences, for two reasons. First, your dog may decide to venture across your property anyway but then refuse to come back so that he doesn't receive a second shock. The second reason is that dogs, other animals, and people can enter your yard freely, but your Golden can't escape unless he's willing to risk being shocked. This means that your dog is much more vulnerable to being attacked by an animal or stolen by a person than he would be without the fence.

Setting Up A Schedule

Raising a Golden Retriever puppy can be chaotic. He's curious about everything, and he's speedy enough to get into mischief in a matter of seconds if you don't keep a close eye on him. He doesn't know about proper bathroom behavior and thus may initially consider your entire house to be his personal potty. And he's just a baby, so that means that he needs plenty of opportunities to eat, drink, sleep, and exercise. How do you keep your sanity while attending to his needs? The answer is simple: Create a schedule.

The schedule will help you organize the many tasks that go into raising a young Golden and will help him make a smooth transition

Multi-Dog Tip

As cute as they are, refrain from buying two Golden Retriever puppies at the same time. Caring for two mischievous puppies requires more effort than you expect—and for all your work, they might bond more closely to each other than to you.

Figure 2.1

7:00 a.m	get up, take puppy to potty spot, put puppy in crate
7:30 a.m	feed puppy, offer water, take puppy to potty spot, play with puppy for 15 minutes, put puppy in crate for a nap
mid-morning	offer water, take puppy to potty spot, play with puppy for 15 minutes, put puppy in crate for a nap
noon	feed puppy, offer water, take puppy to potty spot, play with puppy for 15 to 30 minutes, put puppy in crate for a nap
mid-afternoon	offer water, take puppy to potty spot, play with puppy for 15 minutes, put puppy in crate for a nap
5:30 p.m.	feed puppy, offer water, take puppy to potty spot, play with puppy up to one hour and/or let him hang around with the family in the kitchen
7:00 p.m.	take puppy to potty spot, play with puppy for 15 minutes, put puppy in crate for a nap
Before bed	take puppy to potty spot, put puppy in crate
During the night	take puppy to potty spot if necessary

from his breeder's house to yours. By creating and following a schedule, you'll know when to feed, potty, and play with your Golden puppy—and your consistency in following that schedule will help him learn some of the lessons (like housetraining) he needs to learn to live happily ever after with you.

The best way to organize the schedule is to focus on when your Golden needs a potty break. Generally a puppy less than four months of age needs access to his bathroom first thing in the morning, after naps, after meals, after play sessions, and last thing at night. He may also need a middle-of-the-night break until he's three months old or so.

With those imperatives in mind, you can create a schedule something like that in Figure 2.1. Bear in mind that for the first week or two, your young Golden puppy may not be able to hold his pee and poop for even a couple of hours; in fact, he may need hourly breaks. He will probably also need middle-of-the-night breaks. The good news is that this seemingly perpetual pottying won't last for very long—as he grows, he'll need fewer trips to his bathroom. Chapter 4 offers detailed instructions on how to housetrain your puppy.

Supplies

Every Golden Retriever needs some special gear to feel truly at home—and you'll be one step ahead of the game if you shop for that gear now, before he crosses your threshold. Your shopping list for your puppy should include the following:

Bed

For the first couple of months, the only bed your puppy will need will be the pad you put in the bottom of his crate. (Getting a waterproof pad is a very good idea.) Once he's learned trustworthy bathroom behavior, consider buying him a soft, cushiony bed with a washable cover that will accommodate his stretched-out adult size.

Cleaning Products

No matter how hard you work to housetrain your Golden, he will have accidents. When that happens, you need to use a cleaning product that's especially designed to remove pet stains and odor. Look for a product that says "enzymatic cleaner" or otherwise indicates that it's been formulated specifically to eliminate the residue of puppy accidents.

Clicker and Treats

You'll want to start teaching your puppy basic doggy manners as soon as possible once he settles in, and having a clicker (a small device that makes a clicking sound when you press it) and some tasty treats makes that teaching a whole lot easier. Chapter 4 provides detailed information on clicker training and how it works.

Collar

Every dog needs a collar to hold an identification tag, a rabies inoculation tag, license tag, and leash. Although stores offer plenty of collar styles to choose from, keep things simple for now

Opt for either a soft nylon or thin leather collar that buckles or snaps. To determine your dog's collar size, just wrap a tape measure fairly loosely around his neck. Add 2 inches (5 cm) to the measurement and bingo! You have his collar size.

Crate

No, a crate is not a cage, and it's not cruel to use one. The crate can be your Golden Retriever's best friend—and yours, too, while you're undertaking the all-important housetraining process. For a fast-growing Golden puppy, your best bet is to purchase a crate that's big enough to accommodate his adult size. Make sure, though, that the crate comes with a divider, which will enable you to adjust the size of your puppy's living area within the crate as he grows.

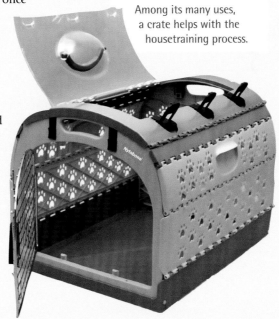

Among its many uses, a crate helps with the housetraining process.

The Doggy Seat Belt

Just as people need seat belts to improve their odds of surviving a car crash, so does your dog. Canine seat belts utilize your car's seat belt system to give your dog the same protection that you get whenever you buckle up. Try to get a seat belt that doesn't have a plastic clasp; such clasps can shatter if your car is hit hard from behind and your dog is sitting in the back seat.

Food

In the beginning, you'll need a week's supply of dog food. Find out what your breeder has been feeding your puppy, and lay in a week's supply of the same. You may decide to change his diet later, but for now his tummy will be happier (and thus your floors will be cleaner) if you keep him on the same food that the breeder's been giving him.

Food and Water Bowls

Your puppy needs two dishes—one for food and the other for water. The best material for such dishes is stainless steel because they're dishwasher safe and can't be damaged by your teething puppy's choppers.

Grooming Gear

For now, your Golden Retriever puppy needs a slicker brush, a mild shampoo formulated specifically for dogs, and doggy nail clippers. Later, when your puppy matures into an adult and develops that glorious trademark Golden coat, you may want to invest in additional grooming equipment. You'll also need a soft toothbrush and a tube of toothpaste made especially for dogs. (Toothpaste for people can upset a dog's stomach.)

Identification

As soon as you know what you're going to name your puppy, invest in an identification tag that contains his name, address, and phone number. You should also plan to have a microchip inserted under his skin during one of his first visits to his veterinarian. The microchip number is entered onto a nationwide registry that helps ensure that if your dog becomes lost, he'll be returned to you.

Leash

Every dog who travels in public places needs a leash to keep him safely tethered to his people. Here again, stores offer lots of different leashes, but your best bet is a 6-foot (2-m) leather leash. Nylon leashes are cheaper, but if your dog pulls and the leash crosses your hand, the nylon leash could leave a nasty abrasion on your palm. Leather is easier on the hands, and it lasts longer too. Retractable leashes are a bad idea for several reasons: They're difficult to control, they encourage dogs to pull, and they can be dangerous to human pedestrians.

Toys

Every Golden Retriever puppy needs toys, but you don't have to buy anything fancy, and you don't need to buy a lot of them either. Empty plastic milk cartons make great toys because they're noisy and bounce around crazily; fleecy toys are great for gumming and cuddling up with; and nylon bones, like Nylabones, are terrific for teething and chewing. Avoid toys that are very small, made of rope (pieces can get caught in the puppy's digestive tract) or that have squeakers (because the puppy can remove the squeaker and swallow it).

BRINGING YOUR PUPPY HOME

At last the big day has arrived: You're bringing

Bringing your new Golden home will be an exciting event for the entire family.

your new puppy home from the breeder. And you're ready with all of the proper equipment, not to mention a puppy-proofed home and yard. You're probably excited and eager to bring home your new family member.

Time-out. Before you go rushing off to the breeder's to bring home your new puppy, put yourself in his paws. Yes, he's starting a wonderful new life with you, but he doesn't understand that. For him, this day will mean that he's suddenly without his mother, littermates, and the human caregiver he's known for his entire life, however short that life has been so far. He may be confused,

disoriented, or even frightened as he tries to understand and deal with what's happening to him. Your job is to help him make his way through this transition and realize that he has a lot to look forward to. That job starts by bringing along the right equipment for the car ride home, including:

- Car Restraint: He's too little to put in a seat belt, but consider buying or borrowing an inexpensive plastic crate to use for the ride home. Place him in the crate, and then secure the crate with a seat belt in the back seat of your car.

Be patient with your Golden puppy as he adjusts to his new life in your home; this young puppy is still adjusting to life at the breeder's.

- **Chew Toy:** Your Golden Retriever may be just a puppy, but he's still a Golden Retriever. This means that he's very oral. A toy to chew on, like a Nylabone, will help release those oral urges and distract him from any stress he's feeling as he makes the trip from old home to new.
- **Leash and Collar:** If your puppy needs a bathroom break on the way home, having him on leash will ensure that he doesn't use the occasion to take off for parts unknown.
- **Paper Towels:** You'll be glad that you brought along a roll of paper towels if your puppy becomes carsick on the way home. And if he makes a pit stop, use a paper towel to gently wipe his bottom and place that paper towel in a plastic bag. You'll use that soiled paper towel to start housetraining him as soon as

you get home.
- **Plastic Bags:** You'll use one to place his soiled paper towel and the other to clean up any poop he produces on the way home.
- **Treats:** You should have one or two treats on hand. You'll use these for when you arrive home.

Once you and your puppy arrive at your home, take him to an area of your yard that you've designated for his outdoor potty area. Place that soiled paper towel on the ground and let him sniff it. He's very likely to eliminate right on top of that paper towel. When he does, praise him gently but enthusiastically and give him one of those treats. Praise yourself, too, for starting to housetrain him before you even enter your home!

Once you enter your home, let him explore

for a little while, and keep other family members from fussing too much over him. Watch to see whether he needs another bathroom break; signs include a sudden halt in whatever he's doing, circling, intense sniffing, or even beginning to squat. If he shows any such behavior, whisk him outside to the spot where he pottied before. When he does his business on that spot, gently praise him again and give him the other treat.

WHAT TO EXPECT THE FIRST FEW DAYS

The most important thing to keep in mind during these next few days is that your new Golden Retriever puppy is trying to make sense of a world that for him has been turned upside down. Start implementing your schedule right away, and keep things as low-key as possible. Spend time with him, but give him time on his own too—like being in his crate to nap.

For the first few nights he's in your home, your puppy is likely to cry—especially the first night. And who can blame him?

He's lonely, and he's missing the warmth and comfort of snuggling with his littermates. To put an end to his nighttime yodeling, empathize with him. Bring him and his crate into your bedroom. That will reassure him that he's not alone. If he continues to cry, bring him and his crate right up to your bed so that the door faces the bedside. Then dangle your fingers in front of the door so that he can sniff them. He will probably quiet down once he's assured that you're close by.

However, if your puppy's cries awaken you in the middle of the night, he probably needs a potty break. Put on your shoes, bathrobe, and (if necessary) a coat and take him to his potty spot. Gently praise him, but then bring him back inside and put him back in his crate. Don't stop to play or frolic unless you want him to get in the habit of demanding a play session at 2:00 a.m.!

CHAPTER 3

CARE OF YOUR GOLDEN RETRIEVER PUPPY

Now your great adventure begins—sharing your life with your Golden Retriever puppy! Your job is to help him grow up into the healthiest, happiest dog he can possibly be, starting with taking good physical care of him, day in and day out. But this job need not be a chore—in fact, it shouldn't be. Just as a mother bonds with her baby by feeding him, changing him, and attending to his other needs, so will you as you meet the needs of your puppy. This chapter will show you how to do just that.

FEEDING A PUPPY

Your puppy needs to eat a nutritious, healthful diet to grow up to be the gorgeous adult Golden Retriever he's meant to be. However, providing him with such fare involves a little more than simply ripping open a bag of kibble and pouring it into his dish. A fast-growing Golden Retriever puppy needs the right kind of food to fuel that growth, and he needs to get that food in the right amounts—not too little but not too much either.

Am I Feeding a High-Quality Food?

How do you know that a food is of high quality? Such food almost certainly lists a meat protein—most commonly beef or chicken—as the first ingredient on the label. That protein should be true meat, not meat by-products, bone meal, or any other derivatives. Pay attention, too, to the nutrients listed on the label. For young Golden Retriever puppies, the protein content should be at least 25 percent.

In addition, some breeders and veterinarians suggest avoiding a food that's high in calcium and phosphorus. The reason is that excessive amounts of those ingredients could lead to bone and joint problems later.

Your Golden needs a nutritious diet to grow up to be a healthy adult.

That said, there are no hard and fast rules about what to feed your little Golden. Any feeding guidelines need to take his age, size, and other factors into account. Here's what you need to know to feed your puppy right.

What to Feed a Puppy

For at least the first week or so that your puppy is home, you should feed him the same food that the breeder was giving him. After all, making the transition from one home to another is stressful enough for your puppy without his having to deal with the added challenge of adjusting to a sudden change in his diet. Moreover, if the breeder's been feeding a high-quality dry puppy food, you might not need to make any changes at all, at least for the next several months.

Although dry dog food, also known as kibble, may not seem very appetizing, you should nevertheless resist the temptation to add table scraps to such fare in an effort to jazz it up. Instead, moisten the kibble with a little water so that it makes a rich gravy.

If you have any doubts about the food the breeder's been feeding your puppy, consult your veterinarian. Make any switches gradually, mixing the new food with the old over a period of seven to ten days.

Consult your veterinarian about whether to continue feeding your Golden Retriever puppy food as he nears his four-month birthday.

Although some vets advocate feeding puppy food to young dogs up until they are a year old or even longer, others suggest switching Golden Retrievers and other large-breed puppies over to an adult food between four and six months of age. Proponents of this switch maintain that continuing to feed a higher-protein-content food to older puppies will cause them to grow too quickly, which could lead to orthopedic problems later in life.

How Much to Feed a Puppy

As for how much to feed your puppy, ask your breeder how much food she's been feeding him and his littermates. From there, take a look at the manufacturer's suggestions for how much to feed your puppy per day—and feed a little less than what's suggested. Manufacturers

Ask your breeder how much food has been fed to your dog and his littermates.

In the beginning, your puppy will have to be fed multiple times a day, just as he was at the breeder's.

are sometimes generous in the portions they suggest feeding dogs—which stands to reason because they are in the business of making and selling pet food. That knowledge and the realization that you'll be using treats to encourage your dog to try everything from being trained to being groomed should prompt you to scale back the portions you feed to your puppy. That said, monitor your puppy carefully. If he starts looking too thin, adjust his portions accordingly.

When to Feed a Puppy

Although puppies need plenty of high-quality food to fuel their rapid growth, they don't need unlimited quantities of such food. That's one reason why most experts discourage making food available 24/7. But that's not the only reason to just say no to this practice, also known as free-feeding. Another reason is that a food-loving Golden whose bowl is always full is likely to become not-so-pleasingly plump. Still another problem is that because it's difficult to monitor how much the free-feeder is eating, it's equally difficult to figure out when that free feeder needs a bathroom break. Finally, that same difficulty in monitoring food intake makes it tougher for the owner to determine when her dog has lost his appetite—and appetite loss is often an initial sign of illness.

That's why, instead of free-feeding, it's better to feed your puppy at the same times each day, every day. A puppy who's 8 to 16 weeks old needs three meals per day: breakfast, lunch, and dinner, along with fresh water at each meal. As for how much to feed at each meal, just give him one third of a full day's ration each for breakfast, lunch and dinner.

Once your puppy reaches 16 weeks of age, you can switch him over to a twice-daily feeding regimen: one meal in the morning and one meal in the later afternoon or early evening. And keep feeding him twice a day for the rest of his life. Although moving him to a once-daily feeding routine at one year of age is acceptable, the dog who eats twice a day is apt to be better behaved during the day, particularly during the latter part of the day, simply because he hasn't had to wait nearly 24 hours for his next meal.

No matter what age he is, though, make sure that your puppy's mealtime is a relaxing time. Children (or for that matter, adults) should not disturb your Golden while he eats. After a meal, take him outside to potty and then let him take a nap. Bypass strenuous exercise; such activity within an hour after a meal can lead to the very dangerous, often fatal condition called bloat, or gastric dilation volvulus (GDV).

GROOMING A PUPPY

You might think that because your puppy is probably just a little fuzz ball right now (although undoubtedly a very cute one), grooming him is not important or even really necessary. But nothing could be further from

With treats and lots of praise, your Golden puppy should learn to enjoy being groomed.

the truth. Good grooming, right from the start, is crucial to the health and well-being of your puppy for a number of reasons.

Why Grooming is So Important

First, grooming your little Golden gives you a chance for the two of you to spend some quality bonding time together. He can relax and enjoy your gently touching and examining him, and you can enjoy his snuggling up to you, offering his belly for a scratch or rub and gazing up at you adoringly. At its best, grooming your Golden can be a two-way love fest.

Second, grooming provides a golden opportunity for you to give your puppy a health check. As you run your hands over his

Training Tidbit

To further accustom your puppy to being touched, examined, and groomed, perform these activities at a quiet time of day. In the evening while you're watching television is ideal.

body and check his fur, you can be on the alert for possible health problems ranging from unexpected lumps to unwelcome signs of fleas. Many canine health problems are much more easily solved if those problems are caught early.

Finally, grooming detangles hair and removes dead hair. Such removal not only reduces shedding (a constant issue in households where Golden Retrievers live) but also stimulates the dog's oil glands, which helps the coat to shine. Of course, brushing your Golden Retriever is just the tip of the grooming iceberg. Like any other breed, a Golden needs weekly ear cleanings, weekly or biweekly nail trims, periodic baths, and daily dental care, all of which are covered in Chapter 6. If all of this grooming seems like a lot of work to you, consider the time you spend grooming yourself (daily shower, hair cleansing and styling, clothing care, nail trims, skin care, etc.). Grooming your Golden will consume a fraction of that amount of time. Doesn't he deserve that?

Grooming Supplies

For now, you don't need much in the way of grooming supplies for your puppy. Start with the following:

- child's soft toothbrush or a toothbrush made for dogs
- mild shampoo formulated especially for dogs
- nail clipper or grinder
- slicker brush
- toothpaste for dogs
- treats

Later, as your Golden Retriever puppy grows up and that fuzzy coat morphs into glorious golden tresses, you'll need to add to that equipment. But for now, that short shopping list is all you need to worry about.

Getting a Puppy Used to Grooming

The benefits of grooming that are so apparent to you may not be as obvious to your puppy. For that reason, it's a good idea to pair grooming sessions with items that your puppy will clearly enjoy—chiefly, treats.

When you want to examine your puppy's nails, touch one and then give him a tiny treat. When you peek inside his ears to make sure that he doesn't have an infection, give him another. Need to lift his lip slightly to look at his teeth or to brush them? Slip him another goodie immediately afterward. As you gently brush his downy puppy coat, let him take a treat from your hand.

The idea here is for your puppy to associate grooming with the occurrence of something pleasant, such as scoring a tasty tidbit. If you're

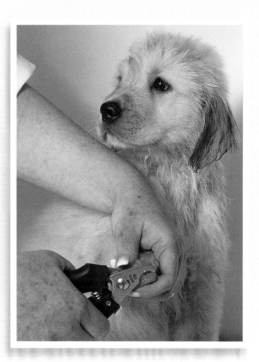

Accustom your Golden to having his nails clipped slowly, one step at a time.

consistent in this practice, your puppy will soon start looking for treats as soon as he sees his brush in your hand.

All these introductory tasks have the following elements in common: starting slowly, keeping sessions short, and using treats liberally. By being patient and not rushing the introductions now, you'll make grooming your adult Golden Retriever a lot easier in the months and years to come.

Later in life, your adult Golden may need more frequent grooming or even the services of a professional groomer. But for now, here's what you should do every day:

Brush the Coat

Use your slicker brush to gently brush your puppy's coat in the direction that the fur grows. After every couple of strokes, feed him a tiny treat. As he becomes accustomed to being brushed and clearly begins to enjoy this activity for its own sake, you can begin scaling back the treats.

Check His Ears

At this point in his life, your puppy shouldn't need any serious ear cleaning unless he either has an infection or makes a habit of rolling in the dirt or mud. All you need to do for now is to lift his ear flap gently, give him a treat, and look for dirt inside the outer ear. As you do, give him another tiny treat. Then lean a little closer, sniff his ear (yes, really), and give him another tiny treat. The ear should have little to no odor; if your puppy's ears smell like bread that's baking in the oven or if they exhibit a truly foul odor, he probably has an ear infection. Call your vet immediately

Ear infections can be very painful to a puppy or dog, and if left untreated, can result in permanent hearing loss.

Do His Nails

Persuading your puppy to accept a pedicure can take a little time and patience. It's worth taking the time to perform this exercise in persuasion slowly and deliberately, with many tiny treats to help the two of you along the way. Begin by getting him accustomed to having his feet touched with your hand, then with the clipper or grinder, and be sure to feed him a small treat every time you touch his foot with either your hand or the instrument. Only when he readily accepts having his nails touched with the clipper or grinder should you attempt to clip his nails—and then only one nail per session and with many treats along the way.

Brush His Teeth

Time and patience are also important when introducing your puppy to getting his teeth cleaned. Begin by wrapping your finger in some sterile gauze, gently lifting his upper lip, and rubbing his gum for a few seconds, followed by a treat. Repeat on the other side and then end the session. Once he accepts your gauze-covered finger readily, add a little doggy toothpaste. Continue the gradual introduction

Multi-Dog Tip

If you own more than one dog, you know how hard it is to keep track of who's gone to the veterinarian when. Keeping written records of each dog's visit to the veterinarian and what occurred during those visits will help you remember which dog gets which medication or special diet. (Actually, this is a good idea for single-dog households too!)

until you're able to brush his teeth with a soft toothbrush and toothpaste.

HEALTH

Keeping your puppy healthy isn't something that you can do all by yourself. You need a partner who's an expert in detecting and treating animal illnesses and who's up on the latest research designed to keep puppies well. That partner, of course, is your veterinarian. This section deals with how to find a veterinarian, what your puppy's first visit to the vet will be like, and the health concerns your puppy is likely to encounter during his first year of life.

Finding a Vet

Ideally, you will have found a veterinarian before you bring your puppy home—but in case you haven't, now's the time to do so. That's because within a day or two of bringing your puppy home, you need to bring him to a vet for his first checkup. That checkup will, hopefully, be the start of a long and fruitful partnership between you and the vet as you both work to keep your puppy healthy and happy.

If you've already had a dog and are happy with the vet you have, you needn't look any further. But if you're new to your community, your Golden is your first pet, or you want to change vets, you need to find a new veterinary practitioner.

Get Some Names

Start by getting the names of a few veterinarians in your area. A good place to start is with your breeder. You can also check online at websites such as Yahoo! or Switchboard. com, in a hard-copy telephone book, or with local breed or kennel clubs. Another option is to search online at the American Animal Hospital Association (AAHA) website (www.

The right vet is crucial to your Golden's good health.

healthypet.com). The AAHA is a national organization that accredits animal hospitals throughout the United States and Canada. The website has a searchable database of animal hospitals that allows you to identify facilities near you.

Visit the Office

Once you've identified a couple of nearby animal hospitals, pay a visit to each. During each visit, try to get answers to the following questions:

- **What are the office hours?** A practice that's open only from 9 to 5 won't be very convenient for you if you're away from home for much of the day. A facility that opens early in the morning or stays open later in the evening, or one that opens on weekends might be a better choice.

- **What forms of payment do you accept?** If your Golden Retriever has an emergency that requires pricey intervention—for example, surgery to remove a sock that he has eaten, which can cost well over $1,000—a practice that accepts credit cards can be crucial.
- **What's the hospital like?** The hospital staff should be courteous and client-oriented (and that means to both the human and the animal clients).The hospital itself should be clean, orderly, and odor-free, except for perhaps a whiff of antiseptic.
- **Is the hospital close to your home?** The closer the hospital is to your home, the more likely you are to be conscientious about taking your puppy in for regular checkups, not to mention getting him to his vet if he's sick.
- **Does the staff keep current?** Veterinary medicine is perpetually changing; new treatments, techniques, and discoveries are constantly emerging. A good veterinarian and vet staff keep abreast of these changes, and clients can see evidence of that effort. Look for certifications and diplomas on the walls; those framed documents show that the vet is continuing her education by learning about new treatments such as laser surgery, which reduces a pet's postoperative pain and recovery time. Other diplomas can indicate that one or more vets in the practice are developing specialties, such as dentistry, internal medicine, or critical care. Finally, the facility itself should be certified; look for a certificate and/or seal that shows that the practice is a member of and has been certified by the AAHA.
- **Are there backup systems?** Ask what procedures are in place if your Golden has an after-hours emergency. Does the practice have a veterinarian on call? Can it refer you to an emergency clinic if necessary?

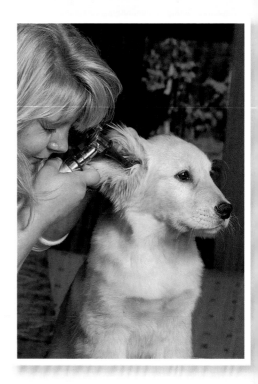

The first visit to the vet is an important one, especially because everyone is getting acquainted.

- **How quickly can the vet see you?** If you need to wait more than two or three days for an appointment, the practice may be too busy or have too few veterinarians to meet your needs. The same may be true if patients and their people consistently spend a lot of time in the waiting room or an exam room before a vet can see them.
- **Does the practice have electronic capability?** A computerized veterinary practice makes it much easier for you to safeguard your puppy's health. You can make appointments online and have access to your puppy's medical records. And by having your puppy's records online, the practice can e-mail you reminders of when your puppy is due for a checkup.

Want to Know More?

For detailed information on illnesses specific to Golden Retrievers, see Chapter 8: Golden Retriever Health and Wellness.

- **Are you comfortable?** Perhaps the most important question you can ask is whether you feel comfortable at the practice. You need to feel able to communicate with the veterinarian, ask any questions that come to mind, and understand the answers the vet gives you.

If the answers to these questions satisfy you, congratulations! By finding a good veterinarian, you've taken a giant step in maintaining your puppy's health. If you're not satisfied, don't settle—keep looking.

First Checkup

Once you've brought your Golden Retriever puppy home (or even before you do), one of your first orders of business should be to make an appointment with the veterinarian for the puppy's first checkup. Set the appointment for no later than 48 hours after your puppy's homecoming.

This first visit to the veterinarian is important for several reasons. First, the visit gives you and your puppy an opportunity to get acquainted with a person who will play a key role in safeguarding your dog's health, and it also gives the vet a chance to meet the two of you. Second, the exam that occurs during this visit

If your puppy is unusually lethargic, take him to the vet.

will allow your veterinarian to learn what your puppy is like when he is healthy, which gives her a baseline against which to compare any readings she takes during subsequent exams. Finally, the exam may uncover hidden health problems besetting your new canine companion, enabling you and your vet to begin solving those problems right away—or if you choose, to return the puppy to his breeder as specified in the purchase contract's health guarantee.

The get-acquainted process will go much faster if you bring your puppy's health records with you to give to the vet. These records will help the vet determine what shots and medications your dog will need, and they will be the foundation of your puppy's medical file. You should also bring a sample of your puppy's stool, which your vet will examine for the presence of parasites, such as worms.

In addition to examining your dog's health records and analyzing the stool sample, the vet probably also will:

- check his body for lumps, bumps, rashes, parasites, and signs of infection
- check the genitals (in males, to see whether both testicles are fully descended; in females, to make sure that there's no discharge from the vagina)
- check the gums and teeth for overall health and proper tooth formation
- listen to his heart and lungs
- look inside his ears for signs of parasites and infection
- measure his pulse and respiration
- peer into his eyes for signs of any abnormalities
- take his temperature
- weigh him

If the stool sample reveals the presence of parasites such as roundworms, hookworms, and whipworms, your veterinarian will prescribe a deworming medication that will rid your puppy of these unwelcome freeloaders. It's important to eliminate worms because they can deplete your puppy's energy and health—and he can also transmit those critters to you. More information about these and other parasites is in Chapter 8.

Vaccinations

Your puppy will also need immunizations to protect him from serious diseases—although, depending on his age, he may not receive those immunizations during this first visit. Many of these diseases are extremely serious, and because your puppy's immune system isn't strong enough to fight off such infections, his chances of survival are not good unless he's received protection from such diseases early in life. Here are some of the diseases that immunizations can protect your puppy from:

Bordetella

This bacterium tends to strike dogs who are in the company of a lot of other dogs, such as at a dog park, a doggy day care, a boarding facility, or a canine-centered event like a dog show, and causes a condition often referred to as kennel cough. Symptoms include a honking cough and discharge from the nose or eyes. Generally the condition isn't serious unless the dog also is lethargic, refuses to eat, or has a fever—which could indicate that he has a much more serious illness. Nevertheless, most doggy day cares, boarding kennels, and even dog training classes require proof of immunization against this condition, as well

The Distemper/Hepatitis/Leptospirosis/ Parainfluenza/Parvovirus (DHLPP) Vaccine

Generally, puppies receive immunization against distemper, hepatitis, leptospirosis, parainfluenza, and parvovirus in a single combined shot commonly called a DHLPP. Puppies receive this shot in a series. The first shot is generally given at around six to eight weeks of age, which means that your puppy should have received his first shot in the series while he was still with his breeder. Subsequent shots are given every three or four weeks until the puppy is around 14 to 16 weeks old. The initial rabies shot is usually given at 16 weeks of age. After this initial series of shots, you and your veterinarian can discuss how often your adult dog should receive immunizations.

as against more serious conditions, before a dog is allowed to enter the premises. The immunization does not always provide full protection but can certainly limit the severity of the symptoms.

Coronavirus

This very contagious virus affects the dog's digestive tract, resulting in diarrhea, vomiting, and depression that ranges from mild to very serious. The condition is particularly dangerous in young puppies because diarrhea and vomiting can deplete them very quickly. The condition can't be cured but may run its course over two to ten days.

Distemper

This deadly, highly contagious virus tends to strike unprotected young dogs. The condition also strikes wild animals such as skunks, foxes, and raccoons. Early symptoms include vomiting, diarrhea, fever, appetite loss, and eye inflammation. Such symptoms may lessen or even disappear after a few days, only to reappear—along with other symptoms such as pneumonia and neurological complications. Treatment focuses on containing the symptoms so that the dog's own immune system has a fighting chance against the disease.

Hepatitis

This highly contagious disease has symptoms that range from a slight fever and congestion of the mucous membranes to severe depression, a significant decrease in white blood cells, and prolonged bleeding time. The condition is especially serious in young puppies. Treatment focuses on giving supportive care to maximize the dog's chances of recovery.

Leptospirosis

This multi-strain bacterial disease mainly strikes unprotected dogs who drink water that's been contaminated by an infected wild animal. Symptoms include lethargy, fever, shivering, vomiting, and dehydration. Golden Retrievers and other dogs who enjoy outdoor activities, particularly swimming, might be especially vulnerable.

Immunization can protect from some strains for up to a year for one of the vaccines. Treatment consists of antibiotics, limiting exercise, and giving fluids.

Lyme Disease

The lowly deer tick is responsible for transmitting this condition to both dogs and people. A bite from an infected tick results in exposure but not necessarily illness; in fact, most infected dogs never become sick. However, those who do may exhibit unexplained joint pain and fever, weight loss, lethargy, decreased appetite, and chronic ear and eye infections that do not respond to medication. They will also test positive for the presence of antibodies, indicating exposure. Complications can include kidney damage. The condition is treatable with antibiotics and can be limited through the use of tick-controlling products.

Parainfluenza

Canine parainfluenza is sometimes mistaken for bordetella, or kennel cough, but is much more serious. Symptoms include not only a cough and discharge but also fever, lethargy, labored breathing, and appetite loss. Complications can include pneumonia, which can be fatal. Treatment focuses on giving an anti pertussis medicine to control the cough and perhaps also antibiotics.

Parvovirus

This extremely dangerous virus attacks the lining of a dog's digestive system, preventing the dog from absorbing nutrients. The result is bloody, foul-smelling diarrhea; fever; lethargy; and appetite loss. Without treatment, most dogs die from dehydration. Unprotected dogs can contract the disease through contact with the stool of an infected dog. Treatment consists of providing fluids and antibiotics, but it is not always successful.

Rabies

Today wild animals such as raccoons, bats, skunks, and foxes are much more likely than dogs to have this disease. That said, a bite from an infected wild animal can pass the disease to an unprotected dog, who in turn can pass the disease to you. Once symptoms appear in either the human or canine victim—in dogs,

those symptoms include erratic behavior and uncharacteristic aggressiveness—the disease is fatal, which is why almost every state in the United States requires that dogs and other pets be vaccinated against rabies. Puppies usually get their first rabies shots at around 16 weeks of age and a booster about one year later. After that, your dog will get a rabies shot every one to three years, depending on local laws.

PUPPY-SPECIFIC ILLNESSES

The immunizations listed in the previous section provide protection from most of the most serious illnesses that can beset young puppies and dogs. However, dogs in these age groups are also those who are most susceptible to other conditions that are usually less serious but also can't be prevented through immunization. These conditions include:

Demodex

Also known as red mange, follicular mange, puppy mange, and demodectic mange, this is a skin disease that primarily strikes young dogs. The cause is one of two types of demodex mites. Although such mites live on the skin of virtually every adult dog, some dogs' immune systems are too weak to keep the mite under control. In such cases, this imbalance results in lesions that feature hair loss, crusty red skin, and perhaps a greasy or moist appearance. The vast majority of dogs with demodex have mild cases and only a few localized lesions. These cases may resolve on their own as the puppy matures and his immune system strengthens. However, to speed the healing process, the veterinarian may prescribe topical treatments such as daily use of a benzoyl peroxide gel.

Other dogs, however, may suffer from a more generalized demodectic mange in which lesions appear all over the body. Such dogs may also suffer from inflamed, cracked skin that oozes a clear liquid. For these dogs, a veterinarian may prescribe periodic dips in an antiparasitic drug called amitraz. Antibiotics may also be given to combat the secondary skin infections that may accompany these more severe cases. Even these severe cases generally resolve, except in dogs with severely compromised immune systems.

Puppy Pyoderma

This condition, also known as puppy impetigo and juvenile pustular dermatitis, is a skin infection that usually causes small pimples and/or crusted areas to appear on the skin. Generally the infection is limited to the abdomen, under the front legs, or the chin.. The veterinarian may prescribe an antibiotic to treat bacteria that cause the infection, as well as an antibacterial spray or shampoo. Most cases resolve with such treatment, but stubborn cases may require further testing to determine whether an underlying condition is causing the problem.

Puppy Warts

Another common condition among puppies, warts are caused by the canine papilloma virus. The warts appear as small cauliflower-

Taking good care of your puppy will help him grow to be a healthy adult.

like growths on the lips or inside the mouth. They resolve on their own over several weeks without treatment, although if they become very large or interfere with the dog's ability to eat, a veterinarian may opt to freeze the warts and then remove them.

SPAYING AND NEUTERING

Spaying or neutering your Golden Retriever puppy carries plenty of advantages. If your puppy is a male, neutering eliminates the risk that he will die of testicular cancer (a very rare cancer) and reduces the risk that he'll suffer from an enlarged prostate, but it increases his risk of prostate cancer. From a behavioral viewpoint, neutering a male can reduce the risk that he'll mark your furniture with his urine and that he'll want to roam beyond your property.

Female dogs who are spayed also experience beneficial changes. Those spayed early in life—generally before their first or second heat cycle—have a greatly reduced risk of developing mammary cancer, which is the most common cancer among female dogs in general, although other cancers such as hemangiosarcoma are more common among female Golden Retrievers. And because the spaying procedure removes the dog's uterus, her chances of developing pyometra (an infection of the uterine cavity) are eliminated. Spayed female dogs no longer go into heat, or estrus, which means that you don't have to deal with the hassles of keeping intact male dogs away from your fertile female.

Finally, for both sexes, early spaying or neutering may be easier than if the procedure occurs later in life. The surgery is easier for

Ask your vet when it's the best time to spay or neuter your Golden.

veterinarians because there's much less fat in the abdominal cavity than may be the case for older animals, and younger animals are believed to recover more quickly and with less pain than might be the case with postoperative patients who have reached adolescence.

Risks

However, spaying and neutering are not without risk. As is the case with any other surgical procedure, the use of anesthesia can lead occasionally to fatal complications, although this already minimal risk is further reduced if the veterinarian runs blood tests on your dog beforehand.

Recent research also indicates that while spaying and neutering decrease the risk of some canine cancers, the procedures may increase the risk that a dog will develop others. One study has shown that dogs neutered before one year of age have a greater chance of developing osteosarcoma, or bone cancer. Another study showed that spayed female dogs could be at a higher risk of developing hemangiosarcoma, a cancer that Golden Retrievers are already more susceptible to than many other breeds. Early (pre-puberty) spaying and neutering before six months of age have

also been implicated in the development of cruciate ligament ruptures, a painful injury that often requires surgery and weeks of recuperation time. Other problems that are more likely to appear after early spaying or neutering include urinary incontinence in female dogs, hip dysplasia, and hypothyroidism. Usually such incontinence is easily treated with a short course of estrogen replacement. Hypothyroidism—a shortage of thyroid hormone that is quite common among adult Golden Retrievers—also is easily treated by giving the dog artificial hormones for the rest of his life.

What does this information mean for you if you don't plan to breed or show your puppy? The answers are not simple. By spaying or neutering your Golden Retriever puppy, you may be decreasing the risks that your Golden will develop some types of health problems, but you may be increasing the risks that he will acquire others—particularly if you have the procedure performed before he reaches adolescence. Ultimately, this is a question that you should discuss with your veterinarian. Together you can determine when's the best time to spay or neuter your Golden Retriever.

CHAPTER 4

TRAINING YOUR GOLDEN RETRIEVER PUPPY

A big part of taking care of your Golden Retriever puppy is training him—but training involves much more than simply taking him to a local obedience class. As much as trainers can teach you, in the end you are your puppy's primary teacher. And you can be the best teacher your Golden will ever have if you take the time to do the job right.

Doing it right doesn't mean that you have to make like a drill sergeant and take your puppy through the canine edition of army boot camp—in fact, as will become clear in this chapter, that's exactly what you *don't* want to do. Good, effective training simply means that you capitalize on the natural instincts and impulses your Golden Retriever already has and use those impulses to guide and direct his behavior. In this chapter you'll see how to do just that.

INTRODUCTION TO TRAINING

Some people don't want to teach or train their dogs to do anything. Perhaps they're reluctant to do so because they don't feel capable of doing the job—or if they're capable, they don't have the time. Others might feel that training a dog is unnatural and manipulative. Those in

the latter category may have a point if they're referring to training methods of yesteryear. Those methods involved coercion, physical manipulation, and at times, even (by today's definitions) mistreatment of the dog.

But using modern positive methods to train your Golden Retriever puppy is an entirely different story. Instead of physically forcing your dog to do something, you show him what you want him to do—and then reward him when he does so. This method is a win-win proposition because by doing something you want, your Golden gets something he wants.

Of course, getting what we want is not the only reason that training is important. Quite simply, dog training saves dogs' lives. A look at animal shelter statistics tells a sobering story. A study by the National Council on Pet Population Study and Policy showed that problem behaviors are the most common reason that people surrender their dogs to animal shelters—and that many such dogs are relinquished to shelters after spending less than three months with their families. Inevitably, some of those dogs are euthanized.

Clearly, then, early training is crucial to ensuring that your puppy grows up to be a well-behaved dog who will spend a long and

Positive training involves showing your dog what you want him to do and then rewarding him when he gets it right.

won't do so happily. Either way, attempting to force your Golden into submission could cause irreparable harm to your relationship with him. Presumably, you've brought your Golden into your life for companionship. That being the case, why would you want to do anything that would diminish that companionship?

Fortunately, there's a better way to train. It's called positive training, and its basic premise is to focus on showing the dog what you want him to do rather than correct him for what you don't want him to do. When your dog does what you want him to do, you reward him, usually with a treat; however, praise, affection and a short play session can also make good rewards.

A dog who's trained with positive methods behaves differently from a dog who's trained the old-fashioned way. The dog who's been reinforced for doing the right thing will work hard to continue such reinforcement. If he's received a treat for sitting when asked, he'll sit again in hopes of scoring another treat. If he's received some playtime for bringing you a tennis ball, he'll keep bringing that ball to you. You'll have an obedient dog, but you'll also have a happy dog who's eager to work with you and engage in new activities with you. In short, by training with positive methods, you'll be bringing out your Golden Retriever's true

happy life with you. And because your dog will grow up to be a big, energetic, sometimes even boisterous Golden Retriever, training during puppyhood is even more important—for both your sakes.

The Importance of Positive Training

But as mentioned earlier, not just any style of training will do. Old-fashioned methods, such as pushing on a dog's rear end to force him to sit or jerking on a leash to teach him to walk politely, don't work well with any dog, but they're especially counterproductive when training a loving, sociable Golden Retriever. Many Goldens will simply shut down—that is, they won't work with their people at all—when confronted with forcible training methods. Others may do what's asked, but they

Positive training uses rewards like treats to achieve the desired result.

nature—happy-go-lucky, sociable, trusting, and eager to be with his people.

Using Rewards

Speaking of positive training and treats, make sure that the treats you offer your puppy are truly tasty and can be broken into small pieces. For training, you need goodies that are especially flavorful so that you can offer your dog a strong incentive to learn—and they need to be breakable into small pieces so that he doesn't turn into a baby blimp during the training process. Tiny pieces of hot dog, canned chicken (drained), cheddar cheese, or meat-roll treats can all provide the incentive your puppy needs to do his best to learn basic good manners. The tastier and more aromatic the treat, the better.

Make sure that you teach any new behavior at a time when your dog is more likely to appreciate those treats. For just about any dog that time is just before mealtime. Because he will be hungry, he'll be more eager to work for the treats that he'll be rewarded with if he performs a behavior correctly.

Using a Clicker

Focusing on the positive without also dealing with the negative—in other words, mistakes—may seem, at least at first, to be a slow or even tedious way to train a dog. You might wonder whether there's some sort of shortcut or tool that helps a dog to instantly recognize that he's done the right thing and is about to be rewarded for it. There is:: It's called a marker. The marker can be either verbal, such as a happy exclamation of "Yes!," or physical, as in the use of a clicker. These days, positive trainers and dog owners alike are finding that the clicker can greatly accelerate the speed at which a dog learns basic good manners or anything else.

Your Golden's Training Environment

Any beginning student, whether human or canine, learns more quickly when he's in an environment with few distractions, if any. For that reason, start teaching any new behavior (what we used to call a command but now call a behavior or cue) in a quiet, distraction-free environment, such as in your home when no one else is around. Later, as your puppy becomes proficient in performing the behavior, you can add distractions, such as being outdoors or having other people milling around. Of course, if you're training outdoors, make sure that he's on the leash unless you're in a securely enclosed area.

The clicker is a small plastic box that's about 2 inches (5 cm) long and 1 inch (2.5 cm) wide. Depending on the way it's manufactured, it contains either a little button or small metal strip on top. By pressing the button or strip, the user produces a clicking noise. Consistent use of the clicker, followed immediately by a treat, will soon help the dog realize that he's just performed a behavior that will be rewarded.

Before you start using a clicker to train, however, you need to show your dog that the sound of the clicker means that goodies will follow. For that reason, your first clicker session with your puppy should be a simple click-and-treat session. Starting with the clicker behind your back (because the sound will be softer), click the clicker and immediately give your puppy a treat. Repeat this procedure until he starts looking for a treat as soon as he hears the

Finding a good dog trainer who uses positive methods is essential, but the whole family must continue training at home as well.

click. If your puppy is like most other Golden Retrievers, that won't take very long!

Remember, though: If you find using the clicker to be difficult (some people do have trouble juggling clicker, treats, and puppy), you can replace the clicker with a word. A good choice for such a word—or in trainer speak, a verbal marker—is "yes!" Avoid using the word "good" as a marker, though, because you're likely to use that word in many other situations. The verbal marker needs to be a word that you're not likely to use with your dog in any other context.

How to Find a Trainer

Finding a dog trainer is not all that difficult. Finding a dog trainer who's truly committed to positive training methods may be a little

bit more of a challenge. Fortunately, several organizations provide searchable online databases to help you begin your search for a positive trainer to help you work with your puppy—either in a group class or one-on-one session. Those organizations include:

- **Truly Dog Friendly** (www.trulydogfriendly. com): This organization was founded by a coalition of dog trainers and behavior consultants who were concerned about the use of electronic shock collars and other coercive equipment in dog training. The Truly Dog Friendly website includes a link to a searchable database of trainers who are committed to using gentle, pain-free methods to train dogs.
- **Association of Pet Dog Trainers (APDT)** (www.apdt.com): This organization, better known by its APDT acronym, boasts more than 6,000 members. Its primary missions are to educate trainers and to encourage trainers to use positive training methods. Like the Truly Dog Friendly site, the APDT site has a searchable database of trainers.
- **International Association of Animal Behavior Consultants (IAABC)** (http:// www.iaabc.org/Divsn/dog.php): This organization's dog division includes among its members not only dog trainers who teach group classes but also professionals who work one-on-one with dogs and their families to address specific problem behaviors. Although the organization does not specifically mention positive training methods, the member-written books listed on its website are all based on these principles.

Once you've identified a few trainers who live near you, your next step is to contact them to see whether their philosophies and services mesh with the needs of you and your dog. Here's what to ask them.

What Is Your Training Philosophy?

Today, most trainers will answer that question by saying "positive reinforcement"— but you shouldn't simply accept a canned answer. Even trainers listed on the websites mentioned earlier may, on occasion, resort to not-so-positive techniques. For that reason, it's a good idea to ask a trainer how she would address specific behaviors. For example, finding out how your prospective trainer will manage a dog who jumps on people can tell you a lot about that trainer's true philosophy. Some trainers will use their knees or the leash to correct the dog's jumping; others will try to teach the dog to seek attention not from jumping but through another action. You want a trainer who opts for the second approach.

What Equipment Do You Use?

The answer to this question will provide additional insight into a trainer's methods and philosophy. A trainer who uses choke chains, prong collars, electronic devices, or anything else that causes discomfort to the animal is not truly positive. Pain isn't necessary to train a dog.

By the Numbers

Don't believe any trainer who tells you to wait until your Golden Retriever puppy is six months old before you start training him. A puppy is never too young to start learning basic good manners. Start teaching him—in short, fun-filled sessions—as soon as you can after you bring him home.

What Is Your Background and Experience?

If a prospective trainer includes an acronym after her name, that means that the trainer has logged in hundreds of hours as a trainer and may have taken an examination to assess her knowledge. The three most common certifications are CPDT-KA (Certified Pet Dog Trainer-Knowledge Assessed), CDBC (Certified Dog Behavior Consultant), and CABC (Certified Animal Behavior Consultant). That said, don't automatically pass up a trainer who lacks such certification. Instead, ask how the trainer's knowledge was acquired. A trainer who claims to have been an apprentice for a positive reinforcement trainer or to have attended one or more behavior academies or seminars offered by such a trainer deserves your consideration.

May I Observe a Class?

Seeing a trainer in action can give you a good idea as to whether you and your dog will be comfortable working with that trainer well as identify the ratio of dogs to students. Ideally, that ratio should be no more than one instructor or assistant instructor for every six dogs. Pay attention to how the trainer explains and demonstrates concepts, deals with owners' questions during class, and handles disruptive dogs. See too whether everyone's having fun. Afterward, don't be afraid to ask some of the students what they think of the trainer and the class.

Do You Have References?

The prudent owner will get independent confirmation that the trainer's methods are what she says they are. Ask the trainer you're considering for references—and if you are given some, use them. (If the trainer won't provide references, cross her off your list.) Ask the people to whom the trainer has directed

Be sure to socialize your Golden to other dogs in a safe setting.

you about their dogs, what they learned, and whether they'd recommend the trainer's class or services.

Do You Offer Both Private and Group Classes?

A trainer who offers both group classes and private instruction may be more experienced and resourceful than a trainer who offers only group instruction. That said, trainers who specialize exclusively in at-home, one-on-one consults are also able to individualize their approaches to solving canine problem behaviors, so don't automatically reject an in-home trainer who doesn't conduct classes.

SOCIALIZATION

Your most important reason for acquiring a Golden Retriever puppy was probably to add a new and very special friend to your life, and you want to be the same for him. But if you are your dog's sole companion (other than other members of your household), and if he never goes anywhere except to the vet's, you may be jeopardizing his emotional health and well-being. That's because no matter how great the food is that you feed him, how cushy his bed is, or how much time you spend with him, he'll still be missing something that's crucial to his becoming a happy, well-adjusted dog. That missing element is a social life—and you need to be his social director.

But being your Golden Retriever's social director isn't very hard. You won't need to establish a Facebook or Twitter account for him, and you certainly don't need to get him his own iPhone or Blackberry. You don't need to overprogram him into a complex set of activities to which you must drive him all over creation. Instead, you simply need to expose your canine companion to people, pets, sights, sounds, and places beyond what's familiar to him in your home. This process—which should continue throughout your dog's life but is especially important to a puppy's mental and emotional development—is what experts call socialization.

What Is Socialization?

Simply put, socialization is the process in which a puppy or dog is consistently and frequently exposed to unfamiliar people, places, sights, sounds, and experiences.

A dog who is well socialized can take surprises in stride. He can face new experiences with poise and aplomb. Visitors to his home, a walk downtown, or a trip in the car to visit your parents are occasions to enjoy, not challenges to fear. In short, the well-socialized Golden Retriever is an easygoing, confident dog who is a pleasure to live with. By contrast, an unsocialized Golden can be difficult and perhaps even dangerous to live with. Without early, frequent, and consistent exposure to new people, places, and situations, your Golden is likely to be much more fearful than his socialized counterpart—all because he hasn't the opportunity to learn that new experiences can be good rather than bad.

If you're lucky, your fearful Golden will express his apprehension at confronting the unfamiliar by hiding behind you, in a corner, or under a piece of furniture. However, he could also react more actively by growling, snarling, or biting. This isn't because he's nasty or combative but because he's scared. To prevent such occurrences—and to ensure that both you and your Golden enjoy a rich, happy life together—you need to make sure that you enrich his life with lots of positive social experiences.

How to Socialize

Hopefully, your breeder has already begun your puppy's socialization process. Something as simple as a car ride to the veterinarian's office for that first round of puppy shots is a stimulating experience for a puppy and provides a good introduction to the world outside the breeder's home. Hopefully, too, the breeder has taken him outside the house so that he has had a chance to experience walking up and down steps (he needs to be taught how!) and to feel a variety of surfaces under his feet, such as concrete, mulch, and grass. The conscientious breeder should make sure that inside the home the puppy meets lots of people and learns to enjoy being handled and living in a family atmosphere.

Once you get your puppy home, though, you need to continue the socialization process.

Socialization involves introducing your Golden to a whole range of things and experiences.

Puppy Kindergarten

A great way to socialize your puppy is to take him to a puppy kindergarten class. A well-run puppy-K class will not only provide your puppy with a safe, controlled way to meet other puppies and people; it will also give you the chance to learn from an expert about puppy behavior in general and how to handle your puppy in particular.

Starting a search for a good puppy kindergarten class is similar to starting a search for a good trainer. Log onto websites such as Truly Dog Friendly (www.trulydogfriendly.com) and the Association of Pet Dog Trainers (APDT) (www.apdt.com), and search their databases for trainers who offer group classes. Once you've narrowed your search down to a few candidates, visit each of their facilities. Then, in addition to finding out basics such as when the classes are held and what they cost, get the following questions answered:

What's your impression of the facility? Here you're looking for a place that's clean and well lighted and has enough room for puppies to run and play but not so much room that the puppies will be too busy exploring the room to bother with each other.

What's the trainer-to-puppy ratio? The more puppies are playing, the more trainers or assistant trainers should be present to supervise the action. The ideal ratio: one trainer or assistant to five or six puppies.

How are the puppies screened? Not every puppy is suited to puppy kindergarten. Large puppies, particularly those over six months of age, don't belong in a puppy kindergarten class. Size compatibility is important; at this stage, big puppies shouldn't be playing with small puppies.

Which vaccinations are required? The trainer should require that every puppy be immunized as is appropriate to his age and should ask for records of such vaccinations before puppies are allowed to play together.

Take him for car rides—and not just to the vet's! Make sure, too, that he meets people of all ages and types and that he has positive experiences with them. The Golden Retriever to whom this book is dedicated still gets excited when she sees a U.S. Postal Service truck or someone in a postal carrier uniform because, during puppyhood, her owner introduced her to the local mail carrier and she scored some treats from him.

During the socialization process, you need to consider your puppy's own very special personality. Although Golden Retrievers are generally happy-go-lucky, gregarious, confident individuals, some are bolder than others. Some may approach a new person, dog, or object with their tails wagging in a relaxed, confident manner, heads up and panting happily. Others may display more apprehension, such as a tail tucked downward or even between the hind legs, ears down and back, and a hesitant demeanor. If your Golden puppy's behavior ever fits the latter category, don't force the issue. Take your time, be patient, and allow him to adjust to a new situation at his own pace.

As important as socialization is, many veterinarians are hesitant to endorse the process. They contend that puppies shouldn't go anywhere or meet any unknown dogs until they've had their full complement of puppy immunizations, which occurs between 16 and 20 weeks of age. They have a point. Until puppies have had all of their shots, they're at risk of contracting serious, highly contagious diseases such as distemper and parvovirus. To sidestep such dangers, your vet may suggest keeping your Golden in your home until he's fully protected—but following those instructions can make socialization very difficult. And without adequate socialization, a dog's mental and emotional health is very much at risk. Fortunately, there's a middle ground between the extremes of this dilemma: Take steps to socialize your puppy without posing undue risk to his physical health. Here are some ideas.

Bring the World to Him

If you're reluctant to take your Golden Retriever puppy outdoors—especially if the areas available to him are visited by other dogs—just bring some of the outside world to him. In other words, invite people and well-behaved, fully immunized dogs over to your home to play with him, and bring your puppy to their domiciles. Until you know more about how your puppy plays with other dogs, though, confine his initial playdates to one-on-one interactions.

Seek Out Dog-Free Zones

You can safely bring your puppy just about anyplace where dogs haven't congregated. That means, however, that you should bypass dog parks, pet stores, and other pet-friendly public places until your puppy has received all of his shots.

Crates are indispensable to Golden Retrievers and their people.

Offer a Lap-Eye's View

If you're not sure whether a place is safe for your puppy, just pick him up and place him on your lap (assuming he's still small enough to be a lapdog). Let him view the world from your entirely safe lap or the comfort of your arms, and he'll be both socialized and safe.

Bring Treats

A Golden Retriever puppy who's taking up temporary residence on your lap can still meet and greet people—all kinds of people. Find a public place, such as a park bench or seat outside a store where people congregate. Then, when people pass by, ask them whether they wouldn't mind feeding treats to your puppy. Most people will happily oblige—after all, who can resist spending some time with a puppy? The Golden Retriever to whom this book is dedicated logged in quite a bit of time on her owner's lap on a bench outside a supermarket when she was a young puppy. Plenty of shoppers stopped to give her a treat

Training Tidbit

An energetic Golden Retriever puppy is likely to learn more quickly if he's had a chance to siphon off some of his near-boundless supply of energy. Play some games or otherwise give him a chance to run around and blow off some steam before holding a training session—especially if you're teaching him something new.

when they entered and left the store—and to this day, this Golden loves meeting any and all human beings.

CRATE TRAINING

Crates are indispensable to Golden Retrievers and their people. The crate greatly reduces housetraining time, gives you a place to put your puppy when you can't watch him, and gives your puppy a place of his own to retreat to when he needs to nap or otherwise chill out. However, some puppies take longer than others to appreciate the joys of being crated. To help the puppies who aren't thrilled with their crates, it's crucial to crate train them before you start crate-dependent lessons, such as housetraining.

What Is Crate Training?

Crate training is simply the process of gently introducing your puppy to the crate before you actually use it for other training. If you're fortunate, your puppy's breeder may have already completed this process—but if the breeder hasn't, you need to undertake his "Love Your Crate" tutorial. The process need

not take long, but when you're done, your puppy will know that his crate is his very own safe, special place.

How to Crate Train

Teaching your puppy to use his crate and love doing so is a simple process. All you need is a little time and a little patience. Here's what to do:

1. Encourage outside exploration. Encourage him to sniff around the exterior of the crate. If he's hesitant, throw some tiny treats around the crate's perimeter.

2. Encourage inside moves. Next, take a small treat and throw it inside the crate, preferably toward the back. If he goes into the crate to get the treat, praise him. If he hesitates, move the treat close to the front of the crate so that he need not enter the crate right away. After he takes treats comfortably at the door, place the treat farther and farther back in the crate until he's completely inside. Each time he takes the treat, praise him lavishly.

3. Close the door—briefly. Once your puppy consistently enters the crate without hesitation, use a treat to encourage him to enter; then, when he's inside, shut the door for five seconds. During those five seconds, speak to him softly and encouragingly. Then open the door and give him another treat when he steps out. Repeat this sequence, increasing the time the door is closed a little bit at a time until your puppy remains comfortably in the crate for about five minutes.

4. Now you're ready to take the next step: leaving the room while your puppy's inside the crate. Time this step to coincide with his next meal. Put his food into a small bowl and place the bowl inside the crate. Then toss a treat inside the crate to encourage

him to enter. When he does, shut the door and leave the room for a minute or so; then check to see how he's doing without seeing you. If he's eating happily, leave again and return in a few more minutes. Once he's finished his meal, let him out of his crate, praise him, and give him a small treat. After he's taken his meal in the crate a couple of times, start enclosing him in the crate without a meal. Gradually extend the time he's in the crate until he stays comfortably for about 30 minutes.

5. Once your puppy can stay calmly in his crate for 30 minutes, he's sufficiently crate trained to begin the housetraining process, and you may find that he'll go to his crate on his own. The Golden Retriever to whom this book is dedicated was introduced to the crate as a puppy in just this way. Even today, at seven years of age, she often heads to her crate for a nap or just to relax. Your Golden Retriever can learn to do the same.

That said, it's vitally important not to overuse the crate. During the first few days of the housetraining process, don't leave your puppy in his crate for more than an hour or two at a time until you have a sense as to how long he can hold his urine. As he matures but continues his bathroom lessons, you can extend his crate time to three or four hours. However, even if your dog is an adult and is fully housetrained, he should not be left in his

When housetraining your Golden, look for signs that he has to go, like sniffing the ground or pacing, and take him outside immediately.

crate for more than five or six hours at a time. In other words, when it comes to crating, one can definitely have too much of a good thing.

HOUSETRAINING

Now that your Golden Retriever puppy has learned to stay in his crate, you're both ready to get into the nitty-gritty of one of the most important lessons you can teach him: housetraining. As essential as this lesson is, it can cause confusion, not to mention consternation, to people and pooches alike. To prevent either result, it's important to understand exactly how necessary housetraining is before you actually try it with your puppy.

What Is Housetraining?

Simply put, housetraining is teaching your puppy to do his business—to poop and pee—only at the times and in the places you want him to. But while the concept is simple, the teaching of that concept hasn't always been so.

A generation or so ago, most people had only the vaguest idea of how to teach a dog basic bathroom manners. We didn't know much about our dogs' basic instincts with respect to bathroom behavior, much less how to capitalize on those instincts. The result was that people would unintentionally give their puppies lots of chances to make mistakes, berate those puppies for such mistakes even though the puppies had no idea what they'd done wrong, and set up a set of conditions that virtually guaranteed the repetition of such mistakes.

Fortunately, now we know better. Now we know that dogs like to have special places, or dens, of their own, and that they'll do just about anything to avoid eliminating in those dens. That's why crates are so important in housetraining. By confining your puppy to his crate when you can't watch him—and by carefully supervising him when he's not in the crate—you've given him his own den, and you're helping him develop the control that's necessary for him to become a housetraining ace. When you housetrain your Golden Retriever puppy in this way, you can say goodbye to rolled-up newspapers, rubbing his nose in his mistakes, and other old-fashioned methods that have never really worked. Instead, you and your puppy will be working together to make him a model of proper potty deportment.

Bear in mind, too, that there's no such thing as "a little bit housetrained." Your puppy either knows his bathroom basics or he doesn't. Even if he's doing his business where and when he's supposed to 80 percent of the time, you're not done being his potty professor. Until he's 100-percent reliable, he's still a housetrainee, not a housetraining graduate.

How to Housetrain

Housetraining isn't a complicated process, but it does require time, patience, and consistency. Follow these steps and your Golden housetrainee will be a housetraining graduate sooner than you think.

1. Establish the puppy bathroom. Ideally, you will have chosen this area before you bring your puppy home. The best place for your puppy's bathroom is outside in your backyard and close enough to your house that he won't have to go too far before he can open his floodgates. If you don't have a back yard, take your puppy to the median strip between the sidewalk and street, have him do his business there—and be sure to clean up whenever and wherever he poops.

2. Make a scent cloth. The very next time your puppy pees, gently blot his sanitary area with a paper towel, and put that

Teaching your dog basic cues will help him become a well-behaved member of the family.

paper towel into a plastic bag. You'll use this soiled paper towel, also known as a scent cloth, to show your puppy where his bathroom is.

3. Show him the bathroom. Once you've created the scent cloth, take your puppy out to his designated bathroom the next time he needs to eliminate, and bring the scent cloth with you. Once you reach the potty place, place the scent cloth on top of it. The scent from the puppy's urine will draw him to the cloth, and in all likelihood he will pee on top of the cloth. Praise him and give him a tiny treat. Bring him to the same spot for all subsequent bathroom breaks.

4. Create a schedule. As a general rule, a young puppy needs to eliminate first thing in the morning, after naps, after meals, after play sessions, and last thing at night. He'll probably also need a middle-of-the-night break until he's at least three months old. This means that he'll need a potty break every couple of hours or so during the day. (More information and a sample schedule appear in Chapter 2.)

5. Supervise closely. Whenever your puppy is not in his crate, you need to watch him carefully to make sure that he doesn't get into any mischief and to prevent accidents. Any time that you can't supervise him, he should be in his crate.

6. Watch for pre-potty signals. The more often you prevent your puppy from having accidents, the faster he will learn his bathroom basics. If you see your puppy suddenly stop what he's doing, sniff the ground intently, start pacing or circling, he's probably about to eliminate. Whisk

him outside to his potty spot as quickly as possible—and if he eliminates there, praise him lavishly and give him a treat.

7. **Expect accidents.** No matter how hard you try or how diligent you are, your puppy will have at least a couple of accidents until he figures out the whole housetraining thing. When that happens, don't scold or berate him, and certainly don't whack him with a rolled-up newspaper or rub his face in the offending puddle or pile. Instead, take him to his crate and clean up the accident without comment. Make sure, too, that you use a cleaner that's formulated specifically to deal with pet stains and odor. Failure to do so could easily prompt your puppy to return to the scene of his accident and perform an encore. Finally, figure out what happened. If your puppy does have an accident, the fault generally lies with you, not the puppy. Did you fail to watch him closely? Did you make him wait too long between potty breaks? Did you fail to heed

a signal that he needed to go? Did you fail to thoroughly clean up the scene of an earlier accident? An answer of "yes" to any of those questions could illuminate the reason behind your puppy's potty foul.

8. **Be patient.** Puppies don't learn proper potty protocol overnight. They need time to figure out where and when they can potty and to develop sufficient physical control to refrain from eliminating until their scheduled bathroom breaks. In fact, most puppies—Golden Retrievers included—don't really master the art of housetraining until they're about six months old, and some take longer. If your Golden Retriever reaches that half-year mark and hasn't had an accident in about a month or so, you can declare victory in the housetraining battle and consider your puppy to be a housetraining graduate.

BASIC GOOD MANNERS CUES

Once upon a time, we taught our dogs so-called "obedience commands." The idea was that we would tell our dogs what to do and they would obey. But that was before we understood that dogs need concrete incentives just as we do and that the ideal way for a human and dog to interact is not about the human's dominating the dog and the dog's submitting to the human. We've learned that it's far better to have a true relationship with our dogs: a partnership that's based on mutual cooperation and respect.

That's why this section doesn't discuss commands. Instead, the discussion centers on cues: prompts that we give our dogs and to which our dogs hopefully respond in the way we'd like.

This section also deals with good manners rather than obedience. A well-mannered dog—especially a well-mannered Golden Retriever—

is a joy to have around. One can enjoy this dog's company in just about any situation, knowing that all he needs is guidance from a cue to handle almost any circumstance with aplomb. The happy-go-lucky, highly intelligent, people-oriented Golden Retriever is especially quick to learn basic cues such as those in this section, which go a long way toward setting a boisterous, out-of-control puppy on a path to becoming a well-mannered dog.

Name and Attention

It's pretty much impossible to train a dog if he's not paying attention to you. So before you try to teach your Golden puppy any basic cues, you need to teach him to focus on you when you ask him to. That's what your puppy's name is for: It's a one-word cue that teaches him to look at you immediately and wait for further instructions.

Consequently, when you choose a name for your puppy, you need to make sure it's something you will enjoy using and that he will enjoy responding to. Consider choosing a short moniker—ideally, no more than two syllables—that's easy to pronounce and is not an object of humor. (In other words, don't name your Golden Retriever puppy Goldilocks just for laughs.)

To teach your puppy his name, have your clicker in one hand and treats in the other or very close by. Then:

1. Wait until your puppy is looking at you.
2. When he does, say his name, click the clicker (or say "Yes!") and give him a treat.
3. Repeat this sequence several times so that your puppy begins to associate his name with the click and treat.
4. Wait until your puppy looks away from you, then say his name. If he looks at you, click and give the treat. If he doesn't, don't repeat his name; instead, make a kissing or

similar noise to get his attention, then click and treat.

Sit

The *sit* cue is just about the easiest maneuver that you can teach your puppy. After all, he knows how to sit already—so all you have to do is help him associate the act of sitting with the word "sit." For that reason, this is a great initial cue to teach your puppy once he knows his name. The ease of teaching this cue will help you both feel successful and will build a foundation for teaching other behaviors later on.

To teach this cue, you'll need a clicker and treats. With the clicker in one hand and a treat in the other, proceed as follows:

1. Start by holding a treat in front of your

The *sit* cue is one of the easiest to teach a puppy.

The *recall* tells your dog to come to you immediately.

puppy's nose, and make sure that he sees it.

2. Move the treat up and back over his head.

3. As your puppy follows the treat with his eyes, he'll automatically sit. As soon as his bottom touches the ground, click the clicker, praise lavishly, and give him the treat.

4. Repeat until you're confident that your dog will sit for the treat.

5. Now you're ready to add the cue. Start saying "Sit" in a cheerful tone of voice as you move the treat over his head and he begins to sit. When he does, click and treat.

6. Repeat 10 to 20 times until he's doing so consistently.

The final step is to simply ask your puppy to sit without using any sort of hand signal.

1. Put your arms behind your back so that he can't see the treat.

2. Say "Sit" in that same cheerful tone of voice.

3. Wait a few seconds to see whether he sits; if he does, click and treat. If he doesn't, use the treat to guide him into the *sit* as you did in the first step, then click and treat.

Your puppy may not learn the cue in one session. That's okay. Keep each session short and sweet—certainly no more than ten minutes.

Down

Many puppies and dogs find it easier to lie down than to sit—so for them, the *down* cue may be easier to learn than the *sit* cue is. That said, your puppy should know how to sit before teaching him to lie down on cue. Once he's sitting, do the following:

1. Hold a treat in front of his face, and make sure that he's looking at it.
2. Say "Down" in a long, drawn-out tone so that you're really saying "Dooowwwwn"— and make sure that you're using a cheerful tone of voice.
3. At the same time, slowly move the treat down to the ground toward his paws; then, when the treat is close to the ground, move it outward several more inches (cm). The effect should be that you move the treat in an L-shaped path.
4. As your dog follows your hand with his eyes, he'll lie down. When he does, click and treat.

Some dogs take longer to learn this cue than others. If your puppy is one such dog, you may need to experiment a bit. For example, if he likes to lie down on one hip, try moving the treat down toward his paws and then outward on the side that's opposite the hip on which he likes to lie down. If he won't lie down at all, move the treat more slowly and perhaps use a different treat (one that's tastier or that he otherwise really wants). Above all, be patient and persistent.

Come

This cue, known in training circles as the *recall*, is just about the most important cue you can teach your puppy: coming when you call him. If you find yourself in a situation where you need him to return to you immediately—such as slipping out of his collar and being about to take off—a rock-solid *recall* can literally save your dog's life. Here are two ways to teach this cue: first by yourself and then with a friend or other human family member.

To teach the cue when it's just you and your puppy, do the following:

1. Have your dog on leash and sitting just a few feet (m) away from you.

2. Say your dog's name and the word "come" in a happy, upbeat tone of voice.
3. As your dog comes to you, squat down and open your arms.
4. When your dog reaches you, welcome him enthusiastically and click and treat.
5. Repeat the process, gradually increasing the distance between you.
6. Once he's mastered the cue with the leash on, try doing it with the leash off. But make sure that you practice in a safe setting, such as inside your own home or within a fenced enclosure. Even when your dog has mastered this maneuver, keep practicing!

To teach the cue with a partner, do the following:

1. Have your dog on leash and have your partner hold the leash.
2. Move a few feet (m) away from your dog and your partner.
3. Say your dog's name and the word "Come" in a happy, upbeat tone of voice. Your partner should let go of the leash so that your dog can come to you.
4. When your dog reaches you, welcome him with enthusiasm, click and treat, and pick up the leash.
5. Repeat, with you holding the leash and your partner calling the dog.
6. Continue calling your dog back and forth between the two of you for five to ten minutes.

Unfortunately, some puppies don't recognize the importance of the *recall*—at least not right away. For such puppies, try the following:

1. Take advantage of your puppy's desire to chase you. Have him sit, then run away from him and tell him to come.
2. Let him catch up to you—and when he does, praise, click and treat.
3. Repeat until he's consistently running to catch you. At that point, switch back to

A well-trained Golden is a pleasure to live with.

squatting a few feet (m) away from him.

4. Make sure the treats you offer are treats that he really likes.

Don't push too far too fast. If your puppy fails to come in an environment with lots of distractions, go back to practicing in a lower-distraction environment.

Very important: Make sure that every time you ask your puppy to come, he'll be rewarded for doing so. In other words, don't call him to come and then scold him, end his playtime, take his toy away from him, or do anything else that would not be pleasant for him. In such instances, go to him so that he doesn't associate coming when called with a negative consequence.

Walk Nicely on Leash

Nothing makes a walk more pleasurable than being accompanied by a Golden Retriever who knows how to behave himself while he's on the leash. Unfortunately, learning to walk politely on leash is a big challenge for many Goldens. With so much to see and smell up ahead, sticking close to you may not seem like very much fun. Your objective is to show him that he's wrong—that fun and goodies result when he stays close to you, not when he attempts to run ahead. Here's how to do just that:

1. Leash your dog, and place the leash loop around your wrist.
2. Grasp the leash with the looped hand just below the loop.
3. Have your dog stand next to you on the side opposite your looped hand so that the leash falls diagonally across your body.
4. Tell your dog "Let's go!" in a cheerful but decisive voice, and start walking. As you walk, chat with your dog so that he pays attention to you.
5. Keep him close to you by clicking and treating him with the unleashed hand every

couple of steps, at least initially. As he gets better at walking politely on leash, you can wait longer between clicks and treats.

6. If he bolts out in front of you, halt immediately so that he can go no farther. This way, he'll learn that he won't be able to go anywhere if he pulls. When he heads back toward you and the leash slackens, resume your walk

7. When you stop, place your unleashed hand a few inches (cm) in front of your dog's face so that he stops too. When he does, click and treat.

Be patient when teaching your puppy this behavior—even if he's really fractious. That said, if mastering this exercise really seems to be beyond your puppy's ability, try the following fixes:

1. When he bolts, don't just stop—turn around and go in the opposite direction. But do so carefully: Do not snap the leash or jerk his head in any way. Simply turn around in one smooth motion. Click and treat him when he catches up and begins walking politely next to you.

2. Let your puppy have some playtime, and if possible, some strenuous exercise before you start teaching this behavior. A puppy who's bristling with energy may find a sedate stroll nearly impossible to perform, no matter now enticing the goodies are.

3. If your puppy pulls continually, invest in a front-clip harness. This handy device is much more effective at arresting the antics of your sled dog wannabe than a choke collar or prong collar or even a head harness. (Plus it's much kinder to the puppy.) Bear in mind that walking nicely on leash is not identical to heeling. The formal heel requires that a walking dog's head be parallel with his handler's left knee and also that the dog must stop and sit next to the handler's left knee whenever the handler stops. The formal heel is beautiful to watch, but most dogs don't need to achieve such precision to be considered mannerly while walking on leash.

Off/Take It

The *off* cue teaches your puppy to refrain from picking up a forbidden object at all. If your puppy is about to pick up something he shouldn't and hears you tell him "Off" (or "Leave it"), he should stop his trajectory and leave the object where it is. The *take it* cue tells your puppy that it's okay for him to pick up or otherwise take an object. Teach him both cues as follows:

1. Sit on the floor with your puppy in front of you.

2. Have a tasty treat in the palm of your hand and show him your palm.

3. As your puppy goes for the treat, shut your hand in a fist so that the treat is not accessible and say "Off."

4. Each subsequent time he noses your hand, repeat the cue.

5. Then after about four or five times, open your fist so that the treat is visible and tell him to "Take it."

6. Practice this cue regularly, even when your puppy seems to have it down pat.

PART II

ADULTHOOD

CHAPTER 5

FINDING YOUR ADULT GOLDEN RETRIEVER

Sure, Golden Retriever puppies are just about the cutest things going. They're wiggly, they're cuddly, and they just about beg to be picked up. Who could possibly resist bringing one into a family? Well—maybe you.

You may not be interested in having to deal with middle-of-the-night puppy potty breaks, cleaning up puppy accidents, and dealing with everyday puppy mischief. And even if those puppy challenges were okay with you, paying $1,000 or more for a purebred Golden Retriever puppy from a reputable breeder might not be. A better choice for you might be an adult Golden Retriever: a dog who's a year old or more.

WHY ADOPTING AN ADULT IS A GOOD IDEA

Let's be honest: living with a puppy can be a gigantic hassle. Although raising a dog from infancy can be incredibly rewarding, such an enterprise is not for everyone.

A prime example is a household in which someone's not home most of the day. Like all other young puppies, Golden Retriever youngsters need a lot of time and attention from their human caregivers. Housetraining them requires that someone be on duty to take them to their potty place every couple of hours or maybe even—in the first week or two—hourly. For the person or family who's at school or work much of the day, adhering to that kind of a schedule is difficult, if not impossible.

And even if someone in your household could stay home to housetrain and otherwise watch the puppy—or make arrangements for outside help, such as a neighbor or doggy day care—to do the job, you may not want to. Just as with a human infant, life with a Golden Retriever puppy may not leave room for much else. New parents are often surprised to find out how all-consuming caring for their infant can be. So too can be the case with owners of young puppies. If you're leading an otherwise busy life, taking on the task of puppy raising may be unfair both to you and the puppy.

But does that mean that the joys of living with a Golden Retriever are off-limits to you and your

Want to Know More?

If purchasing a puppy is more up your alley, see Chapter 2: Finding and Prepping for Your Puppy.

Adopting an adult Golden gives him a second chance at life in a good home.

control needed to hold it between potty breaks—and a lot more time can elapse between those potty breaks too.

He May Already Know How to Behave

Most adult Goldens have already lived in human households and are likely to have acquired some basic good manners training. They may not only understand some basic cues such as the *sit,* the *down,* and coming when called; chances are that they also know that they're not supposed to go raiding the garbage, shredding the toilet paper, or hopping up onto the living room sofa.

He's Probably Calmer

If your adult Golden is older than two years of age or so, he's likely to have passed through the let's-go-crazy period of adolescence that any and all Golden Retrievers seem to pass through. And even if he's still in that period, he can be managed with plenty of exercise, basic training, and astute puppy-proofing.

family? Not necessarily. Instead of dealing with the perpetual challenge of raising a typically mischievous Golden puppy, you can open your heart and home to an adult Golden Retriever.

Regardless of why an adult Golden Retriever finds himself without a home, adopting him gives him a second chance at a happily-ever-after ending. Taking in an adult Golden may not only spare that dog euthanasia but may also make room at a shelter or rescue group for another dog in need of a home. Still need some convincing? Here are some more pluses to offering a home to a grown-up Golden.

He'll Cost Less

As mentioned earlier, a Golden Retriever puppy from a reputable breeder generally costs at least $1,000 and often costs more. By contrast, a Golden Retriever from an animal shelter or rescue group generally costs far less than half that amount—and those charges are levied simply to make up the shelter's or rescue group's expenses in caring for the dog.

You May Save a Life

Most of the adult Golden Retrievers who are up for adoption are homeless—and in many cases, they've lost those homes through no fault of their own. Some are surrendered to a shelter or rescue group (more about those organizations in the next section) because of changes in

He May Be Housetrained

Many adult Goldens already know their bathroom basics. And even if the one you choose doesn't, he can pick up those basics pretty quickly. That's because, unlike a young puppy, the adult Golden has the physical

Although many dogs are are considered to be adults at one year of age, Golden Retrievers generally act like puppies and adolescents until they're two years old or more.

their owners' circumstances that makes it impossible for those owners to care for them anymore. Others find themselves in a shelter or rescue group because they have behavioral problems that their owners didn't know how to solve or didn't want to bother trying to solve. (This doesn't mean that you can't solve such problems, though.) And all too many Goldens

are homeless because they're victims of neglect or even outright cruelty.

ADOPTION OPTIONS

Fortunately, you have several choices if you're looking to add an adult Golden to your life.

Breeders

Occasionally, a reputable breeder will sell an adult Golden Retriever to a family. For example, a puppy whom a breeder thought would be a good show prospect turns out to be a not-so-great prospect after all. Maybe he's oversized or undersized, or the breeder feels that for other reasons he doesn't conform sufficiently to the breed standard to do well in the show ring. Or perhaps she actually did show the dog, only to find that he didn't do well. But no matter what the reason, the Golden Retriever who's

You can obtain an adult Golden through a variety of sources, such as breeders, shelters, and rescues.

Try to be objective when choosing the perfect Golden Retriever for you and your family.

a washout in the show ring could make a fabulous companion for you.

If you're interested in adopting an adult Golden from a reputable breeder, check out the Golden Retriever Club of America's list of regional clubs at http://www.grca.org/thegrca/member_clubs.html. There you'll find a searchable database of state and regional Golden Retriever clubs. Click on the appropriate links to get to one of these local club websites and you're likely to find listings and contact information on breeders who belong to that club. Such clubs also often have breeder referral coordinators who are likely to know whether any of their members are looking to find a home for an adult Golden.

Animal Shelters

Did you think that animal shelters offer only mixed-breed dogs for adoption? Think again! According to the Humane Society of the United States (HSUS), as many as 30 percent of most animal shelter dog populations consist of purebred dogs. And because the

Multi-Dog Tip

If you already have one or more dogs but would like to adopt an adult Golden Retriever, make sure that your resident dogs are okay with this idea. Most shelters and rescue groups allow a prospective adopter to bring current pets to their facilities to meet the new dog before finalizing an adoption—in fact, some insist upon it.

Golden Retriever is among the most popular breeds in the United States, it only stands to reason that your local shelter might have a Golden Retriever available for adoption at least occasionally.

A good way to find out whether shelters near you have Goldens (or Golden mixes) available for adoption is to log onto Petfinder at www.petfinder.com. By following the prompts on the left side of the home page, you'll be able to search Petfinder's nationwide database for adoptable Goldens available from shelters and rescue groups.

Rescue Groups

Many local Golden Retriever clubs have committees that focus on finding new homes for Goldens who, through no fault of their own, find themselves without permanent homes or owners. These committees consist of volunteers who provide foster care for the dogs, screen potential adopters, match dogs and adopters, and raise the money needed to pay for all these activities. Many volunteers take on more than one of these jobs.

Your local Golden Retriever club is likely to have a rescue committee or have a rescue group that's affiliated with the club. By logging onto your local Golden club's website, you can at least find out who heads the rescue committee—or more likely, be directed to the committee or group's website, where you'll see a list of adoptable Goldens. Then you will be able to download an adoption application. Another option is to log onto Petfinder and use the prompts there to search the site's database for available Golden Retrievers.

Note, too, that many rescue groups hold adoption fairs at local pet supermarkets or other venues. At these events, the group's foster caregivers bring the adoptable Goldens to encourage the public to take a look and

Training Tidbit

Although many adult Goldens have already had some training, don't assume that your Golden is one of them. And even if he has learned some basic good manners, the stress of being surrendered from one home and moving to a new one (yours) may cause him to forget those manners temporarily. Not to worry: Just start doing some enjoyable brief positive training as described in this book and he'll remember his training quickly—or learn quickly, if he hasn't been trained before.

to submit adoption applications. Your local Golden rescue group's website probably contains information on upcoming adoption events in your area.

PICKING OUT THE RIGHT GOLDEN RETRIEVER FOR YOU

Once you've identified one or more groups that have adult Golden Retrievers available for adoption and you've found an adoption prospect, it's time to visit the shelter or rescue group foster home and meet the Golden candidate in person. Don't expect this meeting to be easy. You may fall in love with any and all Goldens that you meet, but that doesn't mean that any, much less all, of those Goldens are right for you. It's important to cast an objective eye on the dogs you encounter, ask the right questions, and answer the questions that the shelter or rescue group volunteer asks you.

CHAPTER 6

GOLDEN RETRIEVER GROOMING NEEDS

The Golden Retriever's gorgeous good looks don't happen by accident. They result not only from great genes but also from good health and good grooming. Just as human beings need to care for themselves—bathing their bodies, styling their hair, giving themselves manicures and pedicures, among other tasks—to look and be their best, so too do Golden Retrievers. The difference, of course, is that while human beings can do those tasks for themselves, Goldens need people to perform those tasks for them. And with both species, sometimes the services of specialists can go a long way.

This chapter explains how to groom your Golden all by yourself. It also discusses how to find a grooming pro if the job proves too time consuming for you to do, if you just need a break, or if some grooming chores are too complicated to handle on your own.

BRUSHING

Your adult Golden Retriever's coat needs regular brushing—and not just to look good. Regular brushing also prevents tangling of his coat. Tangles not only look unsightly; if they develop into tight mats, they can also cause considerable discomfort to the dog and irritation to the skin.

Regular brushing also removes surface dirt from your Golden's coat and stimulates the oil glands in his skin, which helps keep his coat shiny. In addition, brushing your Golden Retriever's coat regularly will help keep shedding under control. Goldens are notorious shedders, particularly of their fluffy undercoats. Regular brushing to remove shed hair will help keep your house from being overpopulated by Golden dust bunnies and will save wear and tear on your vacuum cleaner.

Brushing also gives you an opportunity to check your Golden for skin irregularities. As you move your hands over your Golden's body, you can be alert for lumps and bumps. At the same time, you can visually inspect him for fleas, cuts, and rashes.

Finally, regular brushing of your Golden Retriever can be a pleasurable activity for you both. Many Goldens enjoy being brushed. In fact, when the Golden to whom this book is dedicated sees her brush, she comes running to her person and lies down on her side without being asked.

How to Brush

As to exactly how and with what to brush your Golden Retriever—well, there appear to be as many ideas on how to do it as there are

Goldens to be brushed! That said, if you're looking for instructions on how to give your Golden a basic brushing, read no further. A set of instructions is right here. Here's what to do:

1. **Gather your gear.** You'll need a slicker brush or a pin brush, a dematting claw, and perhaps an undercoat rake.

2. **Get into position.** Unless you're using a grooming table, have your dog lie down on his side and either kneel or sit next to him, facing his tummy.

3. **Start brushing.** With your pin brush or slicker brush, start brushing the hair at the base of your dog's tail. Brush gently, from the skin outward, in the direction the hair grows. Brush a little bit at a time, using one hand to hold aside the hair that's immediately ahead of the section that you're brushing.

4. **Start the next row.** When you reach your dog's shoulder, go back to the base of the tail and gently brush the next row up to the shoulder. Repeat, row by row, until you've completely brushed your dog's side.

5. **Lift the front leg.** Gently lift your dog's front leg so that you can see the hair in the armpit. Brush this hair carefully. If you encounter any tangles, use the dematting claw to gently untangle them. Continue brushing the hair on your dog's tummy

Your Golden's thick coat needs regular brushing to look good and keep tangles at bay.

from the skin outward in the direction the hair grows.

6. **Lift the rear leg.** Gently lift the dog's rear leg so that you expose his sanitary area, and carefully brush the hair there and on the inside of the leg—again, from the skin outward, in the direction the hair grows.

7. **Brush the hair on the legs, rear, and tail.** Use the brush to gently tend to the feathers

What if Your Golden Doesn't Like Being Brushed?

What should you do if your Golden Retriever doesn't like being brushed? Introduce him to the pleasures of brushing a little bit at a time, and use treats to further sweeten the deal. Feed your dog a treat, brush for a minute, give another treat, and then end the session. Continue brushing and treating him in very short sessions—even if it takes you a couple of days to do so—until he's completely brushed. The idea here is for your dog to associate being brushed with getting treats. Once he does, he's likely to look forward to being brushed rather than running away at the sight of one.

Multi-Dog Tip

Grooming more than one dog at a time—especially if all of the dogs are Golden Retrievers or other long-haired breeds—can seem like such a huge time commitment that you may hesitate to groom any of your dogs at all. To prevent feeling intimidated by the prospect of having to groom several long-coated dogs, schedule each dog's grooming for a different day. For example, you could designate Monday as Molly's grooming day, Wednesday as Max's grooming day, and Friday as Jasper's day to be groomed.

On the other hand, if you're having all three dogs professionally groomed, consider taking them all to the groomer on the same day—and don't be shy about asking for a multiple-dog discount!

on your dog's legs; then move to the tail and hair on the rear (sometimes known as the dog's pants) on the side that you've been brushing.

8. **Do the chest.** Have your dog change from a reclining to a sitting position. Brush the hair on his chest outward from the skin in the direction it grows.

9. **Reposition the dog.** Have your dog lie down on his other side, and repeat the first seven steps.

If your dog is shedding a lot, you may want to use an undercoat rake on his body before you begin brushing. The rake can remove a lot of loose undercoat hair, making brushing easier and helping to minimize shedding. That said, nothing can make a Golden Retriever stop shedding completely except for shaving his coat—which generally isn't advisable. The only reason to shave a Golden Retriever's coat is if, for some reason, it becomes impossibly matted.

BATHING

Every dog needs periodic bathing, and your Golden Retriever is no exception. In fact, if he's like most other adult Goldens, who delight in rolling themselves in yucky stuff at any opportunity, the periods between those baths may be decidedly short. However, if your Golden's a more fastidious sort—or simply lacks opportunities to roll in gross materials—a monthly bath with a gentle shampoo made especially for dogs will keep him clean and smelling nice.

Where to bathe your dog is a matter of convenience. In warm weather, you can take him outside and hold him on leash while you use a garden hose to wet him down and rinse him. (Just make sure that the water in the hose is neither too hot nor too cold; if you have any doubts, bypass this venue.) There's always a bathtub in your own home—if you have a shower attachment—not to mention self-service dog washes at doggy day cares and some pet-supply stores.

How to Bathe

No matter where you bathe your Golden, these how-to's can help get the job done better and more easily:

1. **Brush beforehand.** Before you start, brush your dog's coat thoroughly to ensure that it has no tangles or mats. Don't skip this step; failure to brush your double-coated

A well-groomed Golden is a pleasure to behold.

Golden before you bathe him could cause his wet hair to clump together into doggy dreadlocks. Such clumps are very difficult to brush out when they dry.

2. **Block his ears.** Place a cotton ball in each of your dog's ears to protect them from water. He'll be very uncomfortable if he gets water in either or both ears.

3. **Dilute the shampoo.** Many groomers suggest diluting your dog's shampoo to help it last longer and rinse more easily. Try adding three or four units of water to every unit of shampoo.

4. **Put him into the tub.** If your dog won't go into the tub on his own (try luring him into the tub with a treat if he's reluctant), lift him carefully and put him there. Lay down a bath mat beforehand to keep his feet steady. If you're using a garden hose, bring him on leash to where the hose is and make sure that the leash is looped securely around your wrist.

5. **Steady as he doesn't go.** Some dogs don't immediately appreciate the pleasures of being bathed. If your Golden is one of them, keep a steady hand on him to prevent him from jumping out of the tub. Make sure, too, that your bathroom door is closed in case he actually does escape from the tub. That way, he won't go running around the house before the bath is finished.

6. **Water him down.** With a handheld shower attachment or the hose, pour warm (never hot) water over your Golden, making sure that the water goes all the way down to the skin. Start at the top of his head and neck, then proceed to wet the length of his backbone. After that, water his sides, chest, legs, and tail.

7. **Bring on the suds.** Once your Golden is thoroughly wet, apply enough diluted

shampoo to work up a lather all over his body—but not such a heavy lather that you see billowy clouds of bubbles in either the tub or on your dog. (If you do, use less shampoo next time.)

8. **Rinse, then rinse again.** Once you've finished soaping your Golden, use the handheld shower attachment or the hose to rinse him off. Wield the water in the same way you did when you wet him down before: front to back and top to bottom. Continue rinsing for five minutes or until the rinse water runs clear, whichever comes last. And no, this isn't meant to be overkill—a less-than-thorough rinse will leave your dog's skin dry, flaky, and itchy.

9. **Wrap him up.** After you've thoroughly rinsed your Golden, wrap him in a couple of extra-large bath towels and remove the cotton from his ears. Gently blot the excess water from his coat and skin. However, don't rub; rubbing could cause the coat to become matted. After you've blotted the excess water, your dog may run around the house a bit. (Most dogs love to indulge in a post-bath breakneck run.) After he's run a few laps, towel him some more or use a blow-dryer set to a cool or low-heat setting if he tolerates it.

10. **Blow-dry carefully.** Don't expect your Golden to take to a sudden introduction to a blow-dryer. Many dogs spook at the loud noise and moving air of these appliances,

and some find the very look of dryers to be menacing when pointed at them. Instead, let your dog sniff the dryer and give him a treat. Then turn on the dryer while it's still lying on the floor and encourage him to come over and inspect it. If he does, give him a treat. Repeat this sequence several times until he's clearly comfortable around the dryer. Only then should you try picking up the dryer and actually drying his coat. Start from his rear end, because that's the part of his body that's farthest away from his head and ears, on a low-heat or a cool setting. Gently brush the hair as it dries. After his rear end is dry (or nearly so), give him a treat. Continue drying and treating, section by section, until the dog is reasonably dry.

11. **Brush him out.** Most Goldens need a post-bath, post-drying brush-out. Just use your slicker brush to brush him the same way you did before his bath. Voilà—your Golden Retriever is now as gorgeous as you know he can be.

EAR CARE

Your Golden Retriever's ears make it possible for him to hear everything you do—and then some—but they can also be a big source of discomfort for him. Those ears are prone to infections, more so than is the case with many other breeds.

One reason for frequent Golden Retriever ear infections is that this breed is allergy prone, and those allergies may manifest themselves as ear infections. Another reason is that the floppy shape of a Golden's ears, plus the hair that surrounds the entrance to the ear canals, make those ears better able to trap moisture, such as during a bath or after a swim. That long-standing moisture can become a breeding ground for infections, and ear infections are

Goldens only need to be bathed every month or so—otherwise, their coats usually stay clean with regular brushing.

more than just a nuisance. They can be very painful to your Golden, and if left untreated, can lead to hearing loss.

For those reasons, weekly ear care should be part of your Golden's grooming routine.

How to Care for the Ears

Here's what to do:

1. **Get an ear cleaning solution.** Pour two parts water to one part white vinegar into a spray bottle, or obtain a sprayable ear cleaner from your vet. You can also purchase a commercial product, which works well.

2. **Lift the flap.** Lift your dog's ear flap and spray a little ear cleaner directly into his ear canal. While you do, inspect the ear to be sure that there's little or no visible dirt or debris.

3. **Rub it in.** Fold over the ear flap and gently massage your dog's ear for about a minute. When you're done, let him shake his head (and he will—vigorously).

4. **Cotton to it.** Use a cotton ball to blot up moisture and gently wipe the inside of the

ear. Afterward, inspect the cotton ball; it should have little or no debris on it, and the debris should not have any sort of odor other than the smell of the vinegar used in your cleaning solution. If that's not the case and/or if your dog's ear is red and clearly bothering him—for example, he's shaking his head frequently or rubbing his ear on the ground—he needs to see his veterinarian.

5. **Give him a trim.** The long hair at the entrance to your Golden's ear canals can further trap debris and moisture, which in

By the Numbers

A Golden Retriever generally doesn't acquire his full adult coat until he's at least one year of age—and many Goldens take longer.

turn can result in ear problems. For that reason, it's a good idea to use some small scissors or grooming shears to trim the hair in that area whenever it's long enough to block the entrance to the ear canal. If you take your Golden to a groomer, ear trims should be part of the service he's given there.

EYE CARE

Your Golden Retriever's eyes are his windows to the world and as such deserve and require your attention and care. Fortunately, there's little you need to do other than be vigilant and use some common sense.

How to Care for the Eyes

More specifically, you should:

- Inspect regularly. Look at your dog's eyes for squinting, cloudy discharge, or redness. Pay special attention if he's been pawing at

Your Golden's eyes require your regular attention and care.

his eye. If you see any of these conditions, contact your vet.
- Clean gently. Each morning, or whenever necessary, dampen a cloth or cotton ball with cool water to wipe your dog's face and eye area. This daily cleansing will remove those crusty "sleepies" your Golden gets after a nap or good night's sleep and will also help keep tearstains at bay.

NAIL TRIMMING AND FOOT GROOMING

Stilettos are gorgeous shoes to look at but very painful for most women to walk in. The shoes do great things for the look of a woman's legs, but they also throw her hips and legs out of alignment and cause her balance to be at least somewhat precarious. So too is the case if your Golden Retriever's nails aren't trimmed regularly. Long nails will throw off his balance in the same way that high heels throw off a woman's balance—and the nails don't look nearly as good as those stilettos do.

That's why regular nail trims need to be part of your Golden's grooming routine. Most experts suggest keeping those nails short enough to be off the ground when he's standing still and keeping the dewclaws (the nails that are found higher up on the leg near the ankle) short enough to keep them from curving back into the skin of the leg. Here's how to do the job.

How to Care for the Nails and Feet

1. **Help him relax.** Pick a quiet time of day, such as when you're watching television in the evening and have your dog with you. Then have him assume either a sitting or reclining position. Sit on the floor with him and pet him for a few minutes.
2. **Lift a paw.** After a lovefest of five minutes or so, when you know your dog is relaxed,

To prepare your Golden for nail trimming, first get him used to having his paws handled.

pick up one of his paws with your hand. Gently press on a toe to extend the nail outward.

3. **Look for the quick.** A dog's toenail has a blood vessel inside that runs almost to the end of the nail. In light-colored nails, the quick is the pink area inside the nail. In dark nails, the quick can't be seen—which means that trims need to be very conservative.

4. **Trim just a bit.** Pick up your dog's nail clippers and place them around the very end of the extended nail. Squeeze the clippers quickly to trim off the nail tip. Continue trimming a little at a time until you see a black dot in the center of the trimmed nail. The black dot signals the start of the quick.

5. **Don't panic.** If you trim too much nail

and hit the quick, don't panic if bleeding ensues. Simply apply some styptic powder (available in pharmacies) to the nail; if you don't have any, just place the nail in a small bowl of ordinary baking flour.

6. **Trim the paw pad hair.** Use a pair of baby scissors or small grooming shears to carefully trim the hair that grows from the paws so that the fur follows the shape of the foot. Then turn the paw over and clip the hair between the pads as short as possible.

If your dog hates having his nails trimmed, a little bribery and a lot of patience can get the job done, albeit at a much slower pace than with a dog who tolerates his pedicures.

Here's how to deal with a pedicure-hating Golden:

1. **Start slowly.** Wait until your dog's relaxed. Have a clicker and some treats on hand, and pick up one of his paws. If he tolerates this, click and treat.

2. **Focus on the toe.** Once your Golden is comfortable having his foot picked up, press gently on one of his toes to extend the nail. Click and treat if he tolerates it.

3. **Introduce the clippers.** Perform the previous two steps, then show him the clippers. If he sniffs at or otherwise investigates them, click and treat.

4. **Touch a nail.** Once your dog is comfortable having the clippers around, pick up the clippers and touch one nail. If your dog tolerates the touch, click and treat. Repeat this sequence until your dog is totally comfortable with having his nail touched.

5. **Perform the first trim.** Trim just one nail, then click and treat. Then end the session for the day.

Once your dog tolerates getting one nail trimmed per day, start adding a second nail to the daily regimen, and again use the clicker and treats to aid the process.

Want to Know More?

For more information on how to use the clicker in training, see Chapter 4: Training Your Puppy.

Taken slowly, even a clipper-phobic dog may learn to tolerate a session with the hated instrument. However, some experts contend that guillotine clippers, which are the most common type of nail clipper, put too much pressure on the nail and don't cut the nail efficiently. They recommend using scissor clippers or a nail grinder instead.

Scissor clippers are stronger and sharper than guillotine clippers and thus put less pressure on the nail. A grinder is an electrical device (some are corded, some cordless but rechargeable) originally intended for precision drilling, sanding, shaping, and detailing of wood and other building materials. Today, however, companies are manufacturing nail grinders especially for dogs.

If your Golden truly won't tolerate your doing his nails, have a grooming pro do the job.

DENTAL CARE

One of the best investments you can make in your dog's health—and it only costs pennies per day—is to brush your dog's teeth. Daily attention to your Golden's gums and pearly whites can go a long way toward preventing canine dental disease, which is a condition that the American Veterinary Dental Society (AVDS) says afflicts more than 80 percent of all dogs by age three. Symptoms of this condition include tartar on the teeth, sore-looking, inflamed gums, and bad breath.

Left unchecked, dental disease can cause the tooth to separate from the gum and may even spawn infections that can spread to other organs in the dog's body. Frequent brushings stave off such problems by removing the food particles, saliva, minerals, and bacteria that form a coating of bacteria-breeding plaque on the teeth.

How to Care for the Teeth

Brushing your dog's teeth need not be difficult. Here's what experts suggest you do:

1. **Get the right stuff.** A child's toothbrush or doggy toothbrush will have bristles that are soft enough to clean your Golden's teeth and gums without irritating them. Make sure, too, that you use a toothpaste made especially for dogs; toothpastes for people could upset your dog's stomach.

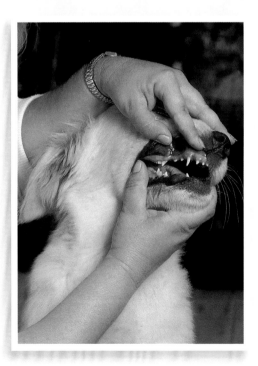

Caring for your dog's teeth is a crucial part of his grooming routine and should be started when your Golden is still a puppy.

2. **Start slow.** Don't feel that you have to start wielding that toothbrush right away. Instead, wrap a little gauze around your finger, lift the dog's lip, and gently rub his gum for a few seconds. If he tolerates the gum rub, add toothpaste to your gauze-wrapped finger, and rub as before. When your dog tolerates the finger and toothpaste consistently, you're ready to move on to the toothbrush.

3. **Lift the lip.** Gently lift your dog's lip on one side of his mouth and brush the teeth for a few seconds. Give him a treat. Repeat on the other side and treat afterward.

4. **Build tolerance.** Over time, gradually extend your brushing sessions to one or two minutes on each side of the mouth.

5. **Make it a habit.** Be consistent about when you brush your dog's teeth. Every day at the same time each day is best.

6. **Have regular checkups.** Your veterinarian should inspect your dog's teeth once a year, and if necessary, schedule a professional tooth cleaning. These routine procedures are similar to those for humans, except that doggy dental cleaning occurs while the dog is under anesthesia. That said, if you brush your Golden's teeth regularly, he won't need professional cleanings very often.

PROFESSIONAL GROOMERS

Although it's certainly possible to groom your Golden Retriever by yourself at home, it's not always easy. Just making sure that all of the shampoo's been rinsed from his massive double coat can be a challenge. (Somehow, the lather has a way of sticking to the undercoat.) Equally challenging are other tasks, such as trimming the hair around the entrance to the ear canal.

If your Golden is a rambunctious sort, bathing and otherwise grooming him may feel more like a wrestling match than an opportunity to bond with him. Other Goldens may be phobic about having their nails trimmed or their ears cleaned by their amateurish owners. And finally, some people don't have the time it takes (a couple of hours, at least) to give their Goldens the full spa treatment.

In any or all of these instances, the services of a professional groomer can help. Being able to drop your dog off at a groomer and know that he'll be brushed, bathed, have his nails trimmed, have his ears cleaned, and have the hair around his paws and ears trimmed can ease the challenges of Golden ownership for busy but loving owners. That said, not all groomers are created equal.

How to Find a Grooming Pro

Here's how to find a grooming pro for your Golden Retriever:

1. **Decide where to go.** Although many groomers have traditional brick-and-mortar enterprises, other groomers have gone mobile; in other words; they've installed grooming equipment in a truck and meet their canine clients at their homes. Figure out which would be more convenient for you.

2. **Ask some experts.** Animal clinics and doggy day cares often have groomers on staff—and even if they don't, your vet or doggy day care provider may well be able to recommend someone to you. Local dog trainers and pet-sitters may also know of competent groomers.

3. **Ask around.** Just as most people love to share the names of their own hairdressers, they're equally happy to share the names of those who tend their dogs' tresses. If you're in a training class, a dog park, or even just out on the street, don't be afraid to query a person whose dog sports a coiffure that you

Some Goldens take to grooming, while others have a little more difficulty discovering the joys of such pampering. Others might enjoy being brushed but balk at getting their nails trimmed. If your Golden Retriever hasn't yet caught on to the joys of doggy spa treatments, give him some incentives: tasty treats. Pairing treats with grooming will help your dog associate grooming with goodies and can help him become more cooperative.

like. Pay particular attention to any Golden Retrievers you see; if you encounter one who looks especially well groomed, ask the owner where the dog gets his locks done (and if the owner says she grooms the dog herself, ask for pointers!).

4. **Visit some groomers.** Once you've obtained the names of a few grooming pros, pick up the phone and have a brief chat with them. Just ten minutes on the phone can yield plenty of information about prices, cancellation policies, and the groomer's experience with dogs in general as well as Golden Retrievers in particular. If you like the answers you get, the groomer may well be worth investigating further.

5. **Visit the shop.** If you like what you've heard from a groomer so far, ask whether you can pay the shop a visit. Once you're there, take a good look around. The shop should be reasonably clean (a little hair on the floor is to be expected, but huge piles of hair are not) and not have overwhelming

smells (the fragrance of dog shampoo is fine; the pungent aroma of doggy accidents is not). Look, too, at how the groomer and the groomer's colleagues interact with their canine clients. Do the dogs seem relaxed? Do the groomer and employees take the time to put the dogs at ease? Are dogs constantly attended when they're on the grooming table? A negative answer to any of those questions should send up a red flag and prompt you to keep looking.

6. **Give it a try.** If, after taking these steps, the groomer and the shop check out, you're ready to book an appointment for your Golden. When you and your dog arrive, pay attention to how the staff interacts with him and what it does to make him comfortable. When you pick him up later in the day, check to make sure that everything you've asked to have done has been accomplished. If you and your Golden are both happy, congratulations. You've found another partner in your dog's care.

CHAPTER 7

GOLDEN RETRIEVER NUTRITIONAL NEEDS

When you were a child, you probably got tired of your mother ordering you to eat your brussels sprouts or your dad commanding you to finish your spinach so that you would grow up to be strong and healthy. The idea behind the adage "you are what you eat" didn't make much sense to you then, but it didn't have to. Your parents knew that the adage was true; consequently, they did their best to put good, nutritious food into your body so that you would attain and maintain optimum health.

The same is true with Golden Retrievers. Just as a balanced diet and good nutrition help a person look and feel her best, so do such a diet and nutrition help a Golden to be the healthiest, handsomest dog he can be. The Golden who gets great grub is likely to have a healthier body and a healthier mind than a Golden whose food regimen is based on cheap eats. Of course, just like a human child, the Golden really doesn't have any idea which food is good for him and which food isn't, but he doesn't need to know. What he does need is a responsible owner—that would be you—to feed him a healthful, well-balanced diet.

This chapter details not only what a Golden Retriever needs to eat to get healthy and stay that way but also describes when and how he needs to do so.

WHY IS GOOD NUTRITION ESSENTIAL?

Golden Retrievers need good nutrition for the same reasons any other living being does: to become and remain healthy and strong and to be able to fight off any and all ailments that might otherwise befall him. For Goldens in particular, good nutrition has been linked to everything from combating fleas to helping to prevent cancer. (The latter condition is one that Golden Retrievers seem especially vulnerable to.) Equally important, good nutrition can keep a Golden lively and alert, help him be more willing to learn, and let him remain the picture of robust good health—in short, help him be the dog you wanted him to be when you welcomed him into your family.

Want to Know More?

For more information on puppy nutrition, see Chapter 3: Care of Your Puppy.

Golden Retrievers need good nutrition to remain healthy and strong.

Think of good nutrition as a building with individual nutrients composing the bricks and mortar of that building. Here are descriptions of those nutrients and their roles in a Golden's diet.

Carbohydrates

Carbohydrates are an energy source that comes from plants such as grains—for example, corn, wheat, and rice—and legumes, mainly soybeans. They're also the predominant form of energy in fruits and vegetables. These plants use sunlight to manufacture carbohydrates from carbon dioxide and water. Carbohydrates are prominent in many commercial dog foods—in fact, quite a few such foods contain 30 to 60 percent carbs—because the plants from which they're derived often represent a cheaper food source than other sources of nutrition. In addition, the starch in carbs adds structure and texture to dry dog food.

However, the actual importance of carbohydrates to dogs is a matter of some controversy. Traditionally, experts have said that carbs are essential for a healthy canine diet, but now that opinion is far from unanimous. That's because some dogs find grains, which are the most prominent source of carbohydrates, difficult to digest. Other dogs may develop allergies to grains, particularly wheat and corn. Still other experts note that wild canines generally don't consume any grains and thus take in far fewer carbohydrates than domestic dogs do; therefore, they reason, dogs don't really need carbs at all.

For these reasons, some veterinarians and breeders recommend that grains be kept out of dogs' diets. The result for such dogs is a far lower carb intake—but often an improvement in their health and quality of life. Check with your vet to see what's appropriate for your individual dog.

Fats

Fats are the compounds that result when a compound called glycerol combines with fatty acids. Although you certainly want to keep your Golden Retriever on the lean side—more information about that topic appears later in this chapter—fats nevertheless should be an important component of his diet. They play an important role in maintaining the health of your dog's skin, brain, eyes, hair, and other tissues; keeping his body temperature stable; and promoting healthy digestion. They also, believe it or not, are very important sources of energy because they contain more calories than either proteins or carbohydrates. Healthy fats come from meats, such as chicken and lamb, and from oils, such as sunflower oil and safflower oil.

Proteins

Proteins are large molecules made from chains of amino acids that contain carbon, hydrogen, nitrogen, and (usually) sulfur. Proteins are the building blocks of many organs, muscles, bones, blood, tissues, nails, and the immune system; they also enable the body to convert food into energy. They're available in many foods, but the best sources of protein are meats, poultry, fish, eggs, and dairy products. Dogs who don't get enough protein may have poor coats, subpar muscle development, weakened immune systems, and low red blood cell counts. Puppies whose diets contain insufficient protein may experience growth problems.

Vitamins and Minerals

Vitamins and minerals are substances that are found in minute amounts in foods. But while foods contain these substances only in very small quantities, those quantities do some very big jobs. They enable the body to process carbohydrates, proteins, and fats properly, help maintain the

Fats in the diet play an important role in keeping your Golden's coat healthy.

immune system and coat quality, and prevent a wide range of physical disorders. Both vitamins and minerals are found in a wide variety of foods and are also available in commercial supplements that can be added to food.

Water

The nutrients contained in food such as proteins, fats, vitamins, and minerals are all important to keeping your Golden Retriever healthy, but water is even more important. A Golden could go for a couple of weeks without much food, but he couldn't last for more than a couple of days without water.

Your Golden needs water—that simple combination of two hydrogen molecules with one oxygen molecule—for the same reasons that you do. Water is critical to regulating body temperature. It's also the foundation of the body's transportation systems: the circulatory system, which moves nutrients within the body, and the urinary system, which transports waste products outside the body.

That said, not all water is created equal. Obviously, clean water is better than water allowed to become scummy and filled with food particles. Tap water is way better than water your dog might lap from a puddle. And some veterinarians and dog enthusiasts believe that bottled or distilled water is better for a dog than water from the tap.

WHAT TO FEED YOUR GOLDEN

Combining all of those nutrients into healthy fare for your Golden Retriever is incredibly easy—or incredibly difficult, depending on how you approach the task. What makes the task easy is that you have plenty of options from which to choose. But that's also what makes the task tough.

Water is critical to regulating body temperature and is also the foundation of the body's transportation systems.

Commercial Food

Simply put, commercial dog food is any food that you can buy for your dog from retail outlets—either in cyberspace or at your local shopping center. But beyond definitions, commercial food doesn't stay simple. That's because there's a dizzying array of commercial dog foods available, with equally varying levels of quality. Among the commercial foods available are dry, canned, and semi-moist options.

Dry Foods

Also known as kibble, this type of food is generally the least expensive of commercial foods—particularly if you buy larger bags rather than smaller ones. Dry food consists of baked bite-sized pellets made from grain, meat, or meat by-products and other ingredients. A dry food meal is easy to fix: All you need to do is pour some kibble into your dog's dish and serve. Another advantage to kibble is that its rough texture makes it an edible toothbrush by scraping

plaque and tartar off the teeth. Still another plus to kibble is that it stays fresh longer than any other type of food once it's opened.

But kibble has some disadvantages too. For one thing, some dogs find an all-kibble, all-the-time diet to be a tad boring, and such dogs may become finicky eaters as a result. Another problem is that kibble often contains a relatively high percentage of grains, which some dogs might have trouble digesting and other dogs might be allergic to.

Canned Foods

Dog food in cans has a much higher moisture content than kibble does and is far more palatable to most pooches than kibble. It's also easier to digest. However, canned food doesn't stay fresh nearly as long as kibble does and must be refrigerated after being opened. Moreover, the high moisture content means that it's less economical; the same amount of canned product is likely to deliver far less nutrition for your food dollar than the same amount of dry food does.

Semi-Moist Foods

This type of food, also called soft/moist food, usually comes in boxes that contain single-serving pouches or bags. They contain more water than dry food but less water than canned. Such foods also tend to be high in salt, sugar, and preservatives in order to maintain freshness while keeping the food soft. For these reasons, experts don't recommend a steady diet of semi-moist foods. However, such foods can be good training treats (broken up, of course) and are convenient for traveling.

Noncommercial Food

Recent concerns over commercial pet food quality, particularly in light of ongoing pet food recalls, have prompted more and more pet owners to bypass commercial fare and prepare their dogs' meals themselves. Other owners—for example, those whose dogs are allergic to ingredients found in most commercial foods—may also opt to fix their canine companions' meals in their own kitchens. Either way, preparing your dog's food yourself holds two big advantages: You have total control over what your dog eats, and you can prepare food that you know pleases his unique palate.

However, prepping your dog's food yourself has some disadvantages too. For one thing, home preparation can be time consuming as well as inconvenient—particularly if you're traveling with your dog and need to feed him en route. Another potential pitfall has been that putting together a meal that not only pleases a Golden but also meets his nutritional needs can be a real challenge unless you're a veterinary nutritionist or have access to one.

Still, for many Golden owners the pluses of preparing meals for their dogs outweigh the minuses. And, happily, some minuses are becoming less of a problem, as can be seen in the following descriptions of the two main methods of home preparation.

Canned food is often more palatable to dogs than is dry food.

Home-Cooked Diet

This diet is exactly what it sounds like: a food regimen that is prepared and cooked in the home kitchen. A typical home-cooked meal for your dog would be a stew that includes meat, fresh fruits and vegetables, and (perhaps) a grain such as rice.

To ensure that the nutritional value of such a diet is as good as the taste, it's a good idea to consult your veterinarian—or, alternatively, other expert sources. One such source is *The Healthy Dog Cookbook* by Jonna Anne (TFH). A good online source is the recipe created by veterinarian and syndicated columnist Dr. Michael Fox. You can find this recipe at www.twobitdog.com/DrFox/Dr-Fox-Homemade-Dog-Food.

In addition, more manufacturers are creating food products to which owners can add fruits, vegetables, or cooked meats to create a complete meal. One such manufacturer is The Honest Kitchen; log onto the site at www.thehonestkitchen.com.

Raw Diet

This diet also is exactly what it sounds like: a food regimen that consists entirely of uncooked food. Raw food enthusiasts believe that uncooked food is better for dogs than cooked food because the raw product is closer than the cooked to what dogs in the wild eat. Among the advantages for dogs cited by raw food proponents are better overall health, cleaner teeth, smaller stools (a big plus with a large dog like a Golden Retriever!), and little to no processing to the food, which can mean fewer allergies and other adverse reactions to food.

Until recently, though, adhering to a raw food diet was even more of a hassle than a home-cooked diet. Devotees needed to visit their butcher to procure raw meats and bones, grind up the meat, add fresh vegetables and fruits,

Feeding a noncommercial diet requires a good bit of planning and preparation.

and keep the product fresh for a few days—at which point the whole cycle would begin again. For a large dog like a Golden Retriever, that would make for a whole lot of food prep.

Also at issue with raw diets is the whole matter of food safety. Raw meat frequently contains a whole host of harmful bacteria such as *Salmonella* and *E. coli*, not to mention parasites as well (such as the *Trichinella* worm in pork, which can cause trichinosis; however, freezing pork at 5°F [-15°C] for 20 days can kill the worm.). Raw diet devotees counter that a dog's digestive tract is much shorter than that of a person, which means that dogs are less likely to be affected by such bacteria than humans are.

Today, in any case, feeding a raw food diet to your Golden is a lot easier than was the case even a decade ago. That's because a growing number of companies are manufacturing raw food products that blend raw meat with vegetables and fruit and selling them in frozen patties or tubes.

If you opt to feed raw meat to your dog, make sure to wash your hands thoroughly with soap and hot water after handling, and clean any utensils and food preparation surfaces thoroughly if they're touched by raw meat. Also, if you're considering this option, check with your vet to make sure that a raw diet is right for your particular dog.

Special Diets

For a variety of reasons, some Golden Retrievers can't or shouldn't eat regular commercial dog food. A big reason to bypass commercial fare is to combat food allergies; more than a few dogs (including the one to whom this book is dedicated) are allergic to one or more common dog food ingredients, such as wheat, corn, beef, and/or chicken. Chapter 8 of this book discusses food allergies in greater detail, including how to detect them and how to choose foods that don't trigger allergenic reactions in your Golden.

Other conditions that may require or benefit from special diets are excess weight; higher-than-normal energy requirements (such as in dogs who compete in sports or who hunt regularly, or female dogs who are pregnant or nursing puppies); cancer; and old age.

If you think that your Golden has a condition that could benefit from a special diet, consult your veterinarian.

Treats and Bones

If you're teaching your Golden Retriever basic good manners (and you are, aren't you?), treats should be an essential part of your dog's diet. Treats come in a dizzying variety of products, some of which are better for your Golden than others. Those products include:

Cookies and Biscuits

Dogs like cookies and biscuits, but these treats are often high in calories and frequently made from grain or grain flour, which can trigger adverse reactions in the allergy-prone Golden. Moreover, because they're hard, it's tough breaking them off into the smaller-sized pieces that make for optimum treats. Some cookies and biscuits may also have dyes—these should be avoided.

Soft Treats

Dogs tend to like these types of treats even more than cookies and biscuits—and they're ideal for training because they break apart easily. What's more, many such treats are grain free and made from novel proteins. So if, for example, your dog is allergic to grains, chicken, or beef, you can find treats made from more exotic substances, such as venison, sweet potato, and duck.

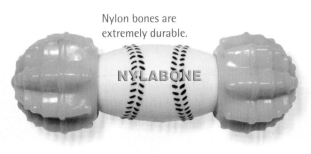

Nylon bones are extremely durable.

Plastic and Nylon Treats

Golden Retrievers are enthusiastic chewers, which makes them prime candidates for enjoying chew toys, such as Nylabones, which are made from plastic or nylon but are completely digestible and extremely durable.

Animal-Derived Treats

Pet manufacturing companies have developed an impressive assortment of chew treats derived from animal parts, including not only rawhide but also pigs' ears, pig snouts, cows' hooves, deer antlers, and even bull penises. For chew-happy dogs like Golden Retrievers, these chews can save countless couches, carpets, and other unauthorized objects from the ravages of Golden teeth.

Straight-From-the-Kitchen Treats

Your own kitchen probably contains a bunch of edibles that your Golden would enjoy. Among the possibilities: low-calorie treats such as sliced apples and carrots and frozen green beans; and high-value treats such as canned chicken (drained), cheddar cheese, and pieces of hot dogs. Chapter 9 explains why high-value treats play such an important role in training your Golden.

Meaty Bones

Veterinarians agree that dogs should never be given cooked bones to chew because they can splinter and injure the digestive tract. However, some holistic veterinarians and many raw-food proponents recommend giving your adult Golden a raw bone with meat on it for chewing. If you choose to give your dog this special treat, do so in a place where the floor can be easily cleaned or where a carpet is covered with tarp or a shower curtain. And never, ever give your dog a raw bone unless you're there to supervise him and to remove the bone if your dog chews it down to a size where he can swallow it and choke.

That never-without-supervision rule applies not only to raw bones but to any type of treat that takes more than a quick chew and swallow; such treats include Nylabones, hooves, pig ears and other animal-derived treats. The reason's the same: You need to monitor your dog's chewing progress and make sure that he doesn't choke on the treat.

WHEN TO FEED AN ADULT DOG

Once your Golden Retriever reaches adulthood, you can settle him into a regular feeding schedule. And while for most Goldens that schedule is pretty simple, that's not always the case. Read on to understand why and to figure out when are the best times to feed your dog.

How Often

You may have heard that an adult dog needs to eat only once a day—and that's generally true. However, the fact that adult dogs, including Goldens, can tolerate having a once-daily meal doesn't mean that that's an optimum feeding schedule for them. The Golden who gets his daily meal in the evening may find himself feeling hungry all day, which isn't a pleasant sensation. A once-daily meal in the morning may cause a Golden to wake up in the middle of the night feeling hungry, which isn't conducive to getting a good night's sleep for him or for you.

Another more serious problem related to feeding once a day is that researchers have discovered that such a regimen increases the odds that large dogs like Golden Retrievers will develop bloat, an extremely serious condition that can result in death if untreated. The condition causes the stomach to swell up from gas and may also cause the stomach to twist as much as 180 degrees.

For these reasons, a twice-daily food regimen is much better for your Golden Retriever. Feeding him twice a day keeps his tummy fuller longer both day and night and is easier on his digestive system than would be the case if that system needed to process a whole day's worth of food at once. The twice-daily meal plan is also great for the Golden who spends time alone during the day. That's because, just as with people, dogs tend to get sleepy after they eat—which means that your home-alone dog may be more interested in taking a nap than in wreaking havoc in your home. The same will apply at night, when an evening meal will help him (and you) get a good night's sleep.

Multi-Dog Tip

Be careful when feeding your Golden and the other dogs in your multi-canine household. If you feed them at the same time, feed each dog in a different location of your house. If you feed them in the same location, feed one dog at a time. Either way, by staggering feedings you'll prevent food fights among your canine family members.

Choosing the Right Food for Your Golden

With so many options, you might find yourself feeling overwhelmed at the prospect of figuring which food(s) are best for your Golden Retriever. Relax. Once you know what to look for, selecting your Golden's grub may not be child's play, but it's a lot easier than you might think. Here's what to do.

Consult Your Breeder. If you trust and respect your breeder, her recommendations may be a good starting point.

Check out product reviews. *The Whole Dog Journal,* a monthly newsletter that doesn't accept any advertising, publishes product reviews of dry and canned dog foods every year. These reviews can save you a lot of time evaluating possible foods for your dog. To learn more, log onto the newsletter's website at www.whole-dog-journal.com.

Look at the ingredient list. For any dog food you're considering, check the ingredients listed on the label. If one or more meats are listed first, that means that the food in question contains more meat than any other ingredient, which is a sign of good quality. Lower-quality foods tend to list grains or grain by-products first.

Study the meat. Not all meats listed on a dog food ingredient label are created equal. "Meat by-products," for example, may mean that your Golden is eating a chicken beak or other equally unsavory part of the animal. A label that simply lists a meat—chicken, beef, duck, ostrich, or other food product derived from livestock or fowl—indicates a dog food that's a much better choice.

Check for additives and preservatives. Look to see whether the listed ingredients include butylated hydroxyanisole (BHA) and/or butylated hydroxytoluene (BHT), two preservatives that have been used to prevent fats in food from spoiling. Studies have shown that high levels of either BHA or BHT can cause a variety of serious problems in animals. Avoid dog foods that list either of these products on the labels.

See how the food affects your dog. Once you choose a food for your dog, your job isn't over. In addition to watching to see whether your Golden likes his grub, see how the food affects his body. Signs that a food doesn't agree with him include bulky, soft stools; flaky skin; flatulence; and weight gain. And if your Golden Retriever turns his nose up at his food, respect his preference and find something else if you can.

Feeding Schedule

Some people might argue that the food regimen that's easiest on a dog's digestive system is not having a schedule at all. But having food available to your Golden at all times—a practice that's known as free-feeding—isn't a good idea for several reasons. If your dog picks at his food throughout the day, you might not notice that he's lost his appetite as quickly as would be the case if he were fed on a twice-daily schedule. That difference can be important because appetite loss is often an early sign of illness. This problem is compounded if yours is a multi-dog household and you leave one bowl out for all of the dogs to eat from. Not only will you find it more difficult to pick up on one dog's loss of appetite, but you'll also have a tougher time figuring out which dog in your pack is having that problem.

In addition, by feeding your dog on a schedule, you can predict when he's going to need a potty break. With free-feeding, it's much tougher to predict when your dog will need to do the doo.

Finally, leaving food out for your dog all day can be an open invitation for other creatures to try sharing that food with your dog. Such creatures—namely cockroaches and mice—not only are a nuisance but also are also unsanitary and may carry disease.

What Times

Plan to feed your adult Golden once in the morning and once in the evening at whatever time is convenient for you. Some dog owners like to feed their dogs before they have their own breakfasts and dinners; others prefer to eat first, then feed their dogs. Either way is fine.

But no matter what time you feed your dog, make sure that mealtime is a good, stress-free time for him. Here are some ideas to help you do just that:

Learn Your Dog's Dining Preferences

Some Goldens like to eat in the kitchen surrounded by other members of the household going about their business. Others prefer to eat in solitude and quiet. Study your Golden to see which conditions he prefers—and once you have an idea of what those conditions are, don't be afraid to cater to him a little. By doing so, you can help him eat better during meals and feel better after meals. Indeed, by feeding him in what he considers to be an optimum environment, he's less likely to suffer after-meal digestive stresses, such as belching and flatulence.

Let Him Eat in Peace

No matter when and how your Golden likes to eat, he has the right to eat uninterrupted. Even if your dog is the most patient sort imaginable, don't let your toddler waddle over to the dog's dining corner while he dining. If you're lucky, the toddler's presence will simply be stressful for your dog; if you're not so lucky, the dog may growl, snap at, or even bite the perceived intruder.

Let Him Linger a Little

Unless your Golden Retriever is a fussy eater (and many Golden owners would express sincere doubt that such a dog exists), don't be too quick to pick up his dish after mealtime. By giving him 15 minutes or so to eat his meal, you'll reduce the likelihood that he'll scarf it down too quickly,

Feeding your Golden twice daily will help him feel fuller and is easier on his digestive system.

which in turn will decrease the odds that he'll get a post-dining tummy upset.

Wash Those Dishes

For the sake of cleanliness, be as conscientious about washing your dog's dishes as you are about washing your own. Ideally, you should include them along with the other items in your dishwasher. At the very least, hand wash the food dish after each meal and the water dish at least once a day.

OBESITY

No question about it, Golden Retrievers are wonderful. Many believe that they are the most wonderful dogs, if not creatures, to grace the planet. But even when it comes to Golden Retrievers—at least individual Golden Retrievers—you can have too much of a good thing. In other words, it's not good for your Golden to get fat. Even plumpness is not pleasing.

But if your Golden is carrying more poundage than he needs to be, he's far from alone. According to the American Veterinary Medical Association (AVMA), as many as 47 percent of American dogs are overweight or obese. Meanwhile, Pfizer Animal Health, a company that manufactures pharmaceutical products for animals, counts Golden Retrievers among those breeds that are more prone than others to packing on too many pounds (kg).

Causes of Obesity

The main causes of excess weight and obesity are the same for Goldens as they are for people: eating too much and exercising too little. More specifically, if a Golden is overweight, the number of calories he takes in through eating exceeds the number of calories he expends through exercising. The difference between what he takes in and what he uses is

Training Tidbit

Mealtimes can be wonderful training opportunities. Once your dog knows how to sit and stay (see Chapter 9 for details on how to teach these cues), have him perform these behaviors before each meal. Hold his food dish off the floor and tell him to sit and stay. Then place the food dish on the floor. Wait a few seconds, then tell him "Okay." By having to wait politely for his meal, you not only avoid having him mow you down as he races to grab his grub, but you also teach him self-control.

excess calories, which his body stores in the form of fat.

However, weight problems in Golden Retrievers and other dogs can also result from other causes. Being spayed or neutered can be a factor; either procedure may slow down a dog's metabolism and result in weight gain if the dog's food intake isn't adjusted accordingly. Another factor can be hormonal disorders such as hypothyroidism, a condition in which the thyroid gland produces insufficient thyroid hormone—and is a condition that Goldens are especially susceptible to. Finally, age alone can cause a pooch to pack on the pounds (kg). Just as people tend to develop a "middle age spread," so can Golden Retrievers by the time they're five or six years of age.

Risks of Obesity

No matter what causes a Golden's excess weight or obesity, however, either condition jeopardizes the dog's health and longevity. An overweight dog is at greater risk than his thinner counterpart for developing a variety of serious illnesses, including arthritis, heart disease, breathing problems, heatstroke, skin problems, spinal problems—and cancer, the number-one cause of death in the breed. Extra weight can also compromise a dog's immune system and heighten the risks associated with surgery and anesthesia. The result may be not only a lower quality of life but also a shorter life: A study by Nestle Purina showed that dogs whose food intake was restricted over their lifetimes—and thus maintained ideal weights— lived 15 percent longer than dogs who were allowed to eat as much as they wanted.

The right amount of exercise will help keep your Golden from becoming obese.

How to Tell Whether Your Dog Is too Plump

So how do you know whether your Golden Retriever weighs more than he should? Sometimes it's hard to tell. A Golden's full, luxuriant coat may conceal a spare tire or two. But if a dog's looks won't tell, his ribs will. Run your hands firmly along the sides of his body; if you can't feel his ribs easily or determine where one rib ends and the other begins, he probably weighs more than he should. Another way to assess your dog's physique is to give him a bath or take him for a swim; with his wet fur matted against his body, you'll find it easier to see whether he is in the shape he should be.

If you're still not sure, check out Nestle Purina's Body Condition System at www.purina.com/dogs/health/bodycondition.aspx. There you'll find nine ratings that can help you determine whether your Golden is too thin, too heavy, or just right.

What to Do if Your Dog Is Obese

If the verdict is "too heavy," you need to take steps to help your Golden recover his sleek physique. Here are some ways to do just that.

Take Him for a Checkup

Your veterinarian may discover that a medical problem, such as hypothyroidism, is causing your Golden to look porky. By uncovering any such condition and correcting it with medication, you could solve your dog's weight problem very easily. And even if your vet finds no medical cause for your dog's weight gain, she can still help you put together a diet and exercise plan that will enable your Golden to take off those extra pounds (kg) and keep them off.

Say No to Free Feeding

If you've been leaving a dish of food out all day for your Golden and filling it up as he empties it, now's the time to end that practice. Many Goldens don't know when to stop eating. If you keep filling up his food bowl, he'll keep filling up his tummy—and then some.

Limit Intake

With your vet's help, gradually reduce the amount of food you give your Golden. Make the reduction significant enough to help him lose weight but not so significant that he's constantly begging for food.

Feed Him More Often

Notice that the suggestion here is not to feed more food—it's to take that reduced amount of food and divide it into two or even three meals per day. Frequent small meals will help your Golden's tummy stay full longer so that he doesn't feel as hungry between meals.

Add Fiber

Putting a few fresh fruits or veggies in your dog's dinner (or breakfast, or both) can help fill his tummy without adding many calories. Good options to try are apples, carrots, frozen brussels sprouts and frozen green beans; and for possible added health benefits, try finely chopped raw broccoli (fresh or frozen), which some studies have shown may also help reduce his risk of cancer. Be prepared, though, for his needing extra trips to the outdoor potty; fiber acts as a laxative for dogs, just as it does for people.

Adjust for Treats

If you're teaching new behaviors to your dog and using treats to do so, reduce the size of your dog's meals to compensate for the extra calories he's consuming while he's learning. Otherwise, your Golden Retriever scholar may also be a Golden Retriever blimp.

Get Moving

Exercise not only mellows out a Golden but also can accelerate weight loss. By pairing decreased calorie intake with increased calorie use, your dog will lose weight faster than with just smaller meals alone.

Go Gradually

Weight that's lost gradually is more likely to stay lost than weight that's shed quickly.

Foods like carrots can help fill up your Golden without adding many calories.

CHAPTER 8

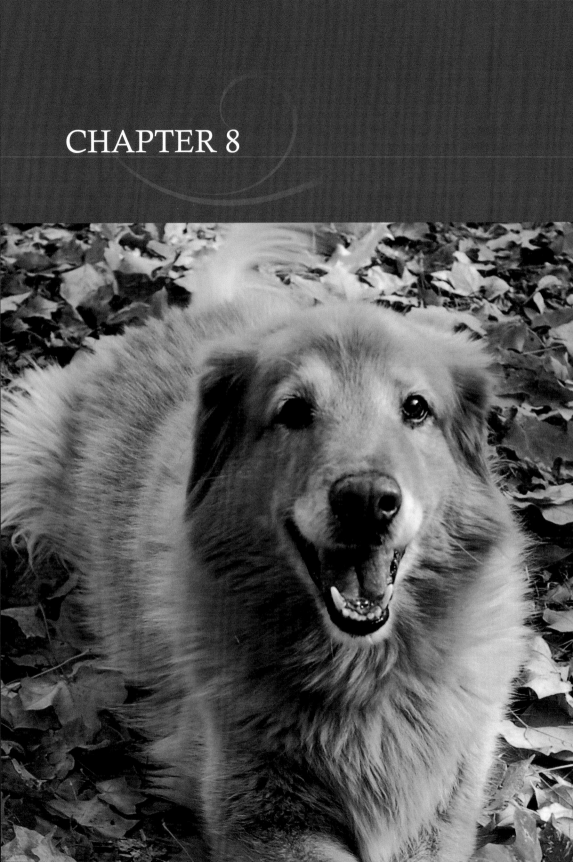

GOLDEN RETRIEVER HEALTH AND WELLNESS

Watching a happy Golden Retriever frolic and otherwise go about his business is pure joy. His glorious coat, joyous disposition, and unabashed appetite for life bring smiles to the faces of all who see him. His whole being radiates good health. Chances are, though, that the good health that Golden epitomizes didn't just happen. In all likelihood, that Golden's owner has worked hard to keep him healthy and has moved aggressively to combat any ills that might befall him. This chapter explains how you can not only keep your Golden Retriever well but also deal effectively during those times (and they will happen) when he's not.

THE ANNUAL VET EXAM

People need regular checkups, or wellness exams, by their doctors, and the same is true with Golden Retrievers. Your Golden needs a wellness exam every year until he reaches his eighth or ninth birthday. At that point, he becomes the canine equivalent of a senior citizen and needs a wellness exam twice a year instead of just once.

The wellness exam is a checkup to make sure that your Golden is doing as well as he appears to be. Generally, a wellness exam includes the following:

- **Measuring weight.** The veterinarian or an assistant will have your dog step on a floor scale to see how much he weighs.
- **Measuring vitals.** The vet will measure and record your dog's temperature, pulse, and respiration.
- **Checking the ears and eyes.** The vet will peer into your Golden's eyes and ears to check for redness, discharge, odor, or any other signs of ear and eye infection or disease.
- **Checking the body.** The vet should run her hands over your Golden's body to see if he has any lumps, bumps, or tender areas. The vet also probably will check to see whether your dog's ribs can be felt easily; if they can't, he's probably overweight.
- **Looking at the skin.** While running hands over your Golden's body, the vet also will

Want to Know More?

If you're wondering how to find the perfect vet for your newly adopted adult dog, see Chapter 3: Care of Your Puppy.

tract infections, nutritional problems, and/or parasites. The vet may also give your dog an immunization if one is scheduled.

Occasionally, a wellness exam reveals problems or illnesses that haven't exhibited outward symptoms. More often, though, the exam gives the veterinarian a baseline against which to measure any bodily changes that your dog might undergo in the future.

PARASITES

Plenty of parasites would love to freeload off your Golden Retriever. Although these critters are very small, they can cause your Golden a whole lot of discomfort, not to mention endanger his health (and perhaps yours). Here is a list of the most common parasites to besiege the inside and outside of your Golden Retriever's body, as well as instructions on how to detect and get rid of them.

Internal Parasites

Some parasites do their dirty work inside your canine companion's insides. Among these inside jobbers are:

Heartworms

The heartworm is a type of worm that is spread via mosquito bites. When a mosquito carrying heartworm larvae bites a dog, the mosquito transmits the larvae into the dog. Once inside the dog's body, the larvae spend the next several months maturing into adult heartworms that reproduce and take up residence in the dog's heart, lungs, and circulatory system. The initial symptom of a heartworm problem is usually a persistent cough; as the worms continue to reproduce, the dog may also become lethargic and experience abnormal breathing. A severely infected dog may also experience fainting.

Although heartworm is treatable, the

Your Golden needs regular checkups, or wellness exams, performed by a vet.

probably check his skin to see whether it's flaky, has a rash, or exhibits anything else that's out of the ordinary.

- **Looking inside the mouth.** The vet will look at your dog's gums to see whether there's any redness or puffiness—both of which are signs of gum disease—and plaque or tartar on the teeth.
- **Drawing blood.** The veterinarian may draw a small sample of your dog's blood, mainly to determine whether he has heartworm.

The vet may also ask you to bring in a sample of your Golden Retriever's urine and stool for analysis to see whether he has any urinary treatment can be debilitating for the dog. The veterinarian may either prescribe an arsenic drug compound—which will require that the dog be hospitalized—or an injection of a compound called melarsomine dihydrochloride. Either way, though, treatment can result in complications. For example, the dead heartworms may obstruct the blood vessels. Such obstructions may cause the dog to develop a fever, a worsened cough, and blood in the liquid the dog coughs up. For this reason, dogs being treated for heartworm aren't allowed to exercise.

Heartworm is much easier to prevent than to treat. Chewable preventives include tablets of ivermectin and milbemycin oxime; topical treatments consist of selamectin and moxidectin. All are usually given monthly.

However, your dog should be tested for heartworm before preventive treatment begins.

Hookworms

The hookworm is, literally, a bloodsucker. The adult hookworms live and mate inside the intestine of their host, usually a dog; the resulting eggs are expelled in the dog's stool. Those eggs hatch in the soil and develop in the environment. The resulting larvae are then ready to infect a new host—either by entering any part of a dog's skin that touches the ground or by being present in soil that the dog licks when he cleans himself—and become adults. Hookworms can also infect people. Hookworm infection is especially common in puppies and can be fatal if not treated. Signs of infection include pallor, physical weakness, iron

Roundworms are quite common in puppies, but a Golden of any age can acquire them.

deficiency, and possibly diarrhea. Getting rid of the hookworms requires two treatments of a dewormer, such as mebendazole, fenbendazole or pyrantel pamoate. A severely infected dog may also need a blood transfusion and/or an iron supplement.

Heartworm preventives are also effective in preventing hookworms.

Roundworms

This parasite is very common in puppies, but a Golden of any age can acquire it. If a dog has contact with an infected animal (for example, a rodent) or steps on soil that has roundworm eggs on it, the eggs enter the body and arrive at the dog's intestinal tract. There the eggs hatch into larvae, and the larvae migrate to other parts of the body and reproduce. The eggs are expelled through the dog's stool. Symptoms of roundworm include coughing, diarrhea, vomiting, and a distended belly. Diagnosis occurs mainly through analysis of a stool sample. To rid the dog of roundworms, the veterinarian may prescribe one of a wide variety of dewormers.

Roundworms can also be prevented if the dog is taking regular flea control or heartworm prevention products.

Tapeworms

A Golden Retriever who has tapeworms is also a Golden Retriever who has fleas. That's because the only way a Golden or other dog can acquire tapeworms is to swallow a flea that has consumed a tapeworm. The tapeworm migrates to the dog's intestine, where it latches onto the intestinal wall. There, the worm sheds segments of its body that are expelled through the rectum. Each segment is the size of a grain of rice, and it's visible in the dog's stool, around the rectum, and even on the dog's bed. Treatment consists of either ingesting or being injected with a dewormer. Prevention requires an effective flea control program.

Whipworms

Another common parasite that lives in the soil in and around dog poop is the whipworm. If your Golden Retriever ingests such soil or has contact with infected stool, he's likely to become infected. Mild cases don't exhibit symptoms, but severe cases result in bloody diarrhea that can kill the dog—especially if he is a puppy—if not treated. The dog may also have otherwise unexplained weight loss. Diagnosis occurs when whipworm eggs appear in a dog's stool. To rid the dog of whipworms, the veterinarian will prescribe one of many deworming medications.

External Parasites

Other parasites don't bother to migrate to your Golden's insides; instead, they get what they need while living on your dog's skin. These unwanted critters include:

Fleas

These almost microscopically small creatures can make your Golden Retriever's life miserable. A single bite can be almost unbearably itchy. If your Golden is allergic to fleas, he may scratch bitten areas so hard that he'll lose his coat and cause the affected area to bleed. And because fleas dine on your dog's blood, without treatment he's likely to become anemic.

Ticks can be prevented by keeping dogs out of high grasses or low shrubs, where these parasites like to congregate.

If your Golden begins to scratch himself almost constantly, suspect fleas and take a look at his tummy to confirm your suspicion. You may see black specks, which are probably flea dirt, on his stomach or groin. To be sure, mix the specks with water. If the specks turn red, your Golden's got fleas. Still not sure? Run a flea comb through your dog's coat; if he has fleas, you'll see them crawling around the teeth of the comb.

Fortunately, you and your dog don't have to put up with fleas, thanks to the pharmaceutical companies that have developed a variety of products to eradicate these freeloaders. Some do their work by stopping flea eggs from developing; others kill adult fleas that bite a treated dog. Even better is that some of these products prevent some internal parasites such as heartworms, hookworms, roundworms, and whipworms from taking hold. However, a vet's prescription is needed for any of these products.

Mites

Mites are very small parasites that tunnel under a dog's skin, causing intense itching; the condition they cause is known as sarcoptic mange or scabies. The affected area—generally on a less hairy part of the dog's body, such as the armpit or belly—may also become inflamed, and hair loss may occur. The edges of the ears and elbow are very often involved. The condition can be difficult to diagnose. A skin scraping may reveal the presence of mites. If that's not the case, the veterinarian may look to other factors, such as a sudden onset of an apparent skin allergy that is actually a sign of sarcoptic mange. In many cases, flea and heartworm preventive treatments are effective in ridding a dog of sarcoptic mange. Such treatments require a veterinarian's prescription.

Ringworm

This condition isn't an actual worm infestation; rather, it's a fungus that infects not only dogs but also cats and people. Direct contact with either an infected animal or a contaminated item (for example, grooming equipment) transmits the infection. The primary symptom is a small round lesion that has no hair, often with scaly skin in its center. These lesions often occur on the head but may also appear on the tail or legs. Sometimes the condition is confused with demodectic mange. The most effective way to diagnose ringworm is to collect scales from the lesion and perform a culture. To treat ringworm, the veterinarian may prescribe either an oral or topical antifungal medication.

What to Do if You Spot a Tick

If you see a tick on your dog, remove it promptly and properly. First, put on a pair of rubber gloves and grab some tweezers. With the tweezers, grab the tick's body and pull it straight off your dog without twisting or jerking as you pull. Examine what you've removed to be sure that you've removed the tick's head as well as the rest of the body. If the head appears to have been left behind, use a needle dipped in alcohol to remove it. Kill the tick by putting it in a bowl of alcohol, and clean the area where you pulled the tick with soap, water, and rubbing alcohol.

For isolated lesions, the hair should be clipped as short as possible, and any equipment used for the clipping or to otherwise groom the dog should be sterilized immediately after use.

Ticks

Ticks come in several varieties, but any type of tick poses a significant danger to both dogs and people. They transmit serious diseases such as Lyme disease, Rocky Mountain spotted fever, and ehrlichiosis. Symptoms of these illnesses in dogs include weight loss, lethargy, decreased appetite, unexplained lameness, and ear or eye infections that don't respond to medication. Antibiotics are used to treat these conditions, but they can also be prevented by keeping dogs out of high grasses or low shrubs, where ticks like to congregate, and (if your veterinarian approves) using topical tick treatments. Another effective preventive is checking your dog regularly for ticks. They're easy to spot: ladybug-sized dark arachnids that cling to the dog's skin.

BREED-SPECIFIC HEALTH ISSUES

Several illnesses seem to strike Goldens disproportionately compared with other breeds. Reputable Golden Retriever breeders are working to eliminate or at least greatly reduce the occurrences of these diseases in their puppies by screening dogs before breeding them and by carefully selecting dogs who overall represent the best of the breed to include in breeding programs. But because the breed is so popular, many less ethical breeders are not testing their breeding stock for these diseases, with sometimes tragic results for those who buy the puppies from such breeders.

That's why it's important to watch your adult dog for symptoms of the following genetic problems. This is especially important if you adopted your Golden as an adult from a shelter or rescue group, where his parentage is probably unknown, or if you purchased him from a breeder that did not supply you with copies of the parents' health clearances for hip and elbow dysplasia, eye problems, and subaortic stenosis (SAS). And if your Golden shows any signs of a problem, bring him to your veterinarian right away. Early detection means early treatment—which in turn could greatly improve your Golden's quality of life, not to mention save that life altogether.

Here are the five most notable conditions that affect the Golden Retriever.

Elbow Dysplasia

This condition occurs when the bones and cartilage of the elbow don't fit together properly. It's commonly seen in young, growing large-breed dogs like Goldens—and like hip dysplasia, is a genetic condition.

Symptoms include obvious lameness in one or both front legs. An X-ray can confirm the diagnosis. Treatment depends on the way the mis-fit occurs: For some dogs, surgery is appropriate; for others, regular low-impact exercise such as walking or swimming can help.

Eye Diseases.

Golden Retrievers are susceptible to a number of eye diseases. These include the following.

Eyelid and Eyelash Problems.

Some Golden Retrievers have eyelids or eyelashes that aren't structured normally, which can result in chronic eye irritation or inflammation. Most common among Goldens is distichiasis, which causes the eyelashes to grow on the inner surface of the eyelids, rubbing up against the cornea and causing the irritated eye to redden and develop a discharge. An affected dog will squint, blink, and rub his eye in an effort to alleviate the irritation; without treatment, the cornea may develop lesions and become infected.

Less common are entropion, which causes the eyelids to roll inward, and ectropion, which occurs when the lower lid is so loose that it droops and forms a pocket in which dust, pollen, and other foreign substances can accumulate and cause irritation. Surgery is the treatment of choice for entropion in order to pull the eyelid into a normal position. To treat ectropion, the veterinarian may prescribe medication to alleviate infections and irritation; for severe cases, surgery can shorten the eyelid and remove the pocket.

Golden Retrievers are susceptible to a number of eye diseases.

Juvenile Cataracts

In this condition, which generally occurs before a Golden is five years of age, the lens of the eye becomes cloudy, which can partially or completely block light from reaching the retina. Some juvenile cataracts resolve on their own; others are so small that they have little effect on the dog's vision. For larger cataracts that don't resolve on their own, a veterinarian may choose to treat the condition with medicated eye drops or may suggest surgery to remove them.

Pigmentary Uveitis

Also known as Golden Retriever uveitis, this condition can lead to glaucoma or cataracts. Symptoms include red, bloodshot, cloudy, or hazy eyes. The condition usually shows up in middle-aged or older Goldens and can be controlled with medication.

Progressive Retinal Atrophy (PRA)

This genetic disorder causes cells in the retina at the back of the eye to degenerate and die, resulting in night blindness. There is no cure for PRA, but fortunately it's relatively rare in Golden Retrievers.

Hip Dysplasia

Hip dysplasia occurs when the two bones of the ball-and-socket joint of the hip don't fit together properly. The condition is genetic; If one or both of a Golden Retriever's parents have the disease, that Golden is more likely to develop the disease than would be the case with a Golden who doesn't have that genetic heritage. For dogs already at risk for developing hip dysplasia, excess weight and forceful exercise such as jumping (as opposed to exercise that provides steady strengthening, such as running and swimming) could increase those risks.

A dog who's developing hip dysplasia will show signs of discomfort during and after exercise and will be stiff when getting up from a reclining position. The dog may hesitate to fully extend his hind legs when walking. Most dogs develop outward signs of hip dysplasia in middle age or older, but some severe cases may exhibit symptoms during puppyhood or young adulthood. A veterinarian can confirm the diagnosis by taking X-rays of the hips.

Treatment depends on the severity of the condition. For some dogs with mild to moderate cases, a combination of proper diet, moderate exercise, and appropriate medication

A Golden with hip dysplasia will show signs of discomfort during and after exercise and will be stiff when getting up from a reclining position.

Many Golden Retrievers feel unsteady when they step onto a veterinarian's scale, and they compensate for that unsteadiness by leaning against a wall if the scale adjoins one. Contact with the wall may help the Golden to feel more secure but also results in an inaccurate reading on the scale. To keep your Golden from performing a scale-induced wall leaning, teach him to walk onto the scale away from the wall. Here's what to do:

- Have your dog sit.
- Take a treat and hold it in front of your dog's nose.
- Keeping the treat at nose level, move it away from him about 2 inches (5 cm) in from the outer edge of the scale.

As he follows the treat, the dog should automatically stand and walk onto the scale without leaning into the wall. When all four of his feet are on the scale, feed him the treat.

can make a big difference. Other dogs may need surgery to repair or even replace the hip.

Hypothyroidism

The thyroid gland regulates a dog's metabolism through the production of hormones. If a dog's thyroid gland fails to produce sufficient quantities of those hormones, hypothyroidism is the result. Symptoms of hypothyroidism include unexplained weight gain, lethargy, hair loss—often symmetrical and on both sides of the body—a dry coat, and excessive shedding. The diagnosis is confirmed with a blood test. Treatment is simple: placing the dog on a daily dose of a synthetic hormone tablet.

Hypothyroidism—and even thyroid production on the low side of normal—has recently been implicated in causing behavioral changes in dogs, such as erratic behavior and unprovoked aggression. This is one reason why, if your dog shows sudden changes in his behavior, a consultation with your veterinarian is in order.

Subaortic Stenosis (SAS)

This condition, also known as SAS, is a hereditary disease that often has lethal results. The cause of SAS is a narrowing of the left ventricle of the heart, which reduces the flow of blood from the organ. The result: sudden death after normal exercise.

That said, a veterinarian can pick up signs of SAS during an examination of an outwardly normal puppy. If the veterinarian hears a heart murmur while examining a puppy under four months of age—particularly if the puppy is a breed prone to SAS, such as Golden Retrievers—the vet is likely to recommend that the puppy be reevaluated in a few months. Some puppies have what are called "innocent murmurs" that disappear by the time they are 16 weeks of age. A heart murmur that persists beyond that time may indicate SAS. X-rays and ultrasound examinations can confirm the diagnosis. A diagnosis that occurs during puppyhood may allow SAS to be managed, which can prolong the affected dog's life. The veterinarian may prescribe medication to regulate the heart's rhythm so that the sequence that causes the death of the dog does not occur.

GENERIC HEALTH ISSUES

Many other health problems that Golden Retrievers face are not necessarily the result of genetic bad luck. Here are some of the most common nongenetic health problems besetting Goldens and how you can help your dog deal with them.

Allergies and Food Intolerance

Allergies and food intolerance have long been prevalent among Golden Retrievers; in fact, experts say that they're the number-one reason that owners seek veterinary help for their Goldens. Symptoms of allergies include ear

infections that don't respond to medication or that recur quickly, frequent licking and/or chewing of the feet, frequent scratching of the armpits, and rubbing of the face. The dog may also bite or scratch his tail, thighs, and groin and develop a rash and even a bacterial infection in those areas if his biting and scratching are severe.

To treat the allergies, a veterinarian is likely to take a two-step approach. The first step is to relieve the immediate discomfort the allergic reaction is causing. This could range from prescribing antihistamines or short-acting corticosteroids to treat skin reactions to prescribing antibiotics, topical treatments, and ear washes for ear infections. The second step is to try to determine what's causing the reaction—but doing so can be challenging. That's because canine allergic reactions can be

If your Golden appears to be not feeling well, take him to the vet.

caused by one or more of a long list of possible offending substances, including pollen, house dust, mold, dust mites, flea bites, and food.

Food Allergy

One clue to a possible food allergy is if the allergic reaction occurs year-round; the dog may also vomit and have diarrhea. If the veterinarian suspects that food is the culprit, she will probably recommend that the Golden be placed on a food elimination trial. This test places the dog on a strict food regimen that consists of one protein and one starch that the dog has never eaten before. No treats, chews, supplements, or chewable drugs are permitted, and you need to make sure that your Golden doesn't score unauthorized table scraps or other foods meant for people. Your Golden will stay on this diet for at least eight weeks and as long as four months, depending on how he responds. If his symptoms have diminished significantly at the end of the trial period, it's safe to assume that at least one of the foods that he customarily had received is the culprit. The test then moves to the second phase: keeping the dog on the current diet but adding his old foods one at a time to see whether the allergic reaction returns. When an allergic reaction occurs, you know that you should eliminate that food from the dog's diet. That said, you may decide not to perform the second step of the trial. Instead, you can keep your dog on the same diet as the food trial diet or feed him other foods that he hasn't had before.

If your Golden's symptoms don't improve during the food trial, your vet may refer you to a veterinary dermatologist, who can test your dog for other allergies. The dermatologist may perform either a blood test or a skin test. Depending on the results, the dermatologist may formulate a program of allergy shots for your dog. Allergy shots, more formally known as immunotherapy, involve injecting progressively larger amounts of the identified allergens into the dog's skin so that the dog becomes less and less sensitive to the allergens. These shots can be very effective but may take as long as a year to show results.

Flea Allergy

If your dog has fleas, your veterinarian is likely to identify his problem as flea allergy dermatitis. To treat the allergy, you need to eradicate the fleas.

Cancer

According to the Golden Retriever Club of America (GRCA), cancer is the leading cause of death among Golden Retrievers. However, it's important to keep these statistics in perspective, as ominous as they sound. That's because, according to the Animal Cancer Center at Colorado State University, 50 percent of all dogs develop cancer if they live ten years or longer. Many dog deaths from cancer reflect the fact that modern veterinary medicine helps our dogs live longer than they did a generation ago or before. However, far too many young or middle-aged dogs, especially Goldens, also find themselves battling cancer.

You can do a great deal to help your dog fight that battle by knowing the signs indicating that he may have one or more cancers. Those signs include:

- **Abnormal swellings** that appear suddenly, persist, or continue to grow. Don't panic: Chances are the lump is harmless. But you can't know for sure that that's the case until the lump a gets look from your vet.
- **Sores that don't heal.** A healthy dog's body heals a cut or sore within a week or two. If a lesion doesn't heal, all's not well within the dog's body, and the reason could be the onset of cancer. Contact your vet.

- **Unexplained weight loss.** Congratulations if your dog is losing weight because of the supervised weight-loss diet you've put him on. But if he's losing weight for no apparent reason, he needs to see his vet as soon as possible.
- **Loss of appetite.** Golden Retrievers are the chowhounds of the canine kingdom; there's practically nothing they won't eat. Consequently, if your Golden shows no interest in food, something's probably wrong. Call your vet.
- **Bleeding or discharge from any body opening.** Blood or any other discharge from the nostrils, mouth, ears, anus, or urethra is not normal and needs a vet's attention.
- **Offensive odor.** Golden Retrievers love to do things that make them stink: rolling in something yucky, eating poop, you

name it. And even if they're not doing something to make themselves stink, other problems can make them smell less than socially acceptable—for example, a yeasty odor from an ear infection or bad breath due to dental disease. However, an offensive odor that can't be explained can indicate that something serious is amiss with your Golden. Call your vet as soon as possible.
- **Difficulty eating or swallowing.** Painful teeth and gums can cause your Golden to have trouble eating or swallowing, but so can a tumor that's blocking the esophagus. Call your vet.
- **Hesitation to exercise or loss of stamina.** Healthy Golden Retrievers are highly energetic individuals. If your normally I-could-walk-all-day Golden suddenly starts

When dealing with an illness like cancer, your vet can make an accurate diagnosis.

Cancer-Fighting Drugs

In 2009, the U.S. Food and Drug Administration (FDA) approved the first drug specifically designed to fight cancer in dogs. The new drug, which carries the trade name Palladia, is to treat mast cell cancers. The drug kills tumor cells and cuts off the blood supply to a tumor.

The development of Palladia reflects the wide range of research that scientists are conducting to learn more about cancer in Golden Retrievers and other dogs and to devise ways to beat this collection of diseases. Several organizations, including the American Kennel Club Canine Health Foundation, the Morris Animal Foundation, and the Golden Retriever Foundation are continually raising funds to pay for research projects that could result in breakthroughs similar to Palladia. For more information on some of the research projects that could benefit Golden Retrievers and other dogs, visit the Golden Retriever Foundation website at www. goldenretrieverfoundation.org.

needing to stop and rest during a walk, he needs a vet's attention.

- **Persistent lameness or stiffness.** If your dog is middle aged or older, don't assume that his stiff gait is a result of aging. Have your veterinarian check to see whether a tumor is causing the problem.

- **Difficulty breathing, urinating, or defecating.** A dog who can't poop may simply be constipated—or may be suffering from a blockage caused by a tumor. A dog who can't pee may have one or more bladder stones or a tumor. A dog who has trouble breathing may indicate a heart ailment or—yup—a tumor. Any sudden problems your dog experiences in performing these vital functions merit your vet's attention.

About half of the deaths of Golden Retrievers from cancer are caused by just two types: hemangiosarcoma and lymphoma. Golden Retrievers also have been known to contract osteosarcoma and mast cell cancer, among others. Here is more information about these particular forms of cancer.

Hemangiosarcoma

This highly aggressive cancer usually starts in the cells that line the spleen or blood vessels. However, a tumor can form almost anywhere in the body because blood vessels are found everywhere. Hemangiosarcoma tends to strike middle-aged dogs or seniors and is more common in males than females. Symptoms of hemangiosarcoma include weakness, lethargy, pale gums, and appetite loss; however, these symptoms may disappear, only to return again a few days later, with several such episodes over a few weeks' time. Other symptoms might include breathing difficulties, unexplained weight loss, and a distended abdomen. If the disease has created a skin tumor, the dog may have a dark rash on his abdomen or a single dark mass either on or under the skin. Treatment may include surgery to remove an affected organ, such as the spleen, and chemotherapy. However, these treatments prolong life at best. Death usually occurs within a few months of diagnosis.

Lymphoma

Also known as lymphosarcoma, lymphoma is a cancer of the lymphatic system. Like hemangiosarcoma, this cancer mainly affects dogs who are middle aged and older. A primary symptom is the presence of enlarged lymph nodes that manifest themselves as lumps underneath the skin. These lumps often appear on the throat, the shoulder, in the groin, or behind the knee. Some dogs may also lose weight, have upset stomachs, act lethargic, and drink more water than normal. If the veterinarian suspects lymphoma, she will check for enlarged lymph nodes and will feel the abdomen to see whether the dog's spleen or liver have gotten larger. The vet may also order blood work to see whether the dog is anemic (as is often the case with this cancer) and to see how the dog's vital organs are functioning (to develop plans for chemotherapy). In addition, the vet will probably order an X-ray in an effort to find internal tumors. Although lymphoma can't be cured, chemotherapy can be very effective in slowing down the progress of the disease and can extend your dog's life span by several months. Approximately one in five Goldens dies from lymphoma.

Osteosarcoma

This condition is a cancer of the bone and is usually found in one of the dog's legs. Treatment generally consists of surgical amputation, perhaps followed by chemotherapy or radiation, to give the dog a few extra months of time. An alternative to amputation may be bone replacement therapy, which consists of surgically removing the diseased part of the affected bone and replacing what's been removed with healthy bone from another part of the dog's body.

A dog who doesn't feel well may experience lethargy and a lack of appetite.

Either way, surgery is just one component of the treatment for osteosarcoma, because by the time the dog shows symptoms—mainly, a persistent limp and a diagnosis confirmed by X-ray—the cancer has probably spread beyond the bone to other areas of the dog's body. Chemotherapy and perhaps radiation can greatly increase survival time and also lessen any pain the dog may be experiencing.

Mast Cell Cancer

This condition is mainly a skin cancer and is one of the most common among all dogs. Like other cancers, it tends to strike older dogs. The most common symptom is an itchy red lump under the skin. The dog may also lose weight, experience vomiting and diarrhea, and lose his appetite. The veterinarian will examine the dog and will probably perform a fine-needle aspirate procedure. This procedure involves inserting a needle into the lump, extracting some fluid, and looking at the fluid under a microscope for cancer cells. The primary treatment for mast cell tumors is to remove the tumor and at least about 1.75 inches (3 centimeters) of surrounding tissue. Chemotherapy and radiation can help slow the spread of any cancerous cells that were not removed during surgery.

Ear Infections

Ear infections can result from infestations of yeast, bacteria, or mites, a foreign body in the ear, and allergies to food or other elements in the environment. For that reason, effective treatment of ear infections may need to be a two-pronged strategy: first, to knock out the immediate infection and, second, to determine and deal with the underlying cause, if possible.

Symptoms of ear infections include persistent head shaking, persistent scratching or rubbing one or both ears, a yeasty or unpleasant odor,

and dark, goopy discharge. Any or all of these symptoms should prompt you to call your veterinarian and make an appointment to have the ear(s) looked at. A physical exam is usually all that's needed to confirm the immediate diagnosis. However, the vet may also examine any ear discharge under a microscope in an effort to pinpoint an underlying cause of the infection, such as mites. To treat a mild ear infection, your vet may suggest a topical over-the-counter product or a prescription cream or ointment and may also prescribe an oral antibiotic to kill any bacteria that may be causing the infection. If ear mites are found, they can be treated with ivermectin, an antiparasite treatment; use of a preventive antiparasite medication should prevent a recurrence.

Chronically recurring ear infections are likely to have an underlying cause—and for the Golden Retriever, allergies are often the culprit. If your Golden's ear infections never seem to go away, or if you rid the dog of one infection only to have another occur within a couple of weeks or less, consider discussing having your dog tested for allergies to food and/or environmental elements.

Eye Infections

A dog's eye problems may be rooted in any one of several causes. Among the more common are:

Conjunctivitis

Also known as "pink eye," conjunctivitis is an inflammation of the tissue that surrounds the eyeball and eyelids. The ailment has multiple causes, including bacterial or viral infections, foreign bodies in the eye, irritation from shampoos and dips, allergies, and a wide range of underlying eye diseases. Symptoms of conjunctivitis include redness in the white parts of the eye and/or the eyelids,

Alternative therapies can be used in conjunction with conventional medical practices.

squinting, and pawing at the affected eye. There may also be a discharge, although the nature of the discharge often depends on the underlying cause of the conjunctivitis. To treat conjunctivitis, the veterinarian tries to determine what caused the condition to occur. If the cause is found, treatment focuses on eliminating the underlying problem as well as alleviating the discomfort from the conjunctivitis itself; if not, the vet generally prescribes a topical antibiotic and/or corticosteroid to reduce irritation and eliminate infection.

Keratoconjunctivitis Sicca (KCS)

This condition, commonly known as KCS or "dry eye," results when the dog's eye doesn't produce enough tears. Symptoms include a red eye, a thick mucus discharge, and squinting. The causes can range from skin allergies to side

effects of certain drugs to age.

To diagnose KCS, a veterinarian gives the dog a test that measures the amount of tears the dog can produce in one minute. If the production is below normal minimum levels, the vet will prescribe a twice-daily administration of cyclosporine cream or liquid, accompanied in some cases by antibiotics, artificial tears, lubricants, or topical corticosteroids.

Glaucoma

This condition results when the fluid within the eye, which normally drains into the circulatory system, is blocked from making such an exit. Consequently, the fluid accumulates and takes up space in the eye, causing intraocular pressure to increase. As the pressure increases, the optic nerve becomes irreversibly damaged. Ultimately the dog loses sight in the eye.

A reddened eye is just one symptom of glaucoma. Other signs include light sensitivity, dilated pupils, loss of vision, eyelid spasms, eye enlargement, discoloration or cloudiness of the cornea, and rubbing or pawing of the eye area. To diagnose glaucoma, the veterinarian or veterinary ophthalmologist measures the amount of pressure within the eye. If secondary glaucoma is suspected, blood and urine tests may be performed to determine the underlying cause; X-rays or ultrasound may be used to locate a suspected tumor. Treatment depends on whether any sight remains in the affected eye. If the eye retains some sight, surgery to either diminish the production of fluid or to bypass the blockage can help. To reduce intraocular pressure, medications such as carbonic anhydrase inhibitors, beta blockers, or miotics can help. If the dog has already lost vision in the eye, the best course of action often is to remove the eye to eliminate any infection or pain that results from the disease.

ALTERNATIVE THERAPIES

Our 21st century is a great time to be a Golden Retriever. That's because, in addition to the wonders that modern veterinary medicine seems to dream up every day (like Palladia for mast cell tumors), there are plenty of additional therapies that can further enhance your Golden's health and well-being. Here are just a few.

Acupuncture

Acupuncture is an ancient Chinese medical practice that is designed to influence the body's energy flow in a positive manner. A key principle of traditional Chinese medicine, from which acupuncture was developed, is that the body's energy flows along unseen pathways called meridians. These meridians are believed to influence other parts of the body. In a healthy dog (or person), the energy, or *chi*, flows smoothly along the meridians. If the flow of the *chi* is disrupted, the individual becomes sick. The goal of acupuncture is to restore the smooth flow of the *chi* by stimulating specific points on the meridians that influence the part of the body that needs help to heal. Acupuncture is commonly used to treat muscle injuries and arthritis. However, the practice may also be helpful in treating other conditions, such as allergies, skin problems, and digestive problems.

A related practice is acupressure, a therapy in which the practitioner places her fingers on the places where acupuncture needles would go to achieve the same effects as acupuncture.

To learn more about veterinary acupuncture or to find a qualified practitioner, log onto the International Veterinary Acupuncture Society (IVAS) website at www.ivas.org or the American Academy of Veterinary Acupuncture (AAVA) at www.aava.org.

Acupuncture is an ancient Chinese medical practice that is designed to influence the body's energy flow in a positive manner.

Chiropractic

Chiropractic is a treatment system in which the practitioner, who is known as a chiropractor, adjusts the spinal column to promote healing and relieve pain. The practice centers on the belief that certain conditions, such as incontinence and arthritis, result from a lack of normal nerve function. To restore normal nerve function, the chiropractor manipulates and adjusts the spine's position by using specific techniques and equipment. Although many chiropractors work on human patients, some work solely with animals. Some of these specialists are veterinarians who have received postgraduate training in chiropractic; others are doctors of chiropractic who've chosen to focus on animals. Either way, a certified veterinary chiropractor has received postgraduate training from one of only five facilities throughout the world, three of which are in the United States, and has passed an examination given by the American Veterinary Chiropractic Association (AVCA). To learn more or to find a veterinary chiropractor for your Golden, log onto the association's website at www.animalchiropractic.org.

Hands-On Therapies

More often than you might think, a knowledgeable touch can heal a Golden Retriever who has mobility or other issues. Here are descriptions of the more common therapies that require a laying-on of hands.

Conventional Physical Therapy

People who have suffered mobility-impairing injuries often decide to undergo physical therapy (also known as rehabilitation) to help them regain that mobility. Such therapy may involve working on a treadmill, underwater exercising, or having a trained therapist work your injured limb for you. Other forms of

> ## Multi-Dog Tip
>
> Check to see whether your veterinarian offers a multi-dog discount if you bring all of your dogs in for their wellness exams at the same time.

physical therapy include heat therapy, to help relax the muscles and loosen the joints; and cold pack, which decreases swelling.

Not surprisingly, physical therapy is becoming a treatment option for companion animals too.

Tellington T-Touch

This special hands-on therapy employs moving the fingers and hands in circular patterns all over a dog's body to have positive effects on the animal's nervous system, which in turn can help relieve problems ranging from aggressive behavior to arthritis. The creator of the therapy, Linda Tellington-Jones, has written several books that explain to pet owners how to practice and use Tellington T-Touch. You can find a professional certified T-Touch practitioner by logging onto the searchable database at www.ttouch.com.

Massage

Massage is probably the most common form of hands-on therapy that people can give to their dogs (not to mention to each other!). The practice requires a person to rub and knead the dog's muscle tissue with the hands. The result, when performed properly, is the loosening of muscle fibers that have become tense or sore during exercise and an increase in the circulation of blood to those muscles. Massage isn't an exotic technique, however;

in fact, simply petting your Golden can be a form of massage if you do it right. Just stroke your dog's head, neck, and body in long, slow motions.

Not every dog is a candidate for a massage. Experts suggest keeping hands off a dog who has a broken bone, broken skin, or cancer. In such cases, massage can make the injury worse or increase circulation in a way that can actually help a cancerous tumor to grow.

To learn more about canine massage and other alternative therapies, check out *The Holistic Health Guide* by Doug Knueven, DVM (TFH).

Herbal

With all of the advances that modern medicine—both human and veterinary—has brought and continues to bring, the ancient practice of using herbs to treat various ills still plays a big part in keeping us feeling good. It's not for nothing that we use aloe vera to soothe sunburned skin or drink chamomile tea to settle an upset stomach. In the same way, many veterinarians find that herbs can help in the treatment of many ailments that beset dogs. Among the many problems that herbs may help alleviate are constipation, skin irritation and injuries, infections, nausea, diarrhea, kidney problems, and bladder problems.

Herbs are available in just about any health food store or high-end supermarket. But just because they're widely available doesn't mean that you should give your dog some chamomile tea the next time he has a tender tummy, nor should you give your dog herbs straight from your garden. Experts strongly

Massage is likely the most common form of hands-on therapy that people can give to their dogs.

recommend that you check with your vet before you give your dog any herbs.

Some veterinarians specialize or at least have had postgraduate training in herbal medicine. If you'd like to find such a specialist, log onto the Veterinary Botanical Medicine Association (VBMA) at www.vbma.org and check out the website's searchable database.

Homeopathy

Another alternative therapy that can be helpful for your Golden is homeopathy. This practice is built around a simple principle: that like cures like. Based on this principle, homeopathic veterinarians give their patients very small diluted amounts of substances that would, in larger amounts, trigger symptoms similar to those the dog already has. The idea is that the administered substances will kick-start the body's natural defenses, allowing the body to heal itself.

The homeopathic veterinarian has thousands of possible remedies at her disposal when treating an animal. The vet will use knowledge and experience to prescribe homeopathic remedies that are designed to address the unique set of symptoms or complaints that that individual animal has. Those symptoms can be wide ranging: from eye inflammation to itchy skin to lack of interest in drinking water.

To learn more about veterinary homeopathy or to find a veterinary homeopathic practitioner, visit the website of the Academy of Veterinary Homeopathy (AVH) at www.theavh.org.

EMERGENCY CARE

Sooner or later, you're likely to face a medical or other emergency that involves your Golden Retriever. Such occurrences are understandably frightening and stressful, and in the midst of your fear and stress, you may not have time to research what you need to do to help your

It's up to you to keep your Golden Retriever in the best health and condition possible.

Golden. That's why it's a good idea to seek out the information you need before any such emergency occurs and to have it at your fingertips.

Keep in mind that getting your stricken Golden to the vet may be more challenging than simply putting him in your car and heading off to your vet's clinic or to an emergency facility. That's because your dog may be too frightened to recognize you, much less understand that you're trying to help him. Experts suggest that you do the following:

- First, stay calm. If you stay calm, your dog will be calmer and easier to deal with.
- Second, get a helper. Another person can drive you to the clinic, and phone ahead to let the clinic know that you're coming.

- Third, ask family members and bystanders to leave you and your helper alone so that you can focus on helping your dog.
- Fourth, handle your dog as little as possible-- and when you do, be gentle.
- Finally, protect yourself. Your normally gentle Golden may bite you or act aggressively because he's frightened and/ or in pain. Put on some thick gloves, and muzzle your dog if necessary.

So what constitutes a medical emergency? Here are some of the most common. If your dog experiences any of these symptoms, he needs immediate veterinary attention. His life could be at stake.

- **Abdominal expansion:** If your Golden Retriever's belly looks as though someone's pumped it full of air over a one-day period or less, he needs to be taken to a vet, pronto. Possible causes include bloat or large-scale leakage of blood or lymph fluid into the dog's abdominal cavity.
- **Breathing problems.** Labored breathing should prompt you to take your Golden to his vet immediately. The problem could be caused by one of several respiratory diseases and injuries, including laryngeal paralysis, pneumonia, bruising of the lungs, or pulmonary tumors.
- **Change in gum color:** If your Golden's normally pink gums either lighten or darken in color, he needs medical attention right away. Depending on how the color changes, he could be in shock, have respiratory problems, be suffering from liver or gall bladder disease, or be experiencing either septic shock or a severe infection.
- **Cold exposure:** Deep shivering, cold limbs, rigid muscles, and lethargy could be signs that your dog has hypothermia, which also requires an immediate trip to the vet.
- **Heat exposure:** A dog who's been exposed to excessive heat may exhibit extreme panting, profound depression, shallow or rapid breathing, and bloody vomiting. These are symptoms of heatstroke, which can result in death without immediate medical attention.
- **Persistent vomiting:** A Golden who's vomited several times over several hours—particularly if what he's vomited contains blood or foreign material—needs to see a veterinarian right away. He might have ingested a foreign object or toxic substance or have pancreatic or kidney disease.
- **Retching:** If your Golden is trying to vomit but can't, he needs immediate veterinary attention. He may have bloat or a blockage where the esophagus opens into the stomach.
- **Significant bleeding:** Bleeding that isn't easily stopped with pressure bandaging after 10 to 20 minutes warrants an immediate trip to your vet. The same goes for any bleeding that spurts or pulses at all because such bleeding indicates an injury to an artery.
- **Sudden collapse.** A dog who collapses suddenly needs to see a vet immediately, whether or not he loses consciousness. He may have a heart problem or have had a seizure.

First Aid

If your Golden Retriever becomes injured or ill, you need to contact your veterinarian and get your dog seen as soon as possible. However, in many such situations, you may need to stabilize his condition yourself before you can transport him to a clinic or animal hospital. Here are some guidelines to dealing with some common medical emergencies.

Bites

After any dog-on-dog altercation, check your dog for bite wounds. Such wounds may not be readily apparent. If you come upon a bleeding bite wound, apply direct pressure to the wound by placing a clean piece of cloth, gauze, or sanitary napkin atop the wound to absorb the blood. Then transport your dog to his vet, pronto.

Bleeding (External)

To stop external bleeding, place a clean piece of gauze, a clean cloth, or a sanitary napkin directly over the bleeding wound. The cloth will absorb the blood and allow a clot to begin forming. Do not attempt to remove the cloth; doing so could reopen the wound. If the wound is on one of the dog's limbs, elevating the limb will also help slow the bleeding. Get your dog to the vet as soon as you can.

Broken Bones

A Golden who's fractured a leg is a Golden in considerable pain. Start by muzzling your dog to protect yourself from being bitten. Stanch any bleeding with direct pressure (see "Bleeding," above). If the fracture breaks the skin, cover the area with sterile gauze dressing if available; if not, use a clean cloth or a sanitary pad. If possible, immobilize your Golden on a large board or similar surface prior to transport. Failing that, and if he still has the use of three of his legs, create a supportive sling by placing a towel under his abdomen and holding the ends above his back. Get him to your vet as soon as possible.

If your Golden has an altercation with another dog, check for bite wounds.

Frostbite

Just like people, Golden Retrievers can develop frostbite if they stay outside too long in cold weather. Signs of frostbite include white skin and a colder-than-normal feel. Bring your dog inside as soon as possible and warm the affected areas with warm wet towels. Then contact your vet for guidance—and if the dog's skin turns dark, get him to the vet immediately.

Heatstroke

Also known as hyperthermia, heatstroke may occur if your dog has been left in a car on a day where the temperature is 70°F (21.1°C) or above or in an area with inadequate shade. (This is just one reason why leaving your Golden alone in a car is never a good idea!) The condition can also occur if you exercise your dog in hot, humid weather. Symptoms include excessive panting, restlessness, excessive drooling, unsteadiness, and bright red or purple gums. To save the dog's life, it's imperative to cool him down quickly. Place cool, wet towels on the dog's armpits, the back of the neck and groin, and wet the ear flaps with cool water. If you have a fan, direct its airflow over your dog to accelerate cooling. Then transport him to your vet.

Poisoning

The proper way to deal with poisoning depends on what toxin your dog has ingested.

Goldens can develop frostbite if they stay outside too long in cold weather.

To obtain that information, call the ASPCA Animal Poison Control Center at 888-426-4435. The center is staffed by veterinary toxicologists who can advise you and/or your vet on how to combat the toxin your Golden may have ingested. Have your credit card ready—there is a fee for the service.

CHAPTER 9

GOLDEN RETRIEVER TRAINING

If you were to perform an Internet search on the phrase "a trained dog is a happy dog," you'd probably come up with hundreds of thousands of hits. There's a simple reason that this phrase is so all-pervasive in the world of dogs and pet ownership: It's true. And yet, that truth might not be self-evident. How could a dog who does what he's told be happier than a dog who's never told anything?

The reason is that the dog who's trained—if that training is done in a manner that's positive and capitalizes on a dog's basic instincts—is likely to enjoy far happier relationships with the people in his life than the dog who doesn't have the benefit of such instruction. A dog who knows how to come when called, sit or lie down when asked, and remain in place when requested (to name just a few desirable behaviors) is a dog who people want to be around. He's a dog who knows how to listen to, communicate with, and otherwise get along with human beings. He's a dog who, by his understanding of human requirements and desires, is generally far more welcome among human beings than his unruly, untrained counterpart. And because he, like other dogs, is a social individual, his being welcome among human beings means that he gets to spend far more time with human beings than a socially clueless and cue-less dog might.

Happily, the humans in a dog's life don't need to act like drill sergeants to teach him what he needs to know. Contrary to the opinions of some, a person doesn't need to dominate a dog to train him. That's because training in a positive, dog-friendly manner is not about demanding obedience; it's about building a relationship. The human shows the dog what is wanted and teaches the dog how to respond as requested; at the same time, the human learns to listen to the dog, heed his signals, and work with him to obtain the results they both want. The result is a win-win situation for both person and pooch. What's not to like? This chapter will show you how to create that win-win situation.

Want to Know More?

For a refresher on training basic cues, see Chapter 4: Training Your Puppy.

A well-trained Golden is likely to enjoy far happier relationships with the people in his life.

REFRESHING THE BASICS

Before you can teach your Golden the moves in this chapter, he needs to know some basics. Specifically, he should be acing the behaviors described in Chapter 4: paying attention when he hears his name; sitting when asked, lying down when asked; coming when called; and walking nicely on leash.

You too need to know some basics. They include:

Understanding Positive Training

You don't need to push, pull, or otherwise physically force your Golden Retriever to do your bidding—and with an adult Golden's weight ranging between 55 and 75 pounds (25 and 34 kg), exerting such force effectively is, at best, problematic. Instead, you can focus on showing your Golden what you want him

to do and reinforce him when he does what you ask. That said, we're not talking about just any reinforcement here; we're referring to reinforcers that give your dog a big incentive to comply with your request.

For most Goldens, the most effective reinforcers come in the form of tasty treats. Other reinforcers of varying degrees of effectiveness include toys, a quick play session, praise, and petting. The bottom line here: You catch your dog doing something right, and when he does, you use reinforcers to reward him for doing the right thing. That way, he'll want to repeat the behavior.

Marking Desired Behavior

How do you make sure that your dog knows that he's doing something right? By giving him a clear, unmistakable signal immediately after he's done that something. Scientists and animal trainers have discovered that one of the most effective ways to convey that signal is with a clicker: a small plastic box that has either a small button or metal strip on top. By pressing the button or metal strip, the device makes a clicking sound. Doing this immediately after your dog does what you've asked lets him know that he's done the right thing—and that a treat or other reinforcer will follow very shortly. Chapter 4 contains an extensive discussion about how to use a clicker (or how to use a marker word, such as "yes!") to maximum effect.

Minimizing Distractions

When teaching any new behavior to your dog, it's best to start in surroundings that have few, if any, distractions. That means teaching initial lessons inside your house at a time when no other family members are around, the television's off, and there's no commotion outside. Once your Golden masters the behavior in this distraction-free environment, you can start adding distractions one at a time as he continues to perfect the behavior you're teaching him.

And we're not talking about just environmental distractions. For example, if your Golden's been home by himself for a while, trying to hold a training session immediately after you arrive home is probably a not-so-great idea. Your dog is too busy being thrilled just to see you and coping with lots of pent-up energy to focus on learning new cues or perfecting old ones. That's why training sessions for a Golden, particularly a young one, generally go better after he's had a chance to blow off some steam with ten minutes or so of strenuous exercise and also after he's had some one-on-one hangout time with you. The workout will siphon off some of your dog's legendary energy, which in turn will help him to focus on learning what you're trying to teach him.

There's only one distraction that's good to have when teaching a new behavior: hunger. If you're using treats to train your Golden, conduct his lessons before mealtimes, when he's most likely to be hungry—and thus, eager to work to earn those treats.

Finally, keep your training sessions short and sweet—no more than ten minutes—and always do your best to end any session with a behavior that your dog already knows. That way, you'll both end the session feeling successful.

Cut Back on Treats

Finally, it's important to realize that you don't have to use treats forever to encourage your dog to do what you ask. Once you're sure that he understands what you want him to do—he should perform the behavior the vast majority of the time that you ask him to do so—it's time to start cutting back the goodies. Instead of giving him a treat every time he performs the behavior, give him one every other time. After a little while, cut back to every third or fourth time, and so on until you give him treats very rarely. That said, don't eliminate treats completely. Giving him a goodie every now and then will keep him eager to work with you and to perform the behaviors that you're requesting.

Once you've both mastered these basics, you're ready to start teaching your dog some fancier moves.

INTERMEDIATE CUES

The cues below not only build on the basics your dog already knows but also can help the two of you deal more confidently and effectively with real-life circumstances.

Stay

The *stay* cue is a great multipurpose behavior to teach your Golden Retriever. When you tell your dog to stay, you're instructing him to remain where he is—and once he understands this, you'll be able to apply the cue to multiple situations. For example, when you feed your Golden his meal, you can ask him to sit (as described in Chapter 4), to stay as you place his bowl on the floor, and to remain in that seated position until you release him. Never again will your dog mow you down as he makes a beeline for his breakfast or dinner.

Here's another situation in which the *stay* works well: if you want your dog to be able to hang out with company without making a pest of himself (which can be a problem with an ever-gregarious Golden). By having him lie down at your feet and then stay in that position, he can be part of the festivities without taking over those festivities.

As the foregoing examples show, the *stay* cue is often paired with either the *sit* or the *down*. But asking your Golden to stay need not be limited to the times when he's in a sitting or reclining position; the cue works just as well if your dog's standing up. For example, if you need to open your front door and your Golden is right there as you do so, a rock-solid *stay* will keep him from darting out the front door. The same applies to when you're traveling: if you've opened the car door, telling your dog to stay can prevent him from exiting the car until you're ready for him to do so.

The *stay* maneuver is also important for your dog to learn if you plan to enter him in competitive obedience trials. These trials, as is explained in Chapter 11, test your dog's ability to perform increasingly complex behaviors in a competitive setting. To succeed at even a novice level, a dog must know how to stay in both a sitting position and a lying position.

That said, don't expect your Golden Retriever to perform the *stay* under such challenging

The *stay* cue asks your dog to remain in place until released.

By the Numbers

The idea that a dog needs to be at least six months old before he can begin training is a myth. When it comes to training, no numbers apply. A Golden Retriever is never too young to learn new behaviors. That's not to say that if your Golden hasn't received schooling during his youth he can never learn. In fact, the opposite is true; a dog is also never too old to learn something new. Training is a process that can—in fact, should—continue throughout your Golden's life.

circumstances until you know that he's mastered the maneuver. As should be the case with any new behavior you teach, start your lessons in an environment that has as few distractions as possible. Then proceed as follows:

1. Have your dog sit or lie down. Have a treat nearby and a clicker in your hand.
2. Say "Stay" in a long, drawn-out tone of voice. The cue should sound like "Staaaaaaay."
3. As you say the cue, open the palm of your clicker-free hand and place that palm at the level of your dog's nose and about 6 inches (15 cm) away from his nose.
4. Withdraw your hand and move back one step. Then return immediately.
5. Click, say the word "okay" (or "free" or "you're done" or any other word or phrase to indicate that he's released from the stay) and give him a treat. Praise him enthusiastically.
6. Repeat the process, moving back two steps this time.

Continue repeating the process, gradually increasing the distance you move away from your dog, the length of time he must stay, and the distractions in his environment. When your dog can hold his *stay* for a good three minutes while you're at the opposite end of the room or outdoors, while other household members

are coming and going, you can consider the cue taught and begin weaning your dog off the treats you've used to teach him.

Stand

The usefulness of the *stand* cue may not seem obvious at first. After all, dogs generally spend a lot of time on all fours, so why would they need to be asked to do so?

An answer to that question may not be clear until you try to have your adult Golden Retriever walk onto the floor scale at your local veterinary clinic. That's because, if the scale is positioned against a wall, your Golden will almost certainly feel that he too must position himself against that wall. The result will be a reading that is many pounds (kg) heavier than your dog actually is. However, if your Golden knows how to stand on cue, you can use that cue to position him on the scale so that he's not leaning

For most Goldens, the most effective reinforcers come in the form of soft aromatic treats, not hard treats like these.

The *stand* cue is a good foundation for the "stack," which all dogs in conformation must learn to perform.

against the wall, which in turn will result in a far more accurate reading.

The *stand* cue also comes in handy if you want your dog to pose for a picture or if you plan to show him in conformation, to begin teaching him to stack (that special standing pose that every show dog must strike).

To teach your dog to stand on cue, do the following:

Preventing Bad Behavior

Some cues can help prevent problem behaviors in your dog, such as guarding food or toys or running off with unauthorized objects. To learn more about these very important cues and teach them to your Golden, check out Chapter 4: Training Your Golden Retriever Puppy.

1. Have your dog sit.
2. Hold a treat at nose level about six inches (15 cm) away from his face.
3. Say the word "Stand." As you say the word, move the treat away from your dog's face, being sure to keep the treat at nose level. As you move the treat away, your dog will stand in order to move forward and follow the treat.
4. As soon as your dog is on all fours, click and treat.
5. Repeat this sequence until your dog is performing this behavior consistently and reliably.

At that point you can begin cutting back on treats. However, if you and your dog are in a real-life situation (for example, when you're facing the veterinarian's scale) that lends itself to using this cue, don't hesitate to use treats. For many dogs, such situations are too distracting to deal with unless they have a tasty incentive to do so!

Place

The *place* cue requires your dog to take himself to a designated area when asked to and to remain there until released. This cue is incredibly useful in a variety of situations—particularly those involving guests in your home. That said, any time you don't want your Golden to be underfoot, either for the sake of your convenience or his safety, knowing that he will go to his place when asked makes life easier for both of you.

Interestingly, many dogs learn this cue (or a variation) without their owners' making a conscious effort to teach it to them. For example, the Golden Retriever to whom this book is dedicated goes into her crate whenever she hears one of her people say "Nighty-night." That's because every time her people put her in her crate while she was being housetrained (see Chapter 4), they would coo "Nighty-night" to her as they did so. Being a typically hyper-smart Golden, this dog didn't take long to associate "nighty-night" with going to her crate. Today, more than seven years later, this now-housetrained Golden continues to trot off to her crate whenever she's told that it's time to go nighty-night.

But if your Golden hasn't learned a similar cue on his own, it's never too late to teach him. (Note: He should know the *down* and the *stay* before you begin teaching this cue.) Here's what to do:

1. Leash your dog.
2. Say the word "Place" (or "Bed," or "Nighty-night," or any other word or words, as long as you use those same words consistently), and lead your Golden to the place where you want him to go.
3. Click and treat.
4. Repeat until he appears to understand what you mean when you give him the cue. At this point, remove the leash and give the cue. If he responds, click and treat. If he doesn't, reattach the leash and lead him to the place where you want him to go.
5. Once your Golden can take himself to his place on cue, ask him to lie down and stay. Have him remain in the *down* position for about 15 seconds. Then click, treat, and give him his release cue.
6. Repeat until your dog can remain in his place for about three minutes.

Touch

The *touch* cue involves asking your dog to touch his nose to your hand or an object. Like so many other cues, this one has multiple applications, starting with being able to direct your dog wherever you want him to go

Keep your training sessions short and sweet, and end each session with a behavior that your dog already knows.

Training Tidbit

Using treats that your Golden really likes can make the training process a lot quicker and more pleasurable for both of you. Do a little detective work to find out which foods really excite him. Chances are, those foods won't be hard, crunchy little dog biscuits; most Goldens and other dogs tend to go wild for soft, flavorful, aromatic treats. Try the following items:

- canned chicken, well drained
- canned dog food that's microwaved so that its texture is dryer and firmer, then crumbled into small pieces
- cheddar cheese, cut up into very small pieces
- hot dogs cut up into very small pieces, served either as is or microwaved
- meat rolls, which are sold in pet-supply stores

By rewarding your Golden with food that really gets him salivating—perhaps literally!—you're helping to create conditions in which he will truly want to work and learn. Just like us humans, dogs need an incentive to work as requested. For us, that incentive usually comes in the form of a monetary salary; for your Golden, the incentive is treats.

without having to apply any force to do so. For example, if you want to move your dog to one side of your body or the other and he knows the *touch* cue, all you need to do is hold out your hand or object at the place where you want your dog to be, say the cue, and bingo! He's there.

This cue is particularly useful if you and your Golden plan to compete in dog sports, especially agility. The reason is that often a dog must touch a precise spot on a course or piece of equipment to earn the maximum number of points or even qualify. For example, a dog who's venturing down a teeter-totter in an agility trial must go all the way down to the end; jumping off the downward ramp to the ground is not permitted. By using the *touch* cue, you can teach your dog to walk or run all the way to the end of the downward ramp.

And for many dogs, the *touch* cue is just plain

fun. Once he has this cue down pat, you can move your hand or object around your body, up high, or down low. Many dogs respond eagerly to these placement variations as though it's a game.

No matter what reason you might have for wanting to apply this cue, here's how to teach it to your Golden:

1. Take a treat and rub it in on your palm so that your hand carries its scent.
2. Hold your palm out no more than 1 foot (0.5 m) from your dog's nose and say the cue word, "Touch."
3. When your dog leans in and touches his nose to your hand to sniff the scent of the treat, click and give him a real treat.

Some dogs are hesitant to touch their noses to an open hand. If your dog is one, try teaching him to touch the top of your closed fist.

Asking to Go Out

Most housetrained Golden Retrievers really try to tell their people when they need a potty break. Some might sit directly in front of their people and stare at them, hoping those people will figure out why they're being stared at. Others might take themselves to a door that leads outside and stare outside; they, too, are hoping that their people will figure out what's going on. Still others lie down in front of those doors, perhaps trying to get themselves as close to their outdoor potties as they can. In any case, unless they can get outside on their own via a dog door, their access to their potties depends on being able to communicate to their people that they require such access. The wise human finds a way to help a Golden do just that. Here's what you can do, step by step:

1. Find something that you can hang from a doorknob within reach of your dog's nose or paw. Sleigh bells or wind chimes (if the chimes aren't sharp) are ideal because they make a pleasant noise that you can hear even if you're in another room of your home.

2. Ring the bells every time you take your dog for a potty break.

Training your Golden well will make him a more valued member of the family.

3. Soon your dog will try to examine the bells. When he does—even if it's a single furtive sniff—click or use a marker word, give him a treat, and take him outside to his potty spot. Repeat every time he examines the bells. The idea here is to associate interacting with the bells to being taken outside to potty.

4. Eventually your dog will go beyond examining the bells to actually trying to manipulate them by tapping them with his paws or nose; when he does, take him out and give him extra treats. Give him a few more treats if he poops or pees.

Multi-Dog Tip

Once your Golden has mastered a behavior in a low-distraction environment, try asking him to perform the behavior while your other dogs are around. The presence of his canine brethren will be a good distraction with which to perfect the behavior—and your other dogs might benefit from a refresher course!

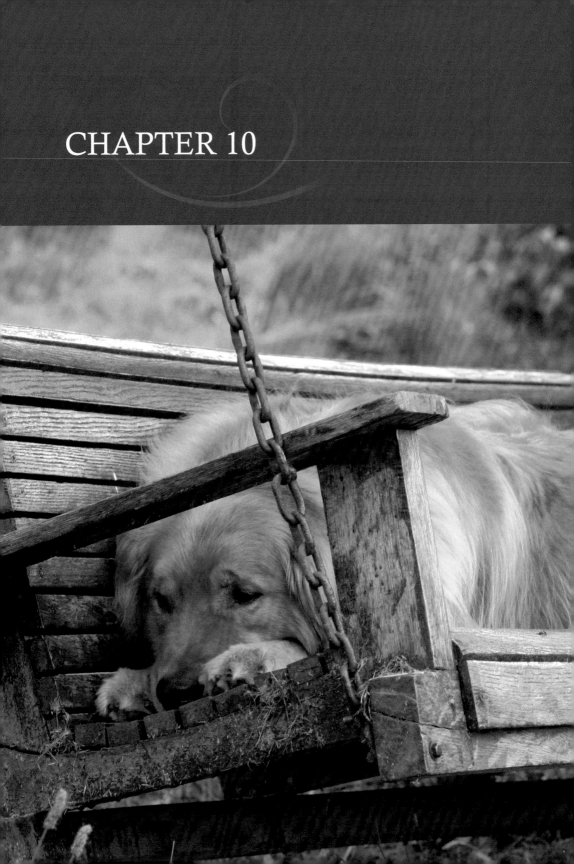

CHAPTER 10

GOLDEN RETRIEVER PROBLEM BEHAVIORS

Golden Retrievers are fabulous dogs, but being fabulous is not the same as being perfect. Like any other breed, Goldens have issues. Some of those issues flow from certain breed tendencies; others may be unique to a particular Golden's temperament or even physical condition; still others may result from mistakes on the part of the owner. No matter what the cause is, though, most such problems can be managed or at least lived with, and many can be totally resolved.

The list below provides basic descriptions of common Golden Retriever behavior issues, outlines ways to combat them, and specifies the times when professional help is needed.

AGGRESSION

According to the *Random House Dictionary* (Random House, 2009), aggression is "the practice of making assaults or attacks." As such, aggression is a catch-all phrase that covers canine threats or attacks in a wide range of contexts. In other words, dogs behave aggressively for many reasons—and often what looks like an offensive action may actually (at least from the dog's point of view) be a defensive *re*action.

Unfortunately, Golden Retrievers are capable of behaving aggressively, and some actually do. Their happy-go-lucky demeanors and reputations for docility are well earned, but under certain conditions those people-friendly characteristics can morph into traits that can be quite dangerous. In this respect, Goldens are no different from any other dog of any breed. All dogs are capable of behaving aggressively—and the wise human being respects this capability and behaves accordingly. In fact, if your Golden behaves aggressively, don't take the matter lightly, and don't delay getting treatment. The sooner you get help for him, the better the chances are of solving this very serious problem.

To help a dog who's behaving aggressively—and, often, to save his life—it's crucial to understand the environment in which the aggression occurs and the circumstances that trigger the behavior. Here are some common circumstances in which aggressive actions or reactions occur among dogs.

- **Aggression around food or toys:** Some dogs become very possessive of their food, treats, or toys—so much so that they will growl, air snap (bite in the air without touching the

How to Find the Right Behavior Pro

A Golden's owner can't necessarily solve every one of a dog's behavioral problems all by himself or herself. Fortunately, the owner doesn't have to. Plenty of knowledgeable individuals stand ready to help a Golden and his person resolve a wide variety of behavioral issues that can get in the way of their living happily ever after. Those specialists include:

Your breeder. Good breeders want their puppies and owners to have a joyful life together and are willing to share advice and guidance based on many years of experience with Goldens and with their line of Goldens. Whether it's a health, training, or behavioral issue, breeders often have insight that may aid in resolving the problem, or they may be able to direct you elsewhere for additional help. A knowledgeable breeder can be one of your best resources for the lifetime of your dog.

Your veterinarian: In many instances, the first specialist you should consult to solve your Golden's behavioral problems should be your veterinarian. That's because many such problems may actually result from a physical ailment. For example, apparently unprovoked aggression may result from a thyroid hormone reading that's on the low side of normal. Deafness or physical pain may also be the culprit.

If your veterinarian is a member of the American Veterinary Society of Animal Behavior (AVSAB), so much the better. This

organization is made up of veterinarians and scientists who are interested in understanding animal actions and conduct. Log onto the organization's website (www.avsabonline.org) to find a veterinarian who belongs to this organization.

A good trainer: If your vet doesn't find any physical problems in your Golden, your next step should be to consult a dog trainer who uses positive, dog-friendly methods when working with dogs. Many trainers not only conduct group classes but also offer one-on-one consultations to help owners solve their dogs' behavioral problems. (Chapter 4 of this book provides detailed suggestions on how to find a trainer.)

A behavioral consultant: The International Association of Animal Behavior Consultants (IAABC) is an organization whose members have considerable experience performing one-on-one consultations for owners of dogs, cats, and other animals. At its website, www.iaabc.org, use the searchable database to find either a Certified Animal Behavior Consultant (CABC) or a Certified Dog Behavior Consultant (CDBC) who can help you with your Golden's problem.

Applied animal behaviorist: An animal behavior professional with the suffix CAAB or AAAB has been certified by the Animal Behavior Society (ABS) to have a graduate degree—at least a master's—in a behavioral science with an emphasis on animal behavior; many of these individuals have doctoral degrees in these disciplines. An applied animal behaviorist is highly qualified to diagnose and treat complex animal problem behaviors but can't prescribe medications for such problems unless she is also a veterinarian. Your own vet can refer you to a certified applied animal behaviorist, or you can contact one yourself by logging onto the Animal Behavior Society website at www.animalbehavior.org/ABSAppliedBehavior/caab-directory.

Veterinary behaviorist: A veterinarian who carries the suffix Dip ACVB after her name has taken postgraduate coursework in animal behavior and completed an internship as well as a residency program with another veterinary behaviorist or at one of only seven veterinary schools in the United States or has completed an animal behavior research project, written three peer-reviewed case reports, and passed a two-day examination. The veterinary behaviorist is particularly helpful if your dog's problem has a physical cause; the behaviorist can conduct a medical exam to determine whether physical factors are causing a problem behavior and can prescribe medications when appropriate. Generally your own veterinarian must refer you to a veterinary behaviorist. A list is available at http://dacvb.org/about-us/diplomates/diplomate-directory/.

Whether you get a behavioral pro's help or not, however, you and your Golden will both benefit by your having some knowledge about his problem.

A veterinary behaviorist can help you deal with serious problem behaviors.

encroaching individual), or even attack the individual whom they feel might be trying to take away their stuff. Experts call this behavior "resource guarding." Such behavior is an important survival strategy among dogs in the wild, but it's not necessary for domestic dogs and can be very dangerous, especially if it's carried to an extreme.

- **Aggression around other dogs:** Although Golden Retrievers are generally very sociable, some—especially older Goldens—may not be all that crazy about being around other dogs. They may express their displeasure by snapping, barking, lunging, or engaging in other nasty behavior, particularly if they believe that the other dog is guilty of a breach of canine etiquette.
- **Aggression when touched:** Some dogs may react in a negative fashion to being touched in a particular place on their bodies, such as

on the ears or on their feet. Such dogs may be experiencing pain on those body parts.

- **Aggression around people:** A dog—even a Golden Retriever—may react in an aggressive fashion to certain people with whom he is unfamiliar or has had a negative experience. For example, a shelter dog who was mistreated by a man may be unwilling to be approached by men even if the males in his new home treat him kindly. A dog who was subjected to ear pulling, tail pulling, or teasing by children as a puppy may take steps to keep children away from him when he reaches adulthood. Still other dogs may become unpredictably aggressive, even if they were fine earlier in life.

Dealing with aggression in a dog is not an enterprise that an untrained or inexperienced person should attempt on her own. Professional help—from a veterinarian, an experienced trainer or behavior consultant, an applied animal behaviorist and/or a veterinary behaviorist—is usually essential for treatment to be both safe and effective.

How to Manage It
That said, an owner can take steps to create an atmosphere that's safer for the Golden, the household, and the owner as treatment begins and progresses.

See Your Vet Right Away
Canine aggression—especially if it's developed suddenly or is unpredictable—may have a physical cause. Among the possible factors are pain—for example, a dog with an undiagnosed ear infection may growl or snap when his ears are handled; head trauma, which can cause behavioral changes; infections, such as Lyme disease; high protein content in pet food; food allergies; epilepsy; exposure to toxins, such as lead; and hormone imbalances, such as

insufficient thyroid hormone production. The latter condition, known as hypothyroidism, is more prevalent in some breeds than others—among the breeds most at risk is the Golden Retriever.

Avoid Triggering the Aggression

If your dog doesn't like being around other dogs, don't take him to the dog park—and if you're walking him and see another dog approaching, cross the street or turn around and walk in the opposite direction. If your dog is possessive about food and toys, don't try to take either away from him. For the sake of your safety—as well as that of your dog—do as much as you can to avoid putting him in a situation in which an aggressive response might occur.

Supervise Children

A dog who's developed aggression issues need to be protected from children and vice versa. Don't let your kids and problem dog interact without your direct supervision, and emphasize to your children the importance of not doing anything that could cause the dog to react in an aggressive manner.

Get a Behavioral Consult

If the vet rules out any physical causes of your dog's behavior, your next step should be to schedule a one-on-one behavioral consultation with a positive reinforcement dog trainer, an animal or dog behavior consultant, applied animal behaviorist, or a veterinary behaviorist. This chapter explains how to find these professionals; Chapter 4 also contains

Be especially diligent about supervising your Golden around children if he has aggression issues.

By the Numbers

Golden Retrievers from six months to two years of age are in the throes of adolescence—a time when misbehavior abounds and problems may surface. During adolescence, your Golden's hormones are surging, he's thrown off the sweet dependence of early puppyhood, he has boundless energy, and he's feeling his oats. Many dogs in shelters or rescue organizations are in this age group—relinquished because their owners gave up on being able to deal with the problem behaviors that often crop up during this time. You can ensure that your Golden avoids this fate by taking the time to train him in basic good manners and working patiently to solve whatever problem behaviors he has.

information on how to find a trainer. The behavioral pro you consult will assess your dog, and if possible, work with you to develop a training plan that will modify your dog's behavior.

ANXIETY

If you acquired your Golden Retriever as a puppy from a reputable breeder and socialized him properly, as described in Chapter 4, he's not likely to grow up into an anxious adult. A socialized Golden is a resilient Golden: able to negotiate novel situations with aplomb, able to bounce back from most setbacks.

But there are exceptions to that general rule. Even a socialized, confident Golden may develop fear following a traumatic event. For example, a dog who's been in an automobile accident may be skittish about car travel afterward. And if your Golden is an adult whom you adopted from a shelter or rescue group, you obviously didn't have the opportunity to socialize him during those optimum first 12 to 14 weeks of his life. Such a dog may have one or more fear issues such as separation anxiety and/ or thunderstorm anxiety.

Golden Retriever anxiety manifests itself in

many ways. Some anxious or fearful Goldens become destructive. Others pant excessively or even drool. Still others begin to bark repeatedly and frantically. Many tremble when confronted with whatever has triggered the fear and will often try to get as far away from that trigger as possible. (See the "Types of Anxiety" sidebar for more information.)

How to Manage It

That said, there's plenty you can do to help your Golden overcome his fears. Here are some ideas.

Build His Confidence

Without exposing your Golden to the issue(s) that trigger his anxiety, do what you can to build his overall self-confidence. Teach him new behaviors, play with him, and introduce him to new experiences that have nothing to do with whatever's giving him the willies.

Wear Him Out

Not only is a tired dog a good dog, but a tired dog is a dog who may actually be too pooped to get scared. Give your Golden strenuous exercise on a regular basis and see whether he doesn't mellow out some.

Making sure that your Golden gets enough exercise can help keep some problem behaviors at bay.

Don't Force the Issue

If your Golden's afraid of a specific circumstance that you can control, such as riding in the car or going for a swim, don't force him to deal with that circumstance. In other words, don't shove him into the car or drag him into the pool. You'll only increase his fear, which is exactly what you do *not* want to do.

See Your Vet

In some cases, medication can help create conditions that make it easier to help your Golden overcome his anxiety. If the measures you undertake on your own don't seem to be helping, book an appointment with your vet to see if she can prescribe meds that can help restore your dog's equanimity.

BARKING

Unlike some breeds—for example, Shetland Sheepdogs and Dachshunds—Golden Retrievers are not known for being nuisance barkers. Consequently, a noisy Golden's vocalizing may reflect the presence of another problem. To truly end the barking, that problem needs to be solved.

What Not to Do

Treating barking effectively means knowing both what you should do and what you shouldn't do. Among the shouldn'ts include not shouting at the dog. Yelling at your barking Golden to be quiet will have just the opposite effect. He'll think that you're barking, too—and will respond by barking all the louder. Also, never use a shock collar. Yes, using a collar

Types of Anxiety

Golden Retrievers can suffer from a few different types of anxiety, including:

Separation Anxiety: A Golden Retriever who refuses to be away from his person, shows signs of anxiety when his owner is about to leave the house, and barks and trashes his house within the first 30 minutes of his owner's departure may suffer from separation anxiety. To remedy this problem, take the following steps:

- Change your dog's perceptions. Give your dog a special toy that's reserved strictly for his times by himself. A food puzzle is ideal. By giving your dog this toy only at these times, you'll help him associate your departures with positive developments, and he'll be too busy to miss you.
- Enrich his environment. Give your dog some stimuli that divert his attention from his unhappiness at being left alone. For example, put him in a room with a window to your back yard so that he can watch birds and wildlife, turn the television on low, play some music, or play a recording of familiar household sounds.
- Set an example. Keep your goodbyes and hellos low-key and matter-of-fact. By keeping your cool yourself, you'll help your dog keep his.
- Reward calm, independent behavior. When you're home, show your dog that he'll be okay when you're not around. Try having him hold sits and stays for a minute or two, then leave the room. Gradually build up to five minutes. Another option: Give him

his favorite chew toy or food-stuffed toy, wait till he's fully engaged with it, and then leave the room.

Thunderstorm Anxiety: Even the calmest Golden Retriever may feel unsettled by the rumblings and flashes of a T-storm. Mother Nature's sound-and-light shows can be unsettling to humans too! Here's how to help your Golden cope:

- Give goodies. Find some treats that your Golden loves and feed them to him during the storm. If he's willing to eat them, try stuffing them into an interactive toy, freezing it overnight, and giving it to him the next time the rumbles start. He might get so absorbed in digging out the food that he'll forget to be afraid of the lightning and thunder.
- Try pheromones. For many dogs, a spray or diffuser that contains dog-appeasing pheromone (DAP), which is similar to the pheromone released by nursing mother dogs, can allay thunderstorm anxiety. The product is manufactured by Central Life Sciences; for more info, log onto www.petcomfortzone.com.
- Wrap him up. A form-fitting garment called the Anxiety Wrap (www.anxietywrap.com) can ease thunderstorm stress; a snug T-shirt may also do the trick. Either way, acclimate your dog to the garment before you try to use it during a thunderstorm.
- See your vet. A veterinarian can prescribe medication to help solve this problem.

Car Anxiety: Most Golden Retrievers love to go car riding with their people—but there are exceptions. If, for example, you and your Golden are involved in a car accident, he may decide that auto travel isn't such a good idea. Here's how to change his mind:

- Time may diminish his anxiety some. Leave it alone. Wait a few weeks after an accident before trying to reacquaint your Golden with the joys of auto travel. Time may have diminished his anxiety some.
- Start car rehab. Start reacclimating your dog to the car in short, five-minute sessions. Start by standing with your dog a few feet (m) away from the car, and click and treat him for calm behavior. Next time, stand a little closer, again clicking and treating for calm behavior. Keep moving closer and closer at each session until he can stand beside your car without any show of stress on his part.
- Open the door. Now try opening the car door and placing the treat on the door ledge; praise him if he picks up the treat. At each subsequent session, move the treat farther and farther into the car until he's jumping into the car on his own.
- Start the motor. Once your dog remains in the car calmly, go to the driver's seat and start the motor. Run it for a few seconds, then click and treat and end the session.
- Start driving. Once your dog remains consistently calm with the motor running, move your car back and forth in the driveway, click and treat—and then again,

end the session. Next try driving around the block. Continue with this sequence until you are able to drive again with your dog safely and happily ensconced in the backseat.

If at any time during this process, your dog hesitates or balks, take heed. He's telling you that you're going too fast and that he's not ready to take the next step. Go back to your previous step, and make sure that he's calm and confident before attempting to progress. Bear in mind, too, that you need to use treats or rewards that your dog goes bonkers for. For some Goldens, the best treats may not be edible ones; instead, they might be a favorite toy. Figure out what really turns your Golden on, and use that to overcome his automobile antipathy.

Water Anxiety: Strange as it may seem, some Golden Retrievers do not like the water. Such a Golden may have gotten a less-than-pleasurable introduction to the life aquatic. For example, he may have leaped off a dock to chase a ball, only to find himself landing in the water and going under momentarily. Here's what to do:

- Don't force the issue. The key to helping a water-shy Golden overcome that shyness is to not force the issue. Let him decide whether to enter the water.
- Encourage him. You can encourage him by standing in the water yourself, holding out a treat or toy, and encouraging him to come and get it.

that provides a mild electrical shock may stop your dog's barking temporarily, but the collar doesn't address the root cause of your dog's particular problem. If you're using one, stop and try to figure out a more humane way to solve your dog's barking problem.

How to Manage It

The following section discusses some common reasons that the normally quiet Golden is barking, as well as some ways to manage the problem. One strategy that covers all your bases is to teach him a *quiet* cue. Catch him barking—but as soon as he stops, say "Quiet" or "Thank you" and give him a treat. Repeat this sequence whenever possible, and soon he'll learn to associate not barking, or barking once then and then quieting, with scoring a goodie.

Boredom

Any dog, including a Golden, who's left out in the backyard alone all day or even for a few hours is bound to get bored—and when he does, he's likely to relieve that boredom by sounding off, doggy style. The solution here: Relieve the boredom by playing with your Golden while he's out there and training him in basic good manners so that he can hang out with you in the house.

Loneliness

If your Golden habitually barks during the night, maybe he's lonesome. Is he made to sleep all by himself in the kitchen or the laundry room? If so, try welcoming him into your boudoir. He'll be happier, and you'll both sleep better. If he's barking during the day while you're away, check out the section on anxiety in this chapter.

Lack of Exercise

The Golden Retriever was bred to be a hunting dog—to run through marshland to fetch fallen game for his human hunting partner. As such, he has prodigious energy. If he doesn't have sufficient opportunity to expend that energy through frequent strenuous exercise, he's likely to try to find a way to use that energy himself. One such way is by barking at human passersby, squirrels who dare to cross your property, falling leaves, and just about anything or anyone else you can imagine. If this behavior describes your Golden's vocalizations, heed the well-known trainer's adage: "A tired dog is a good dog." Give him lots of chances for exercise—and not just walks, either. Goldens and other sporting dogs need to *run*.

You can train your dog not to bark by teaching him a *quiet* cue.

At the end of a sufficiently strenuous session, he'll be too tired to bark, not to mention much mellower.

CHEWING AND DESTRUCTIVENESS

A Golden Retriever is a four-footed love machine. Few people can resist his glorious good looks, his outgoing personality, and his willingness to give affection to anyone and everyone. But among those few who resist—at least sometimes—might be his family if that Golden is chewing, digging, or otherwise destroying their household possessions.

Golden Retriever chewing and destructiveness have many possible causes. Some dogs engage in these behaviors because they panic when they're left alone. Others indulge in these pastimes because they are bored. Still others engage in doggy vandalism because it's the only sure way they know to get attention from their otherwise neglectful people. And still others become demolition dogs simply because the temptation to become one is just too much for them to withstand.

How to Manage It

To end your Golden's chewing and destructiveness, take the following steps:

Determine the Cause

To a large extent, ending your Golden's vandalism depends on what's causing the

One way to keep your dog from chewing your possessions is to make sure he has toys and safe bones of his own to chew.

NYLABONE

vandalism in the first place. That's why it's important to try to figure out what's triggering his rampages. For example, dogs who destroy their homes due to separation anxiety generally engage in this behavior within a half hour of their owners' departures. A Golden who becomes Destructo-Dog while his people are around may be bored or simply trying to gain the attention of those people. Still others engage in the behavior simply because they can; their people haven't bothered to dog-proof their homes. Ask yourself questions and study your Golden's behavior to try to determine what's triggering his rampages in the first place.

Don't Scold

Don't scold—especially after the fact. If you come home to find your place looking like your teenager's bedroom, don't yell at or even scold your dog. He won't have the faintest idea why you're angry. He's not capable of connecting your unhappiness with the mess that he's made. Even if he's sporting a hang-dog look when you walk into a room that looks like a tornado's run through it, don't assume that he feels guilty; instead, realize that he's anticipating your being angry—for reasons he can't fathom.

If your Golden is messing with your stuff due to boredom and you'll only be gone a couple of hours, you can put him in his crate.

Tire Him Out

A Golden Retriever owner can never hear this adage too often: "A tired dog is a good dog." The Golden who gets several exercise sessions each week—and that means running, not walking—is much less likely to trash his home than one who's a couch potato. A tired Golden simply doesn't have the energy to engage in destructive behavior.

Give Him Something to Do

Try stuffing an interactive toy, such as a Nylabone, with food and treats, freezing it overnight, and giving it to your Golden before you leave the house or are otherwise going to be occupied. The effort he expends ferreting out the treats will divert him from expending such effort on destroying your stuff—and afterward, his full tummy might prompt him to take a nap.

Remove Temptation

Study what exactly your Golden is messing with to see whether you can limit his access to those items. Does he like to unroll the toilet paper? Close the bathroom door or put the toilet paper someplace where he can't reach it. Does he overturn wastebaskets and strew the contents all over the floor? Move the wastebaskets to upper-level bookshelves or other inaccessible places. Does he flip open the kitchen garbage can and spread its smelly contents all over the place? Turn the front of the can toward the wall and block it off with some barstools. Does he like to scratch on your sofa? Block off the scratched areas with chairs, boxes, or other items when you can't watch him. Does he chew your shoes? Put those shoes in your closet and close the closet door.

Consider Crating

If your Golden's messing with your stuff due to boredom and you're leaving the house for a couple of hours, put him in his crate. However, do *not* crate him if you'll either be gone the entire day (crating a dog for eight hours or more is cruel) or if his destructiveness results from separation anxiety (because, in such cases, crating will increase his level of panic).

Look for Teachable Moments

Keep a clicker and treats nearby and watch to see whether your dog goes for something he shouldn't. If he does, tell him "Off!" As soon as he backs off, click and treat.

Give Him Attention

If you're super busy and the only attention

you're paying your Golden is to get angry at him for messing with your things, he may decide that the only way to get some face time with you is to turn himself into Demolition Dog. Give him—and yourself—some breaks. No matter how busy you are, taking a few minutes for a tug-of-war session, a quick game of fetch, or even just a mutual lovefest will show him that there are other ways to interact with you besides getting into mischief.

COUNTER SURFING

A Golden Retriever is nothing if not an opportunist. Food left out on the kitchen counter is a Golden Retriever snack waiting to happen. Leave your sandwich on that counter, turn your back for an instant—and poof! when you turn back to look at the counter, that sandwich will have disappeared and your Golden will be licking his lips. Experts have a name for this behavior: countersurfing.

How to Manage It

There's really no reasonable way to teach a dog to refrain from countersurfing. The temptation offered by accessible people food far outweighs his interest in pleasing you or staying out of trouble.

Don't Leave Food on the Counter

Instead, train yourself to never leave anything out on your counter that you don't want your Golden to run off with—or at the very least, block your Golden's access to

the item in question. In other words, deal with your Golden opportunist by denying him opportunities. This same remove-all-temptation strategy applies equally well to Goldens who like to root through the trash, dive into the garbage can, unroll and/or chew the toilet paper, and perform similar antics.

DIGGING

Dogs dig digging, and Goldens are no exception. That's especially true of a bored Golden left to his own devices in his people's backyard. He could care less about the painstaking landscaping that he ruins as he digs to relieve that boredom. That said, some Goldens like to dig even when they have company.

Give your Golden his own digging area so that he doesn't destroy your entire yard.

Want to Know More?

Your Golden needs to know some basic cues to help you train him out of certain problem behaviors. For a refresher, see Chapter 4: Training Your Puppy.

How to Manage It

There are a few strategies you can employ to keep your Golden from digging where you don't want him to.

Keep Him Busy

For the Golden who digs out of boredom and loneliness, the answer is simple: don't let him get lonely and bored. Give him plenty of physical exercise, take the time to train him, and dedicate some time to just hanging out with him. After all, didn't you get a Golden so that you could have some company?

But if your Golden's digging isn't the result of social deprivation, your best strategy is to realize that he's a budding canine archaeologist and give him acceptable opportunities to practice his craft.

Establish a Digging Area

Find an area of your yard that can withstand Golden excavations and encourage your dog to dig there. Just get a few treats and toys, bury them in a few inches (cm) of soil, bring him to the area, and let him have at it. As he digs, praise him to smithereens. Change the buried items every couple of days.

Buy Him a Digging Area

If there's no place in the yard that's suitable for digging, head to your local toy store and purchase a sandbox. Fill it with sand, bury

some toys, and proceed as you would with an in-yard digging area.

JUMPING UP

Oh, how we love to pick up our Golden Retriever puppies! We lift them into our arms, we put our faces to theirs, we give them kisses, and we do all sorts of other mushy things that make us feel good and that the puppies come to appreciate. In fact, the puppies are so appreciative of such attention that as they grow up they'll go to great lengths—or more accurately, heights—to seek out such attention. Translation: They jump.

The trouble is, having a 15-pound (7-kg) puppy at face level in one's arms is very different from having a 65-pound (29.5-kg) Golden Retriever rocketing toward one's face. The Golden's intention is entirely benign, but the possible effect of that intention—knocking a person over—doesn't feel benign at all. For that reason, your Golden Retriever's career as a rocket dog needs to be a very short one. Better yet, you should stop it before it starts.

How to Manage It

Fortunately, you can end that career without resorting to old-fashioned tactics. There's no need, for example, to step on your Golden's paws or give him a knee to the chest. No matter which strategy you employ, though, the key to ending a Golden Retriever's rocket dog career is consistency—not just from you but from anyone he comes in contact with. If a household guest tells you that she doesn't mind whether your dog jumps on her, tell her that *you* mind, and ask her not to interact with your dog until he has all four paws on the floor. Make sure, too, that family members do not tolerate jumping and that they employ at least one of the steps outlined here to end the behavior.

Walk Away

Yes, really. Your Golden is jumping because he wants attention. If you give him that attention—no matter what kind of attention, even if you yell at him—you are rewarding the jumping and encouraging him to repeat the behavior. So to discourage the behavior, you need to quit rewarding him for doing it. In other words, withdraw your attention: Turn your back and walk away from him each and every time he jumps. With consistent repetition of the you-jump-I-leave routine, your dog will eventually learn to keep all four paws on the floor.

Have Him Do Something Else

Another strategy for dealing with jumping is to have your Golden do something that's incompatible with jumping—like sitting. Assuming that your Golden knows the *sit* cue, use it to deflect him the next time he takes a flying leap toward you. As he heads toward you but (ideally) before he becomes airborne, ask him to sit and give him praise and treat him when he does. Consistent repetition of this routine will soon result in your attention-seeking Golden Retriever offering *sits* rather than prepping for takeoff.

Use a Tether

If your Golden's jumping occurs when he greets people who enter your home, show him that greeting people with four on the floor will bring him the attention he seeks. Put on his leash and tie the leash to a sturdy chair leg or table leg. Then pick up your clicker and some treats and walk away about 10 feet (3 m). Now turn and walk toward him calmly. If he tries to jump as you approach, turn and walk away; if he remains on the ground, ask him to sit, then click and treat. Repeat this sequence until he's offering to sit as you approach.

LEASH PULLING

Golden Retrievers grow up to be big, strong dogs. And when they're leashed but want to get somewhere more quickly than their owners are taking them, they put their shoulders into speeding things up. They pull, giving their owners unintended upper body workouts in the process.

How to Manage It

If you want to curb this behavior in your dog, take one or more of the following steps.

Your dog should learn to walk politely and not pull on the leash.

With the right incentives and training techniques, a Golden can unlearn a multitude of bad habits.

Bag the Retractable Leash

Yes, that long wire leash gives your Golden more freedom, or at least the illusion thereof. But the very nature of the retractable leash encourages your Golden to pull. And if he pulls hard enough, he's likely to yank the inflexible handle right out of your hand. Need more convincing? Many municipalities ban leashes that are more than 6 feet (2 m) long—and even if they don't, those wire leashes are hard to see, making them a potential hazard for pedestrians. Opt instead for a standard 6-foot (2-m) leash. Leather is relatively expensive but is easier on the hands and lasts longer than cotton or nylon.

Get the Right Gear

The right equipment can go a long way toward teaching your Golden good on-leash walking manners. Look for harnesses that feature leash clips on the front. Just as important as getting the right equipment is bypassing the wrong stuff. Under that category are choke collars, also known as slip collars or training collars, as well as prong collars. Both of these collars cause discomfort and even pain to dogs, and they're not all that effective at curbing pulling. Head halters, also known as head collars, are more humane, but many dogs don't like them and will work to get them off their faces.

Teach Polite Walking

Head to Chapter 4: Training Your Golden Retriever Puppy for detailed instructions on how to teach your dog to behave himself while on the leash and what to do if he acts up.

Provide Adequate Exercise

Daily walks may not be enough to keep your Golden mellow enough to refrain from pulling on his leash. Find a way to give him vigorous aerobic exercise at least several times a week, if not daily.

Be Patient

Refraining from leash pulling is tough for an exuberant, enthusiastic Golden Retriever. Expect that you will have to continue reminding him for most of his life that he will get to his destination much faster if he doesn't make like a sled dog.

NIPPING

Golden Retrievers are oral creatures, especially during puppyhood. They love to use their mouths and teeth to explore the world around them through taste and touch. Alas, when their desire to taste and touch comes into contact with tender human skin, the results are painful to the human.

How to Manage It

To alleviate that pain, not to mention preventing its occurrence in the first place, do the following.

Teach the *Off* and *Take It* Cues

Teach your Golden the *off* and *take it* cues, as described in Chapter 4: Training Your Puppy. This pair of cues is actually designed to tell your puppy not to pick up a forbidden object. But it's also tremendously helpful in teaching your puppy that human skin is one of those forbidden objects. Here's how to teach them:

1. Sit on the floor in front of your puppy.
2. Put a treat in the palm of your hand.
3. Show him your palm.
4. As your puppy goes for the treat, close your hand in a fist, say "Off," and close your hand into a fist.
5. Each time he noses your hand, repeat the word "Off."
6. After four or five times, open your fist so that the treat is visible, and tell your puppy to take it.

Practice this cue regularly, even if you think that your puppy has mastered it. And once he has, use the *off* cue if his mouth comes into contact with your skin. When he backs off, offer him a treat and tell him to take it.

CHAPTER 11

GOLDEN RETRIEVER SPORTS AND ACTIVITIES

Sure, your Golden Retriever is great to just hang out with. A session with TiVo or Twitter is always nicer when your four-legged Golden pal is curled at your feet under your desk or coffee table, surfacing to solicit some strokes and bestow a kiss or two. But Goldens are so much more than companions in quiet indoor activities. They are dogs to get active with. This chapter outlines some of the many activities that you and your Golden can do together.

EVERYDAY ACTIVITIES

Although plenty of organized sports—and titles denoting accomplishment in such sports—are available to you and your Golden Retriever, nothing requires the two of you to participate in any of them. The two of you can have a great time engaging in everyday activities together. So what if you don't earn any titles? You'll still have high-quality time, which is the whole point of adding a Golden to your life in the first place.

Camping

If you're an experienced camper, why not take your Golden with you on your next trip? Sharing time in the woods with your canine companion can be a great experience; his avid interest in the sights, sounds, and smells around him can reignite your own appreciation of nature. But a successful human/canine camping expedition doesn't happen all by itself. Plenty of prep is needed to make your trip succeed. As you and your Golden prepare to head into the wild, consider the following suggestions:

- **Make sure your dog is welcome.** Not every campground permits dogs. Although many private campgrounds welcome canine campers, campgrounds at state and national parks may not. Call ahead so that you're not disappointed when you get there.

- **Bring the right stuff.** In addition to bringing your dog's food, bring plenty of water from home (don't let him drink from lakes or ponds), a first-aid kit, a collar and leash, and bowls for food and water. A brush to keep your dog's coat untangled, rid it of burrs, and brush away dirt is also a good idea.

- **Check IDs.** Make sure that your dog's identification tags and microchip data are up to date—and don't remove his collar. That way, if he gets lost, you stand a better chance of finding him quickly.

- **Keep your dog under control.** Even at dog-

- **Check your dog over.** At least once a day, check your dog for ticks, cuts, and bruises.

Walking and Jogging

Sure, you walk your Golden three or four times a day so that he gets some much-needed potty breaks. But do you simply take him to his potty spot, let him do the doo, and run back into the house? If so, you're missing out on countless opportunities to spend some special moments with your four-legged friend. You just need to make a little time. Here are some ways to make the most of your walks with your Golden—and how to pick up the pace so that you both get a good aerobic workout.

- **Teach polite walking.** Taking a walk, much less jogging, is no fun if an out-of-control Golden is at the other end of the leash. Check out Chapters 4 and 10 for pointers on how to teach your dog to walk nicely with you when he's on the leash.
- **Potty first.** If you're looking to get some aerobic benefit out of your walk or jog, make sure that your Golden potties first. That way he's less likely to screech to a halt to anoint the stop sign pole just as you're getting into high gear.
- **Leave distractions at home.** When you're strolling the neighborhood with your Golden, make it a point to give that activity—and your dog—your full attention. This isn't the time to be gabbing on your cell phone, chugging your morning cup of coffee, or listening to the latest music you've downloaded to your MP3 player. Not only will you miss some companionable time with your Golden Retriever, but you'll also be less able to respond to unexpected events, such as encountering another dog. Picking up your dog's poop could also be problematic.
- **Mind the temperatures.** Weather extremes

Expending some of your Golden's excess energy by participating in a sport or activity will help keep him out of trouble.

friendly campgrounds, other campers won't be happy if your dog engages in a lot of barking and runs around wreaking havoc. Keep your dog on his leash.

- **Keep your dog with you.** Never leave your dog unattended at your campground, and have him sleep with you in your tent at night. Such precautions will reduce his chances of wandering away, getting lost, and encountering trouble.
- **Clean up.** Make sure that you pick up your dog's poop and get rid of any leftover human or dog food that could attract wildlife or insects.

require adjustments in walking schedules. Just as you don't enjoy walking, let alone jogging, in very cold or very warm temperatures, neither does your dog. When the mercury dips low or shoots high, avoid excessive exercise. By doing so, you'll not only prevent discomfort but also more serious problems, such as heat exhaustion and frostbite.

- **Pay attention to surfaces.** During warm weather, avoid walking your dog on asphalt; the surface temperature can burn his tender paw pads. And consider jogging on a softer surface such as grass (as long as it's not wet) or a trailside shoulder, rather than concrete or asphalt, which are harder on the joints than softer surfaces are.

Swimming

Your Golden Retriever's heritage includes a lot of time in the water; after all, Goldens slog through marshes and wetlands to retrieve fallen game for their human hunting partners. But even if you don't hunt, your Golden can enjoy the life aquatic—with a little help from you. Keep these tips in mind when you take to the waters with your Golden.

- **Go slowly.** Not every Golden takes to swimming right away. Be patient and positive as you introduce your dog to the water. Use treats or toys to entice him, and don't try to make him go into the water before he's ready.
- **Make it a group effort.** Some dogs will go into a pool, pond, or other water body without hesitation the very first time they see one, but many others need a little help from their friends. Hanging out with a dog who loves to swim may encourage your Golden to give the water a go. He may also be willing to follow you into the water if you encourage him and offer him food or toys.

By the Numbers

Don't perform strenuous sports such as agility or jogging with your Golden until he's at least one year old and has had his hips and elbows checked by your veterinarian. The reason: These activities can cause excessive stress to your young dog's developing bones and joints. Wait until he's passed his first birthday, and then introduce the activities gradually.

- **Help him out.** Your Golden may love swimming in a pool but be unable to figure out how to leave that pool. Show him where the pool steps or ramp is so that he can exit. And no matter where he's swimming, watch for signs that he's getting tired, such as heavier breathing or increased splashing while paddling. Finally, never, ever leave your Golden alone in a pool or other water body; he needs your supervision while he's swimming if he's to stay safe.
- **Hose him down.** Pool or pond water can make a Golden's skin and coat feel dry, gummy, and irritated—so after every swimming session, rinse your dog thoroughly and towel him as dry as possible.
- **Dry his ears.** Be sure to dry his ears thoroughly afterward, using a drying powder if necessary.

SPORTS

Golden Retrievers are multitalented dogs. They excel in a wide variety of activities—from conformation to competitive obedience to therapy dog work, to name just a few. Here

Avoid excessive exercise with your Golden when the weather is too hot or cold.

you'll find a list of the dog sports in which Goldens are especially talented and how to find out more about them.

Agility

Does your Golden like to race around the yard, jump on top of the picnic table, or shimmy underneath it? If so, he could be a great candidate for the ever-popular canine sport of agility. In this sport, a human handler guides a dog through a timed obstacle course that consists of tunnels, teeter-totters, hurdles, weave poles, A-frames, and balance beams. And while almost any breed can learn this sport—yes, even big Golden Retrievers can navigate weave poles with aplomb—you might find it difficult to teach your Golden agility moves on your own. Fortunately, plenty of professional dog trainers hold classes for agility beginners of all breeds.

For more information about canine agility, log onto these websites: the American Kennel Club (AKC) at www.akc.org; the North American Dog Agility Council (NADAC) at www.nadac.com; and the United States Dog Agility Association (USDAA) at www.usdaa.com.

Canine Freestyle

If music causes you to tap your feet or bob your head before you even realize you're doing so—and if you're looking to have a lot of fun with your Golden—look no further. Together you and your Golden can trip the light fantastic by taking up canine freestyle.

In canine freestyle, you and your Golden perform maneuvers that are set to music. Your dog might circle around you, jump through your arms, spin, or perform a flip in response to your signals and in time to the music. And some dogs can become incredibly proficient, not to mention creative. One of the best-known canine freestylists was a Golden Retriever named Rookie, who was known for making up some of his own moves when performing with his human partner, Carolyn Scott.

To see whether canine freestyle is for you and your Golden, check out the offerings at your local dog training club or positive reinforcement trainer. If you both enjoy learning freestyle basics, find more info by logging onto the World Canine Freestyle Organization (WCFO) website at www.

worldcaninefreestyle.org and the Canine Freestyle Federation (CFF) at www.canine-freestyle.org.

Conformation

If you've ever watched the annual Westminster Kennel Club extravaganza on television, you've seen conformation in action. That's right: Conformation is simply the formal name for a dog show. That said, the formal name is an apt one because dog shows are designed to measure how well each canine contestant conforms to the standard of his breed, as described in Chapter 1. The dogs who adhere most closely to these standards are the ones who win ribbons in the show ring.

If you're wondering whether your Golden Retriever has what it takes to succeed in the show ring, your best course of action is to

If you want to participate in conformation with your Golden, he should adhere to the breed standard as closely as possible.

Consult a reputable breeder if you want to see if your dog is a good conformation candidate.

find local all-breed clubs by consulting the AKC's website at www.akc.org or regional and local Golden Retriever clubs. And start reading up on the show world. Begin by subscribing to a magazine like the *AKC Gazette*.

One thing to note: If you've already spayed or neutered your Golden, you can't show him. That's because the AKC doesn't allow spayed or neutered dogs to be shown. The original purpose of dog shows was, after all, to showcase prime breeding stock; if a dog can't breed, the reasoning is that there's not much point in showing him. But your altered dog can still compete in other AKC events.

Field Trials and Hunting Tests

The Golden Retriever's original reason for being was to plow through marshland and underbrush and retrieve birds that had been shot by his human hunting partner. Many of today's Goldens still have the ability to perform those tasks. Your Golden may be one of those dogs—and if he is, you can give him a chance to use that ability by participating in AKC field trials.

These field trials vary, depending on the type of dog involved. For example, field trials for Beagles measure the abilities of those dogs to track rabbits and other small game because that is what they were bred to do. Other breeds, ranging from Dachshunds to spaniels, are measured for doing what they were bred to do, whether that involves cornering a quarry in

consult a reputable breeder—maybe your dog's breeder, or if that person's not available, a breeder whom you find by consulting the Golden Retriever Club of America's website. Either way, a breeder can examine your dog and can tell you how closely he conforms to the Golden Retriever breed standard. If the breeder gives you a thumbs-up, try attending a few local dog shows without your dog to get a feel for how dog shows work.

Still interested? Then take yourself and your Golden to a handling class. Local all-breed kennel clubs often offer such classes, as do some local Golden Retriever clubs. You can

Want to Know More?

If your Golden gets especially dirty participating in a sport or activity, he may need a full-on grooming session. See Chapter 6: Golden Retriever Grooming Needs for some pointers.

Many Goldens today have the ability to perform the tasks for which they were originally bred, such as retrieving birds.

a burrow or flushing game out of a bush.

For Goldens and other retrievers (Labrador Retrievers, Curly-Coated Retrievers, Chesapeake Bay Retrievers, Nova Scotia Duck Tolling Retrievers, and Flat-Coated Retrievers), the AKC's field trials consist of measuring a dog's ability to retrieve fallen birds over both land and water under a variety of conditions and levels of difficulty.

For the newbie Golden hunter or for the owner who doesn't cotton to the intensity of retriever field trials, there are hunting tests. Unlike field trials, hunting tests do not require dogs to compete against each other but simply measure each dog being tested against a written standard. Both the AKC and another registry,

the United Kennel Club (UKC), offer hunting tests to Golden Retrievers and other retrievers.

For comprehensive, all-in-one-place information about field trials and hunting tests, consult the Golden Retriever Club of America's website at http://www.grca.org/events/field/gr_field-titles.html.

Obedience

This activity is exactly what it sounds like: a test of a dog's ability to respond appropriately to cues ranging from coming when called to using his sense of smell to discriminate among objects. Golden Retrievers excel in this sport; they've won the AKC national championships more often than any other breed. And of the

20 dogs whose previous year scores were so high that they earned an automatic invitation to the 2009 AKC national championship, 10 (yes, fully half) of those dogs were Golden Retrievers—far more than any other breed.

In an obedience trial, a judge scores a dog for each exercise the dog performs. If a dog scores at least 170 out of a possible 200 points in a single trial, plus at least 50 percent of the points in each individual exercise, he earns a "leg" toward an obedience title. After earning three such legs, he earns his first title: Companion Dog, or CD. If a dog earns additional advanced titles plus high placements in the competition, he can earn points toward the pinnacles of the sport: Obedience Trial Champion (OTCh) and National Obedience Champion (NOC).

The latter accolade is earned by just one dog each year at the AKC National Obedience Invitational.

More information about the world of competitive obedience is available from the AKC at www.akc.org.

Rally Obedience

Some people find competitive obedience to be too dull for their taste, while others find that for them, canine agility requires too much human agility. For these folks—and anyone else who's interested—there's the happy-medium sport of rally obedience.

In rally obedience, you and your Golden complete a course of 10 to 20 stations that's been designed by the judge for the event. At each station is a sign that tells the human-

Find an activity that your dog enjoys; don't force him to participate in somthing that he doesn't like.

Training Tidbit

As you introduce your Golden Retriever to various activities, keep in mind that he is a unique individual—and that his idea of a good time may differ greatly from yours. For example, the fact that Goldens dominate competitive obedience doesn't mean that your Golden will enjoy this activity, and just because most Goldens like swimming doesn't guarantee that your Golden will be among them. Watch your Golden for signs that he enjoys what he's doing: tail wagging; soft, happy expression; eagerness to work. If he shows signs that he's not enjoying himself—reluctance to participate, droopy tail, wanting to leave class, lackluster performance—respect his wishes and try training for another activity.

canine team what the dog needs to do there. For example, at one station, the dog might need to sit; at another, dog and handler might need to walk in a figure-8 pattern; at still another, the dog might be required to lie down from a standing position. In any case, the judge scores the dog and handler on how well they perform each maneuver.

Rally obedience can be a great activity for a Golden Retriever and his person—and in fact, quite a few Goldens compete in this activity and do well. For example, during 2008, which was the most recent year such information was available at the time this book was written, ten Goldens achieved national ranking points in rally obedience from the Association of Pet Dog Trainers (APDT).

Both the APDT and the AKC sponsor rally obedience competitions and titles. Information about the AKC rally program is available at www.akc.org. To learn more about the APDT program, log onto www.apdt.com.

TESTING, TESTING

Most organized dog sports and activities involve some sort of testing in which you and your dog must perform certain maneuvers in front of one or more human evaluators. For many Goldens and their people, training for such tests and basking in the glory of titles won when passing such tests is a lot of fun. For others, test-taking anxiety (remember taking your Scholastic Aptitude Tests [SATs]?) overrides the fun of pre-testing prep and post-testing pride. If you're not sure which category you and your Golden fit into, consider training for one or both of the following tests offered by the AKC.

AKC Star Puppy Program

This program establishes not only that a dog under one year of age has mastered certain behaviors and behaves in a mannerly fashion but also that his owner is fully committed to the dog's care, training, and overall well-being.

To start the program, simply enroll your Golden puppy and yourself in a six-week training class that's taught by an AKC Canine Good Citizen Evaluator. A searchable database of evaluators can be found at www.akc.org/events/cgc/cgc_bystate.cfm.

After completing the course, you and your puppy are eligible to take the AKC Star Puppy test.

The Canine Good Citizen program emphasizes good manners for dogs and responsible behavior on the part of their owners.

AKC Canine Good Citizen® Program

The AKC started the Canine Good Citizen (CGC) Program in 1989 to publicly reward dogs who have exhibited good manners in their homes and communities. Like the AKC Star Puppy program, the CGC program emphasizes not only good manners for dogs but also responsible behavior by dog owners. Training your Golden to pass the CGC test lays an excellent foundation for starting in dog sports such as agility, competitive obedience, and rally obedience and in the process can significantly deepen the bond between you.

Unlike the AKC Star Puppy program, you and your Golden need not take classes from a CGC Evaluator. In fact, you don't necessarily have to take any classes at all, although classes or other expert instruction can be very helpful. However, only an AKC CGC evaluator—whom you can find by searching the AKC's evaluator database at www.akc.org/events/cgc/cgc_bystate.cfm—can administer the ten-component CGC test. Those components are:

- **Accepting a friendly stranger:** This test is designed to show that the dog will allow a friendly stranger to approach him and to speak with his handler in an everyday situation.
- **Sitting politely for petting:** The purpose of this test is to determine whether the dog will allow a friendly stranger to touch him while he's out with his handler.
- **Accepting grooming, exhibiting good**

health: This test demonstrates that the dog welcomes being groomed and examined by a stranger and also that the owner is diligent in caring for the dog and safeguarding his health.

- **Walking on a loose lead:** The test is designed to showcase the handler's control over the dog while the dog is walking on leash.
- **Walking through a crowd:** The purpose of this test is to show that the dog can move politely in pedestrian traffic and is under control in public places.
- **Sit and lying down on cue and staying in place:** This test demonstrates that the dog will respond appropriately to his handler's requests to sit and lie down and will remain in the place specified by the handler.
- **Coming when called:** The purpose of this test is to demonstrate that the dog will come to the handler when the handler calls him.
- **Reacting to another dog:** This test is designed to show that the dog can behave politely around other dogs.
- **Reacting to distractions:** This test aims to show that the dog remains calm and confident when faced with common distracting situations.
- **Accepting supervised separation:** The purpose of this test is to demonstrate that the handler can leave the dog with another person and that the dog will maintain his training and good manners.

More information about the CGC test is available from the AKC at http://www.akc.org/events/cgc/.

THERAPY WORK

The benefits of the human/animal bond have been studied and documented extensively. All too often, though, those who most need those benefits don't receive them. These individuals are patients in hospitals, nursing homes, and other health care facilities; they are children who need an extra injection of confidence to succeed in reading and other challenging activities; they are grieving over the loss of a loved one or are otherwise grappling with difficult personal issues; or they may simply be lonely college students who are away from home for the first time.

For all of these individuals, four-legged therapists can help: specifically, dogs who are trained to provide such therapy. Such dogs might work in libraries, lying down next to

Because of their outgoing personality and affectionate nature, Goldens are naturals at therapy work.

children and listening to them read aloud. Others might visit sick people in hospitals and provide some much-needed unconditional love and cheer. Still others provide similar services to the elderly in nursing homes and assisted living facilities, while other canine therapists are there to provide a loving paw to those who have experienced a death in the family or a traumatic experience or are seeking mental health treatment.

The Golden Retriever's outgoing personality, affectionate nature, and willingness to learn make him ideal for therapy work. However, Goldens are not born therapists. They need training in order to be controllable by a handler, and they need continuing socialization in order to be comfortable in a wide variety of situations.

Although plenty of organizations engage in animal-related therapy work, three such organizations are particularly well known for providing excellent training for canine therapists and their people. Those

organizations are the Delta Society at www.deltasociety.org; Therapy Dogs International (TDI) at www.tdi-dog.org; and Love on a Leash at www.loveonaleash.org.

TRAVELING WITH YOUR GOLDEN

Hitting the road with your Golden Retriever can be a lot of fun—if you plan carefully and put your Golden's welfare ahead of your own desires. Here are some suggestions to keep both you and your dog healthy, happy, and safe when you're hit with some wanderlust.

By Car

Traveling with dogs by auto or other designed-for-the-highway vehicle can be a blast—as evidenced by no less an authority than Nobel Prize winner John Steinbeck in his classic memoir *Travels with Charley*. True, Charley was a Standard Poodle, but there's no reason that the joys that Steinbeck experienced with his dog can't be experienced by you and your Golden Retriever when the two of you hit the open road.

However, planning is essential to keep both of you safe. If you're going mobile with your Golden Retriever, keep the following ideas in mind.

- **No front seating:** As much as you might want to keep your Golden in the front seat next to you, have a care for his safety: If you have an accident and the passenger air bag deploys, the impact could severely injure or even kill him. And even if you don't have an accident, he could try to climb into your lap, distracting you while driving. For his sake and yours, keep him in the back seat.

- **Crate if possible:** Just as you do, a Golden Retriever needs to be secured when in a car so that he's not bounced around in the car—or even out of the car completely—in the event

Allowing your Golden to ride loose in the car, as shown here, is dangerous—make sure that he is secured in a crate or is wearing a seat belt.

of an accident. If your car is large, like a minivan or SUV, you can put his crate in the cargo bed and have him travel in that; make sure that the crate is positioned in a way that it won't move around in the cargo bed.

- **Buckle up:** If your vehicle is too small to permit crating, secure your Golden with a seat belt. Be aware, however, that doggy seat belts are not created equal. The plastic clasps on some seat belts can shatter if a crash occurs. Instead, opt for a clasp-less belt that's made of the same material as seat belts for human passengers.

- **Roll up the windows:** Make sure that the back seat windows are rolled up high enough so that your dog can't hang his head out the window. He may love feeling the wind in his face, but he could be injured by stones or other flying debris in the road.

- **Stop often:** If you're on a long trip, stop at least every two hours so that your Golden has a chance to stretch his legs and take a potty break.

- **Equip yourself:** On any long car trip, bring plastic bags to pick up your dog's poop,

bottled water, and a dish to pour the water into so that your canine traveling companion can quench his thirst.

- **Use the leash:** When having your Golden enter and exit the car, make sure that he's leashed and that you're holding onto it. Doing so will prevent him from bolting and risking getting injured or lost.

- **Don't leave him alone:** Avoid leaving your Golden alone in the car. This is particularly important during warm weather because a car's interior can quickly heat up to a dangerously high temperature, even if the windows are open and the weather's not that warm. And even if the weather is okay, leaving your Golden alone in the car puts him at risk for theft.

- **Curb carsickness:** If your Golden gets queasy in the car, avoid feeding him for at least a couple of hours before you set out. Open the windows a little bit (but not too much) so that fresh air circulates. If those measures don't help, consult your vet about giving your Golden a little Dramamine at least an hour before your departure.

By Plane

Flying with a Golden Retriever can be complicated. That's because commercial airlines don't allow a dog to fly in a passenger cabin with his person unless he can be enclosed in a carrier that fits under the seat in front of the person. With a minimum adult weight of 55 pounds (25 kg), there's no way that a Golden can meet such criteria. That means that in order to fly, a Golden must be placed in a crate and flown as baggage. The U.S. Department of Agriculture's (USDA) Animal and Plant Health Inspection Service (APHIS) offers a fact sheet that describes U.S. government regulations covering the shipment of animals by air. You can download this fact sheet by logging onto: http://www.aphis.usda.gov/publications/animal_welfare/content/printable_version/fs_awpetravel.pdf.

But even if you adhere to all of the USDA regulations, transporting your Golden by air can be a challenge. Most airlines won't transport pets as baggage during the summer, because the cargo area would become too hot while the plane is on the tarmac waiting to take off or coming to the gate after a landing. Some airlines won't transport pets at all. And for those that do, the costs can be prohibitive.

If you absolutely must airlift your Golden, the safest bet is to book him on a carrier that's dedicated to transporting pets in the cabin, not in the baggage hold. One such carrier is Pet Airways, reachable online at http://petairways.com. Bear in mind, however, that you will not be able to accompany your Golden on his trip.

Bottom line: Flying with a Golden Retriever is likely to be complicated at best. You'll save yourself and your dog considerable stress if you find another way to transport him to where you both want to go. Otherwise, leave him at home—either by boarding him with a friend or at a reputable boarding facility or by hiring a pet-sitter.

Lodging for You and Your Golden

Happily, finding a hotel that accommodates you and your Golden isn't all that difficult. Many establishments that once banned dogs now realize that welcoming those dogs means profits and repeat business for them. As a result, more hotels, motels, and even bed-and-breakfasts are saying yes to canine visitors.

To find these pet-friendly lodgings, start by checking out print and online offerings targeted to the dog-owning traveler. Among the best websites are Fido Friendly (www.fidofriendly.com); Pets on the Go (www.petsonthego.com); and Dog Friendly (www.dogfriendly.com).

Once you identify a place to stay, you can start making plans. Those plans should include:

- **Calling ahead:** Call or e-mail the hotel you have in mind to make sure that its pet-friendly policy remains in effect. Check, too, to learn the rules for staying with a pet at the facility and whether the facility requires a pet deposit and/or an extra fee.
- **Pack the right gear:** Bring your dog's crate, dog food, collar and leash, immunization record, and plastic bags.
- **Bring some comforts from home:** When your dog's in an unfamiliar place, some familiar objects can be comforting. Pack two or three of his favorite toys—and also, perhaps, an old T-shirt with your scent on it. The latter may be of considerable help if you have to leave him alone in his crate.

If You Can't Take Your Golden With You

Sometimes bringing your Golden Retriever with you isn't in the interest of you or your

Even if you don't want to participate in a formal sport or activity, just spending time together will strengthen your bond.

Golden. If you're flying—especially during the summer—or going someplace where you'll be touring around and leaving him alone all day, both of you may be happier if he stays home while you hit the road. But of course, you can't just leave him home alone; you need to arrange for someone else to care for him in your stead. Here are some options.

A friend: If your circle of friends includes a dog lover, consider asking whether she'll either come and stay with your Golden while you're gone or is willing to care for him at her home. This option is particularly good if you'll be away for more than a day or two. Make sure, though, that she has the information she needs to care for your Golden properly—and if she has other dogs, make sure that they get along with your Golden.

Your dog's breeder: If your Golden's breeder lives near you, ask if she'd be willing to put up your dog while you're away. She may welcome the chance to get reacquainted with her "baby."

A boarding kennel: A good boarding kennel is your best option if you can't take your Golden with you on your trip and you have no friends who can care for him. Your veterinarian, groomer, or dog trainer may be able to suggest some kennels. Before you make a reservation, though, pay a visit to the kennel. Make sure that it's clean and escape-proof and has staff on the premises 24/7. Make sure, too, that the kennel staff is knowledgeable about dogs and attentive to those who are in their care.

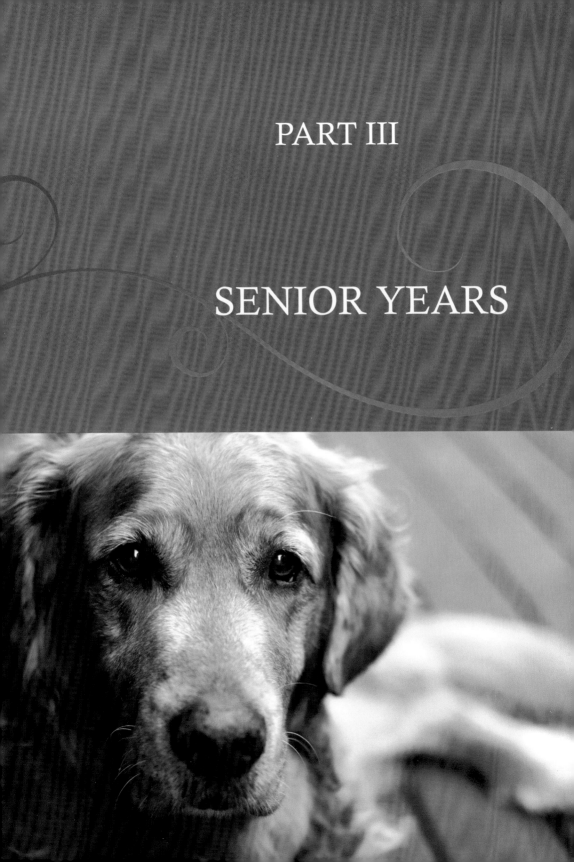

PART III

SENIOR YEARS

CHAPTER 12

FINDING YOUR GOLDEN RETRIEVER SENIOR

Like a fine wine, the Golden Retriever ages well. The bouncing out-of-control puppy, the sometimes fractious adolescent, and the highly enthusiastic (read: energetic) adult give way to a sweet and mellow kind of dignity by the time a Golden turns eight years of age or so. That maturity and other pluses are probably obvious to those who have had the privilege of living with and loving Golden Retrievers since puppyhood. But if you're thinking about welcoming a senior Golden into your home for the first time, you may have a hard time figuring out how anything can outweigh the possible disadvantage of perhaps having only a few years together with your Golden. This chapter will help you figure out why adopting a senior Golden offers plenty of advantages over adopting his younger counterpart.

THE PROS OF ADOPTING A SENIOR

Rescue groups often have quite a few senior Goldens available for adoption—but as appealing as those dogs may be, they often take longer to find homes than younger Goldens do. Would-be adopters may hesitate to bond with

Want to Know More?

If adopting an adult is more your speed, see Chapter 5: Finding Your Golden Retriever Adult.

an older Golden Retriever because they fear that the dog will have only a few years with them before succumbing to the ravages of old age.

That fear is understandable, but it's not entirely rooted in logic. Life doesn't have any guarantees, and Golden Retrievers are no exception. You can welcome a young puppy into your home only to experience the heartbreak of having that puppy or young adult passing away. Conversely, you can welcome a healthy older Golden into your home and find that he's with you for far more than just a couple of years. Although the average Golden's life expectancy is 10 to 12 years of age, it's not uncommon for a Golden to live to be 13 or 14, and some live even longer.

Need more convincing? Here are some other advantages that the mature Golden Retriever offers.

By the Numbers

A Golden Retriever is considered to be a senior citizen at about eight years of age—but with good luck and good health, he can live well into his teens.

He's Probably Housetrained

Older dogs do need to potty more often than their younger colleagues do—but at least they know that they're supposed to do their business only at certain times and places. By adopting a senior Golden, you're bypassing the tedium of housetraining.

He Won't Destroy Your Possessions

The mature Golden has probably lived for many years in one or more human homes, so he knows that he's not supposed to get into your stuff. In other words, you need not fear coming home to find that your dog has trashed your home in a fit of boredom, loneliness, or panic.

There's no Mystery

Puppies—even purebred Golden Retriever puppies—are a little bit of a mystery. A person can't know for sure if that little Golden butterball will grow up to be undersized, oversized, light in color, or darker in color. (Coat colors can vary widely even within a litter of Golden Retriever puppies.) A puppy's temperament is not always predictable either; the puppy who was a shy little darling may grow up to be Mr. Hell on Wheels, especially if he doesn't have appropriate training. A senior Golden is exactly who he appears to be, which means that you don't need to worry about unwelcome surprises.

He'll Already Know How to Behave

Even if he hasn't had all that much training, a senior Golden isn't likely to indulge in very many puppy antics, if any. He's too dignified to jump up on people, and counter surfing may be too much of an effort for him.

He'll Be Easier on Your Bottom Line

Generally, adopting a senior dog costs considerably less than adopting a younger one, much less buying a puppy from a reputable breeder. For example, the fee for adopting a Golden Retriever from GRREAT, a Washington DC-area Golden rescue group, is $300 for a dog under four years of age, $250 for a dog from four to seven years of age, and $175 for a dog eight years of age and up. A reputable breeder is likely to charge at least $1,000 for a Golden puppy—and often considerably more. The discount for senior dogs doesn't mean that such dogs are inferior in any way to youngsters—it simply reflects recognition of the fact that many people bypass the joys of adopting an older Golden in favor of one who's younger.

He'll Like Being With You

Adolescent and young adult Golden Retrievers certainly love their people, but they have additional priorities. After all, there's a whole world out there for them to explore! Consequently, if you let a younger Golden off leash in an unprotected area, that Golden may decide to take off on an exploratory expedition. And youthful Goldens are surprisingly speedy—they have no problem outrunning their humans. However, the older Golden not only doesn't possess such speed, but he isn't at all unhappy about it. He's no longer beset with wanderlust; his idea of a good time is to hang out with you.

Many older Goldens are a pleasure to live with because they're better behaved than their younger counterparts.

He'll Give you a Rest

The countersurfing, garbage-raiding, paper-shredding, sock-stealing Golden Retriever puppy or young adult is a total hoot—but boy, he'll keep you busy dealing with such antics. The senior Golden is way beyond such mischief; it's beneath his dignity—and the more dignity he has, the more rest you get.

He'll Know When to Leave You Alone

Although an older Golden will tend to stick closer to you than a young Golden will, that doesn't mean that the oldster is a pest. As long as he knows where you are, he'll be cool with whatever you're doing. If, for example, you're

playing around on your computer, a senior Golden will be perfectly happy just taking a snooze at your side—or at most, discreetly signaling you that he needs a potty break. Such discretion can be a welcome alternative to dealing with a puppy who relentlessly tries to get you to play, gets himself into trouble when you won't play, or just can't settle down while you update your Facebook or Twitter page.

He'll Pay Attention

Adolescent and young adult Golden Retrievers don't always appear to hear what you're asking them to do. They may be guilty of a kind of selective deafness: They don't seem to hear you tell them to get off the couch or to come when

The fact that a Golden Retriever is a senior citizen doesn't mean that he can't continue to learn. Help your senior Golden keep his mind sharp by teaching him new cues and playing games with him (for example, hide the toy or hide-and-seek) that require him to exercise some brainpower.

every word and, if possible, do what you've asked. If a senior Golden appears not to hear what you're saying, the reason may be real deafness, not the selective kind.

He'll Appreciate You

Puppies and young adult Golden Retrievers are the cutest, most infectious beings to grace the planet, hands down. That said, their cuteness doesn't really extend to being affectionate. Instead, they entertain us with their playful behavior and their unabashed *joie de vivre*. They're too busy enjoying life in general to pay a whole lot of attention to you in particular (although spending time training and socializing a young Golden can help change that). But a senior Golden is different—especially if you've adopted him as a senior from a shelter or rescue group. He knows

called, but they magically appear before you if they hear words like "cookie" or "treat." But with senior Goldens, such hijinks are a thing of the past. They're happy to hang onto your

An older Golden will tend to stick closer to you than a younger Golden.

An older adopted Golden will truly appreciate you.

how good his life is with you. He's grateful for cuddle time, an extra treat, and—most of all—extra attention. Many adopters of rescued or shelter Goldens (and for that matter, other breeds) strongly believe that their dogs know how fortunate they are and that they greatly appreciate the second chance at happiness that their adopters have given them.

He'll Teach You What Really Matters

The writer Milan Kundera wrote that "Dogs are our link to paradise. They don't know evil or jealousy or discontent. To sit with a dog on a hillside on a glorious afternoon is to be back in Eden, where doing nothing was not boring—it was peace." Crazy, active young Golden Retrievers certainly contribute to the glory of an afternoon; there are few things more beautiful than seeing a Golden run with the afternoon sun shining on his coat. But real peace and joy come from sitting down in that afternoon sun with a senior Golden. The older dog is much more likely to settle down enough to enjoy that activity (or more accurately, inactivity) than his younger counterpart is.

Multi-Dog Tip

As with any plans to adopt a dog, do your best to make sure that the senior Golden you want to adopt will get along well with the other dogs in your family.

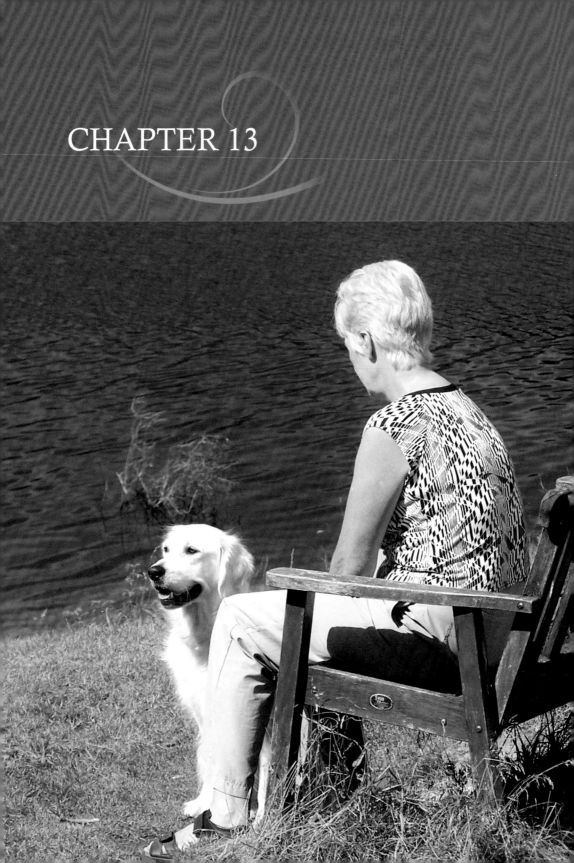

CHAPTER 13

CARE OF YOUR GOLDEN RETRIEVER SENIOR

Taking care of your senior Golden Retriever doesn't have to be all that different from taking care of a younger Golden. Just like any other dog of any age, the mature Golden needs good food, good grooming, good health care, and good training to be at his best. That said, he requires some minor adjustments to those four essential elements as he ages. This chapter describes those adjustments.

WHEN DOES A GOLDEN BECOME A SENIOR?

On average, Golden Retrievers begins to show signs of aging when they reach their eighth birthdays, but within that average is considerable variation among individual Goldens. Some of that variation may be due to sheer genetic luck, but some Goldens age more rapidly than others for reasons their humans can control.

For example, an overweight Golden is likely to age more quickly and have a shorter life span than a Golden with a sleek physique. By keeping your dog lean and giving him plenty of exercise, you could add months or even years to his life. And whatever your Golden does eat should be the highest-quality food that you can afford.

Good dental health is also an important component to maintaining health and extending the life of your Golden. That's because dental disease can morph into serious infections of a dog's vital organs, not to mention diminish his quality of life.

But in any case, it's important to bear in mind that reaching the age of eight does not suddenly mean that an individual Golden Retriever is a senior citizen. Instead, the wise owner looks for concrete signs of aging such as:

- **Slowing down:** A Golden who can claim the title of senior citizen won't move as quickly as he did when he was younger. He'll probably take more time going up and down stairs, getting up from a nap, and just getting around than he used to. He's also likely to be less interested in—or to need—the kind of strenuous aerobic workout that he required when he was younger.

- **Whitening up:** An older Golden Retriever will start sprouting white hair around his muzzle and eyes. His coat may also become less luxuriant and drier than it was when he was younger. (But note that many Goldens

Senior dogs can make wonderful companions.

begin graying around the muzzle and eyes far before they are seniors, often by three to four years of age!)

Having accidents: Many people find that their bladder control diminishes with time, and the same is true with Goldens. Urinary incontinence is often an issue for older spayed female Golden Retrievers (but can often be corrected). Other aging Goldens of either sex may forget their bathroom manners because they've developed canine cognitive dysfunction syndrome (CDS), which is similar to Alzheimer's disease in humans.

Getting lumpy: Aging Goldens often develop soft spongy lumps on their bodies—but don't assume that any lumps that your Golden develops are age-related. Get them checked.

Appearing to ignore you: If you call your Golden Retriever or give him some other cue to which he doesn't respond, don't assume that he's exhibiting selective deafness. He may truly be going deaf—which happens fairly often among senior dogs.

Becoming disoriented: Some senior Goldens appear to not know where they are even when they are in what had been familiar places. Such disorientation can be a symptom of CDS.

Exhibiting more fear: Age can cause some Goldens to become apprehensive or even frightened of occurrences that didn't bother them in their youth. If your dog was previously impervious to thunderstorms, loud noises, or other startling occurrences but now whines, trembles, or becomes clingy, his age could be catching up with him.

FEEDING YOUR SENIOR GOLDEN

Just because your Golden Retriever is now a senior citizen doesn't mean that you necessarily need to change what he eats. If he's healthy and thriving on his current fare, there's no reason not to continue feeding that fare. However, if your Golden develops health problems—whether or not those problems are age related—a change of diet might be in order. That's because certain conditions may well respond to adjustments in the diet.

However, before you make any changes in your senior's diet, consult your veterinarian. Your vet not only can help you identify foods that will optimize your dog's health but also can suggest dietary supplements that can help bring about improvements. For example, the vet might suggest the addition of fatty acid capsules to improve the quality of your Golden's skin and coat and strengthen his immune system.

How to Feed Your Senior

Whether you change your senior Golden's diet or not, it's a good idea to at least consider the way you feed him. Sometimes a dog's dining needs and preferences change as he ages. The wise Golden Retriever owner takes those changes into account and accommodates them as much as possible. Here are some tips to consider.

Be Consistent

Senior dogs, like senior people, generally don't welcome sudden changes in routine. Feed your mature Golden at approximately the same times each day.

Feed Twice a Day

If you've been feeding your Golden only once a day, split that meal in half so that you're feeding him twice: morning and evening. A twice-daily regimen will be easier on his digestive system than if he's fed only once a day.

Heed the Hunger Strike

A hearty eater who suddenly refuses to eat may be sick. Call your vet if your dog's hunger strike goes on for more than a couple of meals.

Pamper the Picky Eater

If your dog isn't eating his grub with much enthusiasm—and if a checkup doesn't show any problems—consider making a gradual change in his food. Dry food can be jazzed up with a little warm water to make a gravy. Also, any regimen will benefit with a little bit of fresh non-fatty meat such as white meat chicken mixed in.

Cater to His Dining Preferences

Dogs, like people, may have dining preferences. Some prefer to dine in solitude; others like having a person around. Pay attention to

Feed your senior Golden at approximately the same times each day.

how your Golden behaves while he eats—for example, does he stop eating when you leave the room?—and go from there to see whether any adjustments are needed.

Be Careful Around the Food Bowl

No matter how unpossessive your Golden is about food, make sure that you don't surprise him while he's eating. Many Goldens lose some of their hearing as they age and may react in a negative fashion if you surprise them from behind. If your Golden wants you around while he eats, that's fine. But don't mess with his food bowl while he's dining—and don't let anyone else do so either.

Minimize Stress

Above all else, try to keep your Golden's dining experience as stress-free as possible. Now more than ever, he needs to eat nutritious fare, and if he finds mealtimes to be tense-laden affairs that prompt him to toss his cookies later,

he won't benefit from the nutrition you're attempting to provide.

GROOMING YOUR SENIOR

Just because your Golden Retriever has crossed the threshold of seniorhood doesn't mean that you shouldn't continue to help him retain his fabulous good looks. An aging Golden needs just as much attention to his coat, ears, teeth, feet, and other body parts as his younger counterpart does. And because the older Golden is generally calmer and more dignified than a puppy or younger adult is, he's better able to appreciate the joys of having someone tend to him than his youthful compatriot is.

How to Groom Your Senior

For the most part, you can groom your senior Golden the same way you did when he was younger. Only a few minor adjustments are needed to maximize his comfort. Those adjustments include:

When grooming your senior, make sure that your bathtub is slip-proof.

Make Your Bathtub Slip-Proof

If you bathe your Golden in a bathtub at home, make sure that the bottom of the tub is secure so that he doesn't slip. A simple bathmat will do the trick.

Let Him Lie Down

Brushing will be much more comfortable for your Golden if you allow him to lie down on his side during the procedure. To make this easier, you can teach him the *dead* cue.

You will simply sit down on the floor, have your dog perform a *down*, and then tell him "Dead." He should respond by rolling onto his side, ready to be brushed and otherwise pampered. In fact, if you pair this cue with grooming often enough, your Golden may assume this position as soon as he sees you pick up his brush! Until then, though, you can teach your dog this cue as follows:

1. Ask your dog to lie down.
2. Hold a treat a couple of inches (cm) away from your dog's nose—just close enough that he can't grab the treat from you.
3. Move the hand with the treat away from your dog's nose at a two o'clock angle (if his left-paw side is facing away from you) or at a ten o'clock angle (if his right-paw side is facing away from you) and toward the floor.
4. As your hand reaches the floor, your dog should lie down on his side. When he does, click and treat.
5. Repeat until your dog is consistently lying on his side to follow the treat. Once he does, add the cue word "dead" as you begin to move your hand.

Give Him a Once-Over

Use the time you spend grooming your Golden to also give him a little checkup. As you brush him, be alert for any lumps or bumps under the skin—and if you find one, call your

Want to Know More?

For a refresher on how to teach the *down*, see Chapter 4: Training Your Golden Retriever Puppy.

veterinarian. (Don't worry; it probably isn't cancer, but checking with your vet is a good way to make sure that that's not the case.) When you clean his ears, peer inside to see whether there's any discharge, and give them a sniff to see whether they have an offensive or yeasty odor. Notice, too, whether he's had any undue hair loss and whether he has bad breath. All of these conditions may signify the onset of a serious health problem—but by catching it early, the chances of solving that problem multiply exponentially.

Savor the Experience

Living with a well-loved senior Golden is a uniquely sweet experience, and there's no better time to savor that experience than when you're grooming him. Let your gentle strokes and loving attention provide some quality time together for the two of you, as well as a brief respite from the stress of day-to-day living.

SENIOR HEALTH CARE

Older people tend to have more health issues than younger ones, and the same is often true of older Golden Retrievers. Living longer exacts a certain amount of wear and tear on the human and canine body—plus the longer one lives, the greater the odds that something will go awry. Not to worry, though: More often than not, whatever goes awry can be put right.

How to Care for His Health

An important weapon in the fight against senior dog illnesses is to catch those illnesses

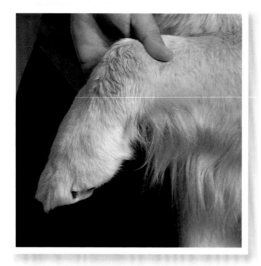

Preventive health care will help your senior stay healthier longer.

in their early stages—and for that effort, preventive care is indispensable.

Employ Preventive Care

You can perform some of this preventive care yourself by checking your dog frequently for lumps, bumps, and other signs of trouble; by feeding him the best-quality food you can afford; by keeping him slim and trim; and by giving him opportunities to get sufficient exercise. But you can't and shouldn't be the sole guardian of your senior Golden's health. You need a partner: your veterinarian.

More specifically, you need to continue to take your Golden Retriever to your veterinarian not only when he shows signs of illness but also for regular wellness checkups. Until he reaches the age of seven or eight, an annual checkup is all that's needed. But once your Golden reaches seniorhood, you should plan to increase those exams to twice a year. Veterinarians recommend the twice-yearly exam for seniors because such diligence can

enable them to spot signs of trouble even earlier than would be the case with an annual physical. The earlier a problem is found, the greater the odds that it can be solved or at least managed.

At a wellness exam, the vet will measure your Golden's temperature, pulse, and respiration; listen to his heart and lungs; check his eyes and ears for discharge, redness, inflammation, or other signs of trouble; run hands over the dog's body and palpate the abdominal area to check for lumps, swellings, or tenderness; examine the skin for rashes, flakiness, and undue dryness or oiliness; and check the teeth and gums for redness, inflammation, plaque, and tartar.

The vet is also likely to want to a sample of your Golden's urine to check for problems in the urinary tract and also for signs of chronic conditions that affect the urine. Finally, she will probably also draw a sample of your dog's blood to analyze for the presence of a wide variety of diseases ranging from hypothyroidism (insufficient production of hormones from the thyroid gland) to diabetes.

The costs of such an exam is not cheap—expect to fork over a few hundred dollars. However, many veterinary practices offer yearly promotions that involve senior pets. A common promotion is to designate one month per year "Senior Pet Month" or "Geriatric Pet Month" and offer a discount on either lab tests or an entire senior pet exam.

Common Senior Dog Illnesses

Certain conditions tend to strike older Golden Retrievers more often than younger ones. Among these illnesses are the following:

Arthritis

Arthritis is one of the most common illnesses faced by older Goldens. The disease involves the bones; the joints, which are where the ends of bones come together; cartilage, which covers the bones that form the joints; and fluid, which lubricates the cartilage. When the cartilage deteriorates over time, the bones that form the joint rub up against each other instead of gliding smoothly over each other. To make matters worse, there's less fluid to lubricate the joints, which causes the joints to become inflamed. The painful result is arthritis. Risk factors for arthritis include not only age but also excess weight, joint abnormalities like hip dysplasia, previous injuries, and a previous case of Lyme disease. Size matters too: Larger dogs like Goldens are more likely to acquire arthritis than smaller dogs are.

Symptoms of arthritis include mobility difficulties—particularly in the morning, on stairs, lying down, or getting up from a reclining position—reluctance to exercise, morning stiffness, and favoring one limb over the other three if only one limb is affected. However, these symptoms can also signal the onset of other diseases, and arthritis can result from other conditions such as hip dysplasia and Lyme disease. For those reasons, it's important to consult your vet to confirm the diagnosis and determine whether there's an underlying cause of your Golden's condition.

Fortunately, a variety of treatments can alleviate arthritis. Nonsteroidal anti-inflammatory drugs (NSAIDs) can be very helpful but should be given only under your vet's supervision. Other helpful remedies include certain nutraceuticals, which are nutritional supplements designed to relieve

Senior Goldens should have an annual checkup twice a year.

Training Tidbit

Your senior Golden will enjoy food rewards as much now as he did when he was younger. However, his metabolism has probably slowed down somewhat—which means that those rewards are likely to result in his putting on extra weight. Prevent such weight gain by giving much smaller portions of the treats you're currently using, or switch to low-calorie fare, such as small pieces of apples, bananas, frozen green beans, or carrots.

diseases. Among these, glucosamine and chondroitin are especially beneficial for treating arthritis. Another possible remedy: acupuncture, which is discussed in Chapter 8.

If your arthritic Golden is also overweight, your veterinarian will probably help you put together a weight-loss diet to reduce the stress on your dog's joints. Exercise can help too, even though your dog may be reluctant to try; gentle movement a couple of times a day can keep him from getting even stiffer.

In extreme cases of arthritis, a veterinarian may recommend surgery such as hip replacement to relieve pain and restore mobility.

Canine Cognitive Dysfunction Syndrome (CDS)

Just like aging human beings, aging dogs often experience a decline in brainpower. Extreme declines in humans are called dementia; for dogs, the term is canine cognitive dysfunction syndrome (CDS). This condition is believed to occur when proteins form deposits of plaque on the brain, similar to what happens with people who have Alzheimer's disease.

Symptoms of CDS include behavioral changes such as new fears or phobias; a sudden onset of separation anxiety—especially if such anxiety occurs at night; housetraining lapses; confusion and disorientation; failure to recognize familiar people; changes in the sleep cycle (often dogs with CDS sleep most of the day and wake up at night); uncharacteristic aggressiveness; diminished interest in people; unexplained vocalizing; forgetting how to navigate stairs or around obstacles; and failure to respond to known cues or directions.

To confirm a CDS diagnosis, a vet will perform a variety of tests to rule out other conditions. Those tests might include a neurological examination, blood tests, a urinalysis, and perhaps imaging of the brain. There's no cure for CDS, but there are some options available to control symptoms. One is Anipryl, a drug approved by the U.S. Food and Drug Administration (FDA) to reduce CDS symptoms. Another comes from Hills Pet Foods: Prescription Diet Canine b/d, which the company says can combat the effects of aging on a dog's brain. Both products are available only with a veterinarian's prescription.

Cataracts

Cataracts are simply a clouding of the lens of your dog's eye. The clouding occurs when too much water enters the lens. There are several types of cataracts, some of which are primarily conditions besetting senior dogs. In any case, the primary sign of cataracts is a whitish cloudiness to one or both eyes accompanied, possibly, by signs of vision loss. This cloudiness differs from the blue-gray color on the eyes that almost all older dogs develop; that condition is called nuclear stenosis, which—unlike cataracts—has little effect on a dog's vision.

To confirm cataracts, a dog needs an examination by a veterinarian or perhaps a veterinary ophthalmologist. The veterinarian may also order blood work to rule out the possibility that the cataracts result from an underlying condition such as diabetes.

Surgery to remove the affected lens is the only cure for cataracts, but in many cases such surgery isn't advisable. A frail senior dog or a diabetic dog is not a good candidate for surgery. For such dogs, treatment of the inflammation that cataracts may cause may

be a better option. In any event, healthy older dogs whose owners can commit to weeks of postoperative care and to restricting their dogs' activities can do well with such surgery. In the long run, though, many cataracts are best left alone, especially if they're small and not interfering with the dog's vision.

Cushing's Disease

Also known as hyperadrenocorticism, Cushing's disease is a common condition among older dogs that results when a dog's adrenal glands produce too much cortisone. Golden Retrievers are among the breeds that are thought to be especially vulnerable to this condition.

Cushing's disease results from one of the following scenarios: if a dog has been given steroids over a long period of time to treat

Dogs suffer from more illnesses as they age.

another health problem; if the dog has a small tumor—usually noncancerous—on his pituitary gland; or if the dog has a tumor on the adrenal glands themselves. Of these three scenarios, the pituitary gland tumor is the most common.

Symptoms of Cushing's disease include increased appetite; increased water consumption; increased urination; a distended belly; unexplained weight gain; weakening of the legs; hair loss on both sides of the body, and darkened, thinning skin. The condition can also cause behavioral changes such as lethargy, excessive panting, nighttime restlessness, and seeking cool surfaces on which to lie down.

Because the symptoms of Cushing's disease are similar to those that signal the onset of other diseases, a veterinarian needs to conduct several tests before arriving at a diagnosis. The vet is likely to draw a blood sample to determine what your dog's white blood cell, liver enzyme, and cholesterol levels are. If those readings are higher than normal, additional testing is likely to confirm the diagnosis.

The treatment for Cushing's disease depends on the cause. If the condition results from a pituitary gland tumor, the veterinarian will prescribe a drug to reduce the level of cortisol in the blood. To treat Cushing's disease that results from a tumor on the adrenal gland, the vet may choose to remove the tumor surgically. For Cushing's disease that results from steroid medication, treatment consists of ceasing the steroid treatment and finding another way to treat the condition that prompted the steroid regimen.

Vestibular Syndrome

An older Golden Retriever who acts as if he's had one alcoholic beverage too many or has suffered a stroke may well be suffering from vestibular syndrome. This condition causes a dog to lose his balance, lean to one side, and keep his head tilted. He may also attempt to walk straight ahead but actually walk diagonally. Other symptoms include vomiting and a refusal to eat or drink. A physical exam by a vet is usually all that's needed to confirm a diagnosis.

There's no cure for vestibular syndrome—but while it's frightening to watch, it's usually not serious. Treatment focuses on keeping the dog comfortable. To prevent the dehydration that may result from the dog's vomiting and refusing to drink water, the vet may insert fluids through a tube into an area under the skin. The dog's body will then slowly absorb the fluids. The dog should also get plenty of rest. Generally the symptoms disappear after a few days.

TRAINING YOUR SENIOR

You *can* teach an old dog new tricks—in fact, doing so is a very good idea. Teaching a dog something new helps keep his mind sharp and greatly improves an older dog's quality of life. Bear in mind that it's important to adjust your training techniques to both the physical and mental capabilities of your mature Golden Retriever.

A nutritious diet can do wonders for your Golden's health.

How to Train Your Senior

Here are some specific ideas for making training your senior Golden a bit easier.

Keep up the Positive Attitude

Employing positive reinforcement in your training technique is just as important for a senior Golden as it is for a puppy. Make sure to keep your sessions with your dog happy and upbeat. Rather than focus on what he's doing wrong, catch him doing something right—and when he does, reward him for it in the form of a tasty tidbit, verbal praise, a short play session, or any combination thereof.

Keep It Real

Understand that a senior Golden Retriever may have physical limitations that preclude certain types of training. For example, a Golden whose face is turning white may do better at rally obedience than at agility. One great training goal for a senior Golden is to prepare him to pass the AKC Canine Good Citizen test, as explained in Chapter 11. The behaviors your dog needs to perform to pass this test are not physically difficult, but learning them may offer him a mental challenge that can give him a new lease on life.

Teach Hand Signals

If your dog is showing signs of losing his hearing, start teaching him hand signals now so that he can respond to cues even when he can no longer hear your voice. For example, when you ask him to sit, pair the verbal cue with placing your hand on your chest. If you want

him to come when called, pair the word "come" with a clap of your hands. (He may be able to feel the vibration from the clapping even if he can't hear either the clapping or the cue.)

Keep Sessions Short

A senior dog's attention span may be shorter than it was when he was younger. Adjust accordingly—don't let any training session go longer than five or ten minutes.

End on a Good Note

Always end a training session by asking your dog to do something you know that he'll do well. When he responds to your request, give him lots of positive feedback. You'll both end the session feeling proud of what you've accomplished, even if you suffered some setbacks earlier.

Multi-Dog Tip

If you acquire a new puppy, make sure that your senior Golden Retriever doesn't feel neglected or that his place in the household has changed. Your senior Golden needs to know that you still love him best. The new puppy, who's already had to share human attention with his mother and littermates, won't mind continuing to share such attention for a little while longer.

CHAPTER 14

GOLDEN RETRIEVER END-OF-LIFE ISSUES

A list of the joys that come from living with a Golden Retriever could fill up a book and then some. An exuberant personality, loving nature, outsized intelligence, and breathtaking good looks are just a few of the characteristics that make this breed among the most popular in America. But there is one unmistakable downside to living with these wonderful dogs—or for that matter, any dog.

The disadvantage is that your Golden Retriever will probably die before you do. The joy that you're experiencing now in living with your Golden will, in time, be halted by the pain you'll experience when his life ends. And if you've loved your Golden well, that pain will be surprisingly sharp and deep. That said, you can temper your pain by making the most of your time with your Golden now and by planning ahead to make the end of your Golden's life as painless as possible for both you and for him.

WHEN IS IT TIME?

For many Golden Retriever owners, the question "When is it time?" has two meanings: deciding when to end treatment for a terminal condition and deciding when the time has come to euthanize a dog. Here are some thoughts to help you answer both questions.

Deciding to End Treatment

Veterinary science has come up with some amazing ways to extend the lives of dogs whose diagnoses would have been death sentences just a generation ago. Surgery, radiation, and chemotherapy can prolong the life of a canine cancer patient. A wheelchair can provide mobility for a dog who has lost the use of his hind legs. A dog with heart disease can be given new drugs that can give him an additional year of life—and a high-quality life at that.

But the availability of these life-extending options doesn't make them appropriate for every dog and every situation. Sometimes an owner—in consultation with the veterinarian— may conclude that she should end aggressive treatment of the dog's illness and shift the focus to keeping him comfortable for the remainder of his life.

Of course, making such a decision can be extremely difficult. To help you make the right choice for your Golden Retriever, try answering the following questions:

Canine hospice is one option that can help your dog remain comfortable until it's time.

- Has your dog's quality of life improved since he began treatment?
- Does your veterinarian favor continuing treatment—and if so, why?
- Do you think that continuing treatment will be good for your dog?

If the answer to any of these questions is no, you might want to consider whether the time has come to end aggressive treatment of your Golden Retriever's illness.

Creating a Canine Hospice

If you've decided that stopping aggressive treatment is what's best for your Golden, you may still be able to take steps to keep him happy and content for awhile. Basically, you'll be giving your Golden hospice care: providing him with a safe, comfortable, and caring end-of-life experience after efforts to cure a life-threatening disease are no longer viable. Such care can be good not only for your Golden, because he no longer has to endure arduous treatments, but also for you, because providing your dog with hospice care gives you time to come to terms with your dog's impending death and to say goodbye.

That said, providing hospice care in a way that minimizes stress for both you and your dog takes some preparation. Here are some steps you can take:

Consult Your Vet

Ask your veterinarian whether your Golden is a candidate for hospice care and what such care might entail. Some dogs in hospice care require extensive nursing, while others simply need a couple of meds and some tender loving care. Your vet and you are in the best position to make the right decisions regarding hospice care for your Golden.

Study Up
The veterinary profession is paying more attention to the idea of hospice care for pets than was once the case. Check out the American Association of Human–Animal Bond Veterinarians (AAH–ABV) hospice web page (http://aah-abv.org/Net/Home/Hospice.aspx); the Nikki Hospice Foundation for Pets (www.pethospice.org); and the American Animal Hospital Association (AAHA) hospice page (www.healthypet.com/library_view.aspx?ID=9&sid=1).

Be Honest With Yourself
In some cases, providing hospice care for a dog could involve providing fluids intravenously, giving regular injections, and/or preparing special food. And no matter what you do, the end result is likely to be either eventual euthanasia or death from natural causes. Ask yourself whether you are up to the financial and emotional costs of providing such care—and also whether you have the time to do so.

By the Numbers

The average life span of a Golden Retriever is 10 to 12 years of age.

Deciding When to Euthanize
At some point in your Golden's life, whether you provide hospice care or not, you may need to decide that the time has come to end his life in a compassionate, humane manner. However, figuring when that time has arrived can be incredibly difficult—not only because you love your dog and don't want to lose him but also because your dog doesn't have the words to tell you that he's ready to go. But your pain and your dog's lack of verbal language skills don't mean that you can't figure out when it's time to say goodbye. Ask yourself the following questions and answer them as honestly as you can. The answers will help you make the right decision at the time.

It's up to both you and your vet to decide when it's time to euthanize.

How Is My Golden Doing?

A dog who's still engaged with the world around him—eating, interacting with you—may want and be able to stick around a little longer. A dog who's clearly miserable—refusing to eat, apathetic, not interacting with his people—may well be ready to call it a day.

How Am I Doing?

If providing hospice care for your Golden is proving to be more emotionally draining than you had anticipated—or if such treatment is depleting your bank account and his prognosis is poor—it may be time to consider euthanizing him. If this is your situation, don't feel guilty. You're doing the best you can, and you need to consider the needs not only of your Golden but also of you and the rest of your family.

What About the Rest of the Family?

If you're not the only adult or near-adult human in the household, you shouldn't make the euthanasia decision on your own. Find out how the other members of your family feel, and take their ideas into account. Ideally, you'll all agree that now's the time—or if not now, what the criteria for a "yes" decision would be.

EUTHANASIA

Deciding to euthanize a dog is always emotionally painful, no matter how many times you've had to make that decision in the past. However, that pain can be lessened if you do everything you can before and during the procedure to make sure that your dog has a good death and that you and your family aren't traumatized. To ensure both outcomes, consider taking the following steps:

Decide on a Place

If you want to euthanize your Golden at home, find out whether your vet is willing to make house calls. (Not every vet will provide this service.) If the vet doesn't do so, ask for a referral to a vet who can.

Book and Pay Ahead

Whether you have your dog euthanized at home or at the vet's, pay ahead of time so that you're not having to deal with financial matters just after you've had to say goodbye to your Golden. And if you're euthanizing your dog at the vet's, book the last appointment of the day so that your vet can give you and your dog full attention and not have to rush off to another appointment.

Ask for Privacy

Most clinics will let you bring your dog to an exam through an employee entrance so that you don't have to face other people and their pets before the procedure takes place.

Don't Drive Alone

Have a friend or someone else in your family drive you and your dog to the clinic if you're having your Golden euthanized there. You're likely to be too distracted to drive safely, which could pose a danger not only to you but also to other motorists.

The memories you have of your senior Golden can help comfort you during this difficult time.

Bring the Comforts of Home

If your dog is being euthanized at the vet's, bring his bed with you so that he can be more comfortable during the procedure.

Consider Staying

A wonderful last gift to give your Golden is your familiar presence during the procedure. Most veterinarians allow family members and children of school age and above to remain with their pets during euthanasia. Being there for your Golden can comfort him and can give you a sense of closure and completeness.

DEALING WITH GRIEF

In the days immediately before and after your Golden Retriever's death, you will undoubtedly be full of sorrow. That's okay—as horse enthusiast Gretchen Jackson said upon the death of her beloved race horse Barbaro, "Grief is the price we pay for love." During this time, your objective should be not to rid yourself of grief but to cope with it—and to help the other members of your family, human and nonhuman alike, do the same.

Coping With Your own Grief

For many people, losing a dog is no less painful than losing a human family member. If that's the case for you, it's important for you to take care of yourself—and to give yourself permission to acknowledge and grieve for your loss. Here are some suggestions to help you deal with the immediate aftermath of your Golden's death.

- **Take time off.** Take a day or two off from work so that you have the time and space you need to cope with the immediate shock of your dog's passing.
- **Keep your routine.** Even if you don't feel like doing so, try to eat three square meals a day, get regular exercise, and take one day at a time.

Multi-Dog Tip

If possible, allow your other dogs to view your Golden Retriever's body after he has been euthanized. Dogs do understand death, and seeing that life has left your Golden will help the surviving canine members of the family come to terms with his passing.

After your Golden is gone, you will need time to work through the grief.

- **Expect delayed reactions.** If you were nursing your Golden through a long terminal illness, you may actually feel relief immediately after his death. That's okay. However, be prepared to feel deep grief and sadness weeks or even months later—and know that that's okay, too.
- **Ask for help.** If you're having trouble coping with your grief, consider contacting a pet-loss support hotline. Your veterinarian and local animal shelter should be able to give you contact information for such groups.

Explaining Pet Loss to Children

When your children must experience any painful event, including the death of your Golden Retriever, your first instinct may be to limit your child's pain as much as you can. However, such protectiveness is not in a child's best interest. Experts counsel that the better course of action is to be honest with your child about what's happening. Here are some tips for helping your child deal with the impending death of your Golden and its aftermath.

Be direct: Tell your child that your dog is dying or will die soon. Using euphemisms such as "putting our dog to sleep" can backfire because after your dog dies, your child may become afraid to go to sleep.

Don't lie: Don't tell your child that your Golden ran away or was given to someone else to take care of. Sooner or later, the child will know what really happened—and the realization that you lied could cause serious repercussions in your relationship.

Show that you're sad: By showing your own sadness—occasional tears, acknowledgment of your feelings—you give your child permission to show her grief and affirm that your Golden has been a beloved family member.

Tell other caregivers: If your child is 12 or younger, tell her teachers what's happening. That way, the teacher can monitor your child's behavior, offer comfort if necessary, and keep you informed about how the child is doing.

Helping Other Pets

If there are other animals in your household, they probably know that something—or rather, someone—is missing. For dogs and cats, the sudden departure of a family member can trigger an emotional tailspin that has both physical and behavioral effects. The grieving animal may lose his appetite, forget his bathroom manners, or just plain act lethargic. To help him, take the following steps:

- **Resume your routine as soon as possible:** Often a dog or cat is less upset by the absence of another animal than by the change in routine that absence may cause. Returning as soon as possible to the routine

You'll know when and if it's the right time to add another Golden to your family.

Want to Know More?

If and when you're ready to add a new dog to your home, see Chapter 2: Finding and Prepping for Your Puppy or Chapter 5: Finding Your Adult Golden Retriever for some pointers.

your pet is accustomed to can help him get back to normal.

- **Tempt his taste buds:** If your dog or cat isn't interested in his regular food, try making that food a little more interesting. Add a couple of treats or flavorful pieces of lean meat to his meal, or try warming it up in the microwave before serving.

- **Get moving:** Exercise can help both you and your pet feel better. A brisk walk or run with your dog will take his mind off what's troubling him; a session with an interactive toy and you can have the same effect on your cat.

- **Consult your vet:** Some apparent signs of grief may actually signal that your pet is sick. If your dog or cat hasn't eaten anything for two days; your cat fails to urinate for several hours or starts missing the litter box; or your dog starts having consistent housetraining lapses, consult your vet. A call to the vet is also in order if other symptoms such as lethargy, whining, crying, or wailing persist for more than two weeks.

As you, your children, and your family grieve over the loss of your Golden Retriever, remember that time can go a long way toward healing your wounds. A time will come—it really will—when your sorrow over your Golden's death will give way to happy memories of the time you spent together.

50 FUN FACTS EVERY GOLDEN RETRIEVER OWNER SHOULD KNOW

1. Golden Retrievers are among the most popular dog breeds in the United States.

2. In 2008, New Orleans is the only major city in which the Golden Retriever did not rank among the top ten most popular breeds.

3. Two now extinct breeds were among the Golden Retriever's ancestors: the Wavy-Coated Retriever and the Tweed Water Spaniel.

4. Other breeds used to develop the Golden Retriever included Irish Setters and Bloodhounds.

5. The two dogs whom Sir Dudley Marjoribanks bred to begin developing the Golden Retriever were named Nous and Belle.

6. Golden Retrievers were once known as Golden Flat-Coated Retrievers.

7. The Golden Retriever was developed to work with humans in rugged terrain and in marshland to retrieve fallen birds during hunts.

8. The Golden Retriever is a member of the Sporting Group of the American Kennel Club (AKC).

9. More Golden Retrievers have won the AKC National Obedience Championship than any other breed.

10. The first three dogs to win AKC Obedience Trial Championships were Golden Retrievers.

11. Golden Retrievers' coats can range in color from pale blond to almost russet—even within the same litter.

12. The Golden Retriever breed standard calls for a "friendly, reliable, and trustworthy" temperament.

13. Although Golden Retrievers can't fly, the hair on their tummies, tails, and legs is called feathers.

14. When Gerald Ford was president, a Golden Retriever named Liberty lived at the White House.

15. Despite the breed's striking looks and consistent popularity, no Golden Retriever has ever won Best in Show at the Westminster Kennel Club Dog Show.

16. The best showing by a Golden Retriever at Westminster was in 2006, when a Golden named Ch. Chuckanut Party Favour O Novel won the Sporting Group competition.

17. A Golden Retriever named Houston won the Bred by Exhibitor Best in Show ribbon at the 2006 American Kennel Club/Eukanuba Classic dog show.

18. A Golden Retriever named Aruba not only won plenty of dog shows but also whelped 32 Golden Retriever champions.

19. Fifty Golden Retrievers walked in a procession to the Concord, MA, church where the funeral of Golden Retriever enthusiast Rachel Paige Elliott was held in 2009.

20. An expert in canine intelligence, Dr. Stanley Coren, ranks the Golden Retriever fourth in intelligence among all dog breeds.

21. Cancer is the leading cause of death among Golden Retrievers.

22. Of the cancers that befall Goldens, the two most common are hemangiosarcoma and lymphoma.

23. The two dogs who appear in Bush's Baked Beans commercials are Golden Retrievers.

24. The multi-talented Golden Retriever can excel in competitive obedience, agility, flyball, rally obedience, tracking, and field trials.

25. The Golden Retriever Club of America (GRCA) offers a Triathlon award to Goldens who distinguish themselves in conformation, field trials, and performance.

26. Goldens who distinguish themselves in conformation, field trials, and performance can also earn a Versatility Certificate from the GRCA.

27. Goldens who excel in both conformation and field trials earn a place in the GRCA Dual Dog Hall of Fame.

28. Pennsylvania Governor Edward Rendell and his wife, Judge Marjorie Rendell, share their home with rescued Golden Retrievers.

29. The first Golden Retriever registered in the United States was Lomberdale Blondin, in November 1925.

30. Goldens have been characters on television shows such as *Mad Men*, *Full House*, and the *Drew Carey Show*.

31. The GRCA was formed in 1938.

32. Golden Retriever puppies are generally ready to go home with their permanent owners at around eight weeks of age.

33. Most Golden Retrievers don't achieve their full growth until the age of two and may act like puppies or adolescents even longer.

34. A Golden Retriever doesn't acquire his full adult coat until he's at least one year of age—and often older.

35. Golden Retriever puppies need three meals a day until they're 16 weeks of age.

36. A Golden Retriever should have one wellness exam each year until he's seven to nine years of age, after which he should have two such exams annually.

37. Golden Retrievers are teenagers from six months to at least two years of age.

38. A Golden should not perform strenuous sports such as agility until he's at least one year old so that he doesn't put too much strain on his bones and joints.

39. A Golden is considered a senior citizen at between seven and nine years of age, but with luck and good care can live well into his teens.

40. The myth that Golden Retrievers originated from Russian circus dogs is just that—a myth.

41. A Golden Retriever who is more than 1 inch (2.5 cm) under or over the height specified in the breed standard must be disqualified from the show ring.

42. The AKC recognizes only the "Golden Retriever"—not "white Golden Retrievers" or "Golden Labrador Retrievers."

43. The dog featured in an iconic photograph of a search-and-rescue dog being ferried across a canyon of debris at the World Trade Center after the September 11 attacks is a Golden Retriever named Riley.

44. A Golden Retriever named Rookie and his owner/handler, Carolyn Scott, did much to popularize the sport of canine freestyle.

45. Golden Retrievers who are bred to hunt are called field Goldens.

46. Some common health issues for Golden Retrievers include hip dysplasia, elbow dysplasia, eye problems, hypothyroidism, subaortic stenosis, and allergies.

47. Young Golden Retrievers need a strenuous aerobic workout daily or at least several times a week.

48. Among the many celebrities who own or have owned Golden Retrievers are Pamela Anderson; Mary Chapin-Carpenter; Joe Cocker; Jamie Lee Curtis; Kristin Davis; America Ferrara; Sally Field; Nick Jonas; Ashton Kutcher; Matt Lauer; Arnold Palmer; Anna Paquin; and Betty White.

49. Author Dean Koontz's late Golden Retriever, Trixie, inspired several of his books.

50. The Land of Pure Gold website contains dozens of tales of Golden Retriever heroes: http://landofpuregold.com/heroes.htm.

ASSOCIATIONS AND ORGANIZATIONS

Breed Clubs

American Kennel Club (AKC)
5580 Centerview Drive
Raleigh, NC 27606
Telephone: (919) 233-9767
Fax: (919) 233-3627
E-Mail: info@akc.org
www.akc.org

Canadian Kennel Club (CKC)
89 Skyway Avenue, Suite 100
Etobicoke, Ontario M9W 6R4
Telephone: (416) 675-5511
Fax: (416) 675-6506
E-Mail: information@ckc.ca
www.ckc.ca

Federation Cynologique Internationale (FCI)
Secretariat General de la FCI
Place Albert 1er, 13
B – 6530 Thuin
Belqique
www.fci.be

Golden Retriever Club of America (GRCA)
www.grca.org

Golden Retriever Club of England (GRC)
www.thegoldenretrieverclub.co.uk

The Golden Retriever Club of Canada (GRCC)
www.grcc.net

The Kennel Club
1 Clarges Street
London
W1J 8AB
Telephone: 0870 606 6750
Fax: 0207 518 1058
www.the-kennel-club.org.uk

United Kennel Club (UKC)
100 E. Kilgore Road
Kalamazoo, MI 49002-5584
Telephone: (269) 343-9020
Fax: (269) 343-7037
E-Mail: pbickell@ukcdogs.com
www.ukcdogs.com

Pet Sitters

National Association of Professional Pet Sitters
15000 Commerce Parkway, Suite C
Mt. Laurel, New Jersey 08054
Telephone: (856) 439-0324
Fax: (856) 439-0525
E-Mail: napps@ahint.com
www.petsitters.org

Pet Sitters International
201 East King Street
King, NC 27021-9161
Telephone: (336) 983-9222
Fax: (336) 983-5266
E-Mail: info@petsit.com
www.petsit.com

Rescue Organizations and Animal Welfare Groups

American Humane Association (AHA)
63 Inverness Drive East
Englewood, CO 80112
Telephone: (303) 792-9900
Fax: 792-5333
www.americanhumane.org

American Society for the Prevention of Cruelty to Animals (ASPCA)
424 E. 92nd Street
New York, NY 10128-6804
Telephone: (212) 876-7700
www.aspca.org

The Humane Society of the United States (HSUS)
2100 L Street, NW
Washington DC 20037
Telephone: (202) 452-1100
www.hsus.org

Royal Society for the Prevention of Cruelty to Animals (RSPCA)
RSPCA Enquiries Service
Wilberforce Way, Southwater,
Horsham, West Sussex RH13 9RS
United Kingdom
Telephone: 0870 3335 999
Fax: 0870 7530 284
www.rspca.org.uk

Sports

International Agility Link (IAL)
Global Administrator: Steve Drinkwater
E-Mail: yunde@powerup.au
www.agilityclick.com/~ial

The World Canine Freestyle Organization, Inc.
P.O. Box 350122
Brooklyn, NY 11235
Telephone: (718) 332-8336
Fax: (718) 646-2686
E-Mail: WCFODOGS@aol.com
www.worldcaninefreestyle.org

Therapy

Delta Society
875 124th Ave, NE, Suite 101
Bellevue, WA 98005
Telephone: (425) 679-5500
Fax: (425) 679-5539
E-Mail: info@DeltaSociety.org
www.deltasociety.org

Therapy Dogs Inc.
P.O. Box 20227
Cheyenne WY 82003
Telephone: (877) 843-7364
Fax: (307) 638-2079
E-Mail: therapydogsinc@qwestoffice.net
www.therapydogs.com

Therapy Dogs International (TDI)
88 Bartley Road
Flanders, NJ 07836
Telephone: (973) 252-9800
Fax: (973) 252-7171
E-Mail: tdi@gti.net
www.tdi-dog.org

Training
Association of Pet Dog Trainers (APDT)
150 Executive Center Drive Box 35
Greenville, SC 29615
Telephone: (800) PET-DOGS
Fax: (864) 331-0767
E-Mail: information@apdt.com
www.apdt.com

International Association of Animal Behavior Consultants (IAABC)
565 Callery Road
Cranberry Township, PA 16066
E-Mail: info@iaabc.org
www.iaabc.org

Veterinary and Health Resources
Academy of Veterinary Homeopathy (AVH)
P.O. Box 9280
Wilmington, DE 19809
Telephone: (866) 652-1590
Fax: (866) 652-1590
www.theavh.org

American Academy of Veterinary Acupuncture (AAVA)
P.O. Box 1058
Glastonbury, CT 06033
Telephone: (860) 632-9911
Fax: (860) 659-8772
www.aava.org

American Animal Hospital Association (AAHA)
12575 W. Bayaud Ave.
Lakewood, CO 80228
Telephone: (303) 986-2800
Fax: (303) 986-1700
E-Mail: info@aahanet.org
www.aahanet.org/index.cfm

American College of Veterinary Internal Medicine (ACVIM)
1997 Wadsworth Blvd., Suite A
Lakewood, CO 80214-5293
Telephone: (800) 245-9081
Fax: (303) 231-0880
Email: ACVIM@ACVIM.org
www.acvim.org

American College of Veterinary Ophthalmologists (ACVO)
P.O. Box 1311
Meridian, ID 83860
Telephone: (208) 466-7624
Fax: (208) 466-7693
E-Mail: office09@acvo.com
www.acvo.com

American Holistic Veterinary Medical Association (AHVMA)
2218 Old Emmorton Road
Bel Air, MD 21015
Telephone: (410) 569-0795
Fax: (410) 569-2346
E-Mail: office@ahvma.org
www.ahvma.org

American Veterinary Medical Association (AVMA)
1931 North Meacham Road, Suite 100
Schaumburg, IL 60173-4360
Telephone: (847) 925-8070
Fax: (847) 925-1329
E-Mail: avmainfo@avma.org
www.avma.org

ASPCA Animal Poison Control Center
Telephone: (888) 426-4435
www.aspca.org

British Veterinary Association (BVA)
7 Mansfield Street
London
W1G 9NQ
Telephone: 0207 636 6541
Fax: 0207 908 6349
E-Mail: bvahq@bva.co.uk

www.bva.co.uk

Canine Eye Registration Foundation (CERF)
VMDB/CERF
1717 Philo Rd
P O Box 3007
Urbana, IL 61803-3007
Telephone: (217) 693-4800
Fax: (217) 693-4801
E-Mail: CERF@vmbd.org
www.vmdb.org

Orthopedic Foundation for Animals (OFA)
2300 NE Nifong Blvd
Columbus, Missouri 65201-3856
Telephone: (573) 442-0418
Fax: (573) 875-5073
Email: ofa@offa.org
www.offa.org

US Food and Drug Administration Center for Veterinary Medicine (CVM)
7519 Standish Place
HFV-12
Rockville, MD 20855-0001
Telephone: (240) 276-9300 or (888) INFO-FDA
http://www.fda.gov/cvm

PUBLICATIONS
Books
Adamson, Eve. *The Golden Retriever.* Neptune City: TFH Publications, 2005.

Anderson, Teoti. *The Super Simple Guide to Housetraining.* Neptune City: TFH Publications, 2004.

Anne, Jonna, with Mary Straus. *The Healthy Dog Cookbook: 50 Nutritious and Delicious Recipes Your Dog Will Love.* UK: Ivy Press Limited, 2008.

Boneham, Sheila Webster, Ph.D. *Golden Retrievers.* Neptune City: TFH Publications and Discovery Communications, Inc., 2006.

Dainty, Suellen. *50 Games to Play With Your Dog.* UK: Ivy Press Limited, 2007.

Morgan, Diane. *Good Dogkeeping.* Neptune City: TFH Publications, 2005.

Magazines

AKC Family Dog
American Kennel Club
260 Madison Avenue
New York, NY 10016
Telephone: (800) 490-5675
E-Mail: familydog@akc.org
www.akc.org/pubs/familydog

AKC Gazette
American Kennel Club
260 Madison Avenue
New York, NY 10016
Telephone: (800) 533-7323
E-Mail: gazette@akc.org
www.akc.org/pubs/gazette

Dog & Kennel
Pet Publishing, Inc.
7-L Dundas Circle
Greensboro, NC 27407
Telephone: (336) 292-4272
Fax: (336) 292-4272
E-Mail: info@petpublishing.com
www.dogandkennel.com

Dogs Monthly
Ascot House
High Street, Ascot,
Berkshire SL5 7JG
United Kingdom
Telephone: 0870 730 8433
Fax: 0870 730 8431
E-Mail: admin@rtc-associates.freeserve.co.uk
www.corsini.co.uk/dogsmonthly

Websites

Nylabone
www.nylabone.com

TFH Publications, Inc.
www.tfh.com

Boldfaced numbers indicate illustrations.

PHOTO CREDITS

DEDICATION

To Allie, who always shows me her brains as well as her beauty

ACKNOWLEDGMENTS

Any book is a group effort, and this one's no exception. I'd like to thank:

- Stephanie Fornino, who asked me to take on this project;
- All the dog professionals—too numerous to name—from whom I've learned so much about dog care, health and training;
- Most of all, my family: my husband, Stan Chappell; my daughter, Julie Chappell; and our Golden Retriever, Allie, who were (as usual) incredibly patient while I was writing this book, especially when I was close to deadline.

ABOUT THE AUTHOR

Susan McCullough writes about dog behavior and health for media outlets all over the United States and is also the author of several dog care books. She has won six Maxwell Awards from the Dog Writers Association of America (DWAA) for her work. Susan and her Golden Retriever, Allie, live with their family in Vienna, Virginia.

VETRINARY ADVISOR

Wayne Hunthausen, DVM, consulting veterinary editor and pet behavior consultant, is the director of Animal Behavior Consultations in the Kansas City area and currently serves on the Practitioner Board for *Veterinary Medicine* and the Behavior Advisory Board for *Veterinary Forum*.

BREEDER ADVISOR

Rhonda Hovan has been a breeder/owner/handler of Golden Retrievers under the "Faera" prefix for more than 30 years, producing more than 60 Champions. As a health and genetics writer, she has won the Veterinary Information Network Health Education Award and the Eukanuba Canine Health Award. Rhonda is the Research Facilitator for the Golden Retriever Club of America, founded the Starlight Fund at the AKC Canine Health Foundation to support Golden Retriever health research, and is an Emeritus Director of the Orthopedic Foundation for Animals. She is a frequent speaker on topics of canine health, and lives in Akron, Ohio, with four Goldens and a rescued raccoon. Rhonda invites correspondence at rhondahovan@aol.com.

NATURAL with added VITAMINS
Nutri Dent ®MD
Promotes Optimal Dental Health!

360° Design

Cleaning Action!™

Dogs Love'em!™

AVAILABLE IN MULTIPLE SIZES AND FLAVORS.

Nylabone®

Trusted For Over 40 Years

MADE IN THE USA

Our Mission with Nutri Dent® is to promote optimal dental health for dogs through a usted, natural, delicious chew that provides effective cleaning action...GUARANTEED to make your dog go wild with anticipation and happiness!!!

Nylabone Products • P.O. Box 427, Neptune, NJ 07754-0427 • 1-800-631-2188 • Fax: 732-988-5466
www.nylabone.com • info@nylabone.com • For more information contact your sales representative or contact us at sales@tfh.com   A275